Cybersecurity and Privacy Law Handbook

A beginner's guide to dealing with privacy and security while keeping hackers at bay

Walter Rocchi

<packt>

BIRMINGHAM—MUMBAI

Cybersecurity and Privacy Law Handbook

Group Product Manager: Mohd Riyan Khan
Publishing Product Manager: Khushboo Samkaria
Content Development Editor: Nihar Kapadia
Technical Editor: Arjun Varma
Copy Editor: Safis Editing
Project Coordinator: Deeksha Thakkar
Proofreader: Safis Editing
Indexer: Manju Arasan
Production Designer: Prashant Ghare
Marketing Coordinator: Ankita Bhonsle

First published: December 2022
Production reference: 1241122

Published by Packt Publishing Ltd.
Livery Place
35 Livery Street
Birmingham
B3 2PB, UK.

ISBN 978-1-80324-241-5

www.packt.com

To my children, Bianca, Maria, and Enrico, and to those who supported and believed in me.

– Walter Rocchi

Contributors

About the author

Walter Rocchi, with 24 years of activity and ISO 27001 Lead Implementer, ISO 27001 Lead Auditor, CISA, CEH, and IAPP CIPP/E – CIPT certifications, is a seasoned freelancer and has acted as CISO and in similar roles for several companies, mostly in finance, retail, telecoms, utilities, Big Pharma, and government agencies. He has consulted with big corporations and funded start-ups and he's always looking for new challenges.

He spends his free time reading, hiking, and enjoying his time with his two children. He's also an avid blues listener and is addicted to TV series (especially Marvel and horror series).

I want to thank the people who have been close to me and supported me, especially Roberta Carolina Ainara Bermúdez, for her invaluable help in simplifying the GDPR for mere mortals. Moreover, thanks to Francesco Tonin, who always reminded me of the frameworks that needed to be mentioned. Finally, all the guys at Packt, who gave me the opportunity to write a book, especially my editor Nihar Kapadia, and Safis, for their patience in dealing with my poor examples.

About the reviewer

Francesco Tonin is a senior information technology professional and expert in IT audit, risk, and compliance with over 14 years of working in highly regulated markets such as financial services, insurance, and healthcare. He is broadly skilled in relation to cyber security, IT auditing, IT risk, and governance but also in relation to business process design, SAP FI, CO, and MM and data warehousing, and data analytics for audit and process improvement. He's a certified professional (with CISA, CISM, ISO 27001LA, and CIPP/E for GDPR and Data Privacy certifications) and took part in a part-time master's program focused on planning and control in corporate finance.

Table of Contents

Preface xiii

Part 1: Start From the Basics

1

ISO27001 – Definitions and Security Concepts 3

The 27k family of standards 3
Confidentiality, integrity, and availability 6
Information security concepts and definitions 8
Governance, policies, and incident management 11
- Governance 11
- Policies and procedures 12
- Incident management 14

Differences between ISO 27001 and NIST 14
- What's NIST? 14

Summary 17

Part 2: Into the Wild

2

Mandatory Requirements 21

iSMS, controls, commitment, context, scope policy, and objectives 21
- iSMS 21
- Statement of applicability, risk treatment plan, and action plan 23
- Controls 25
- Commitment and project management 25

Identify, Protect, Detect, Respond, and Recover 26
- Identify 26
- Protect 27
- Detect 28
- Respond 28
- Recover 29

Can ISO 27001 and NIST coexist? 29
Summary 35

3

Data Protection 37

What is privacy (and why do we desperately need it)? 38
GDPR and his brothers 40
Territorial scope 41
The GDPR, CCPA, and LGPD each define personal data differently 42
The importance of anonymous, pseudonymous, de-identified, and aggregated information 43
Legal bases for data processing 44
Data access privileges 45
Fines and penalties 46
Why deal with data protection? 46
The six principles of the GDPR 48
Summary 51

4

Data Processing 53

The data controller 53
The data processor 54
Accountability 54
Recommended documents 55
The privacy dashboard 55
Training materials 56
Mandatory documents 56
Data protection – the last warning 61
EU–US Privacy Shield 61
Brief summary 62
Schrems II ruling 62
The frequently asked questions issued by the EDPB 63
What occurs next? Vade mecum for entities 64
Conclusions 66
Summary 67

5

Security Planning and Risk Management 69

Security threats and challenges 69
What are the different types of security threats? 70
What is risk and what is a threat? 70
Implementing a risk management program 72
Why is risk management so important? 73
Traditional risk management versus enterprise risk management 73
What are the steps involved in risk management for information security? 75
From the top-down to the bottom-up 76
Benefits and challenges of risk management 76

Building and implementing a risk management plan 77
Qualitative risk analysis 79
Quantitative risk analysis 79
Difference between qualitative and quantitative risk analysis 80
When to perform a qualitative and quantitative risk analysis 80
Summary 80

Part 3: Escape from Chaos

6

Define ISO 27001 Mandatory Requirements 83

ISO 27001 operations 83
The ISO 27001 standard – what it is and what requirements it establishes 84
How to structure an iSMS 85
ISO 27001 support requirements (or Clause 7) 88
7.1 – Resources required to establish and operate an iSMS 89
7.2 – Competency 90
7.3 – Awareness 93
7.4 – Communication 94
7.5 – Documented information 97
Summary 102

7

Risk Management, Controls, and Policies 103

Elements of project risk management 104
The risk management plan 104
Fundamental notions 104
Risk evaluation 105
Risk characteristics 105
Risk heatmaps 107
Risk mitigation 108
Best risk mitigation strategies 108
How to establish risk mitigation strategies 110
Data classification 110
Why is the classification of data important? 111
What are the four levels of data classification? 111
What are the various types of data classification? 111
Difficulties with data classification 112
Effects of compliance standards on data classification 112
Data classification levels 113
Developing a policy for data classification 114
Data classification procedures 115
ISO 27001 controls 116
Control Category A.5 – Information Security Policies (1 objective and 2 controls) 116

Control Category A.6 – Organization of Information Security (2 objectives and 7 controls) 117
Control Category A.7 – Human Resource Security (3 objectives and 6 controls) 117
Control Category A.8 – Asset Management (3 objectives and 10 controls) 117
Control Category A.9 – Access Control (4 objectives and 14 controls) 118
Control Category A.10 – Cryptography (1 objective and 2 controls) 118
Control Category A.11 – Physical and Environmental Security (2 objectives and 15 controls) 119
Control Category A.12 – Operations Security (7 objectives and 14 controls) 119
Control Category A.13 – Communications Security (2 objectives and 7 controls) 120
Control Category A.14 – System Acquisition, Development, and Maintenance (3 objectives and 13 controls) 121
Control Category A.15 – Supplier relationships (2 objectives and 5 controls) 122
Control Category A.16 – Information security incident management (1 objective and 7 controls) 122
Control Category A.17 – Information security aspects of business continuity management (2 objectives and 4 controls) 123
Control Category A.18 – Compliance (2 objectives and 8 controls) 123
Who is charged for implementing Annex A controls? 124
Using the ISO 27001 controls 125
Identification of ISO 27001 controls to implement 125

Summary 125

8

Preparing Policies and Procedures to Avoid Internal Risk 127

Company policies 127

How do you determine the appropriate policies for your business? 128

Policy writing instructions 129

What about procedures, then? 130
The importance of policies and procedures versus their pain 130
How to physically write a policy? 132
Selecting a method for managing the process 133
Establishing a policy management group 133
Prioritizing a policy list 133
Creating a preliminary draft 134
Verifying the processes 134
Sending a draft out for review 134
Obtaining final approval and signatures 135
Employee Code of Conduct example draft 135
Template for the Employee Code of Conduct 135
Cloud hosting policy 141

Company procedures 144

When is a procedure necessary? 145
When a process requires a procedure 145
How to write a procedure 146
Step 1: gathering information 146
Step 2: beginning to write 147
Step 3: evaluating design elements 147

Summary 149

9

Social Engineering, Password Guidance, and Policy 151

The starting point 151
OSINT 152
Social scientist 152

Common social engineering attack methods 152
Pretexting 152
Misdirection theft 153
Phishing 153
Targeted phishing 153
Vishing 154
Smishing 156

Have you got a M.A.P.P.? 158
Step 1 – learn how to recognize social engineering attacks 158
Step 2 – develop realistic and implementable policies 159
Step 3 – conduct periodic real-world audits 161
Step 4 – implement applicable security awareness programs 162

Summary 162

10

The Cloud 163

How did the cloud emerge? 163
What exactly is the cloud? How does it work? 164
What is cloud security? 164
Types of cloud services 165
Distribution models 165
Cloud security – examples of measures that can prevent risks 166

The seven pain points of cloud computing 166
Reduced visibility 167
Compliance violations 167
Absence of a strategy and architecture for cloud security 167
Internal threats 167
Contractual violations 168
Unprotected user interface (API) 168
Errors in the configuration of cloud services 168

Cloud and GDPR concerns 168
Security concerns specific to the cloud 169
What effect is GDPR having on the cloud industry? 169
Requirements for cloud service providers under GDPR 169
Normative requirements 170

The GDPR code of conduct for CSPs 172

Summary 173

11

What about the US? 175

The US status of privacy 175
What the current national privacy laws (don't) do 176
The FTC 178
An overview of Section 5 of the FTC Act 179
NIST and FTC 179
BYOD 180
Benefits of BYOD 181
Disadvantages of BYOD 181
Managing mobile devices 181
Criteria and recommendations 182
Remote working 182
Security issues 183
Important ramifications 183
Keeping a remote workforce secure 183
A multifaceted strategy 184
Assisting the transformation 185
Computer safety 185
What privacy rights are available to employees? 186
What exemptions exist to worker monitoring? 186
Do employees know what information employers can access? 186
Should employees bring personal equipment to work? 187
Summary 187

Appendix 189

ISO 27002 189
What is different? 190
Is it superior to the previous version? 190
Is it a standard set of controls for information security? 191
What must you do at this time? 192
Privacy 193
VA/PT 194
VA 194
PT 196

Index 201

Other Books You May Enjoy 210

Preface

Focusing on evolving frameworks? This book helps you to implement a fully working cybersecurity and privacy program to safeguard your company from hackers and malicious attacks.

Who this book is for

If you are a seasoned manager who wants to see how external cybersecurity consulting impacts your company's profits, or a novice willing to learn how to deal with cybersecurity and privacy smoothly, this book's for you.

What this book covers

Chapter 1, ISO27001 – Definitions and Security Concepts, describes in a clear and understandable way the 27k family of standards, confidentiality, integrity and availability, information security concepts and definitions, governance, policies, incident management, and differences within **NIST**, the **National Institute of Standards and Technology**.

Chapter 2, Mandatory Requirements, explores iSMS, information security management system, controls, commitment, context, scope policy, and objectives of the ISO 27001 and NIST framework.

Chapter 3, Data Protection, delves into the history of privacy, **General Data Protection Regulation** (**GDPR**), and other privacy laws, territorial scope, anonymous, pseudonymous, de-identified, and aggregated data, legal basis (or justification) for data processing, data access privileges, and fines, the six principles of GDPR, and, finally, why we have to deal with data protection.

Chapter 4, Data Processing, discusses the roles involved in data processing, looking at data controllers, data processors, accountability, privacy dashboards, a **Data Protection Impact Analysis** (**DPIA**), treatment register, the EU-US Privacy Shield, and Schrems II.

Chapter 5, Security Planning and Risk Management, focuses on risk management. We will understand what the security threats and challenges are, the various security threats, how to implement a risk management program, the differences between traditional risk management and enterprise risk management, and why risk management is so important.

Chapter 6, Define ISO 27001 Mandatory Requirements, dives deep into the ISO 27001 framework and its Annex A controls, with all the clauses within the ISO program.

Chapter 7, Risk Management, Controls and Policies, looks at how risk management interacts with controls and policies. We will be focusing on risk heat maps and risk mitigation techniques. Then, we'll deep dive data classification and policies.

Chapter 8, Preparing Policies and Procedures to Avoid Internal Risk, discusses how to write policies and procedures in a corporate way.

Chapter 9, Social Engineering, Password Guidance, and Policy, reveals the most important social engineering attempts to steal your credentials and how to avoid them by using complex password management.

Chapter 10, The Cloud, deals with the cloud, from the basics to how it works now, in our quest for frameworks and privacy processes.

Chapter 11, What About the US?, discusses social engineering, password guidance, and privacy policies in the US, including local and national laws and bills. We'll also be taking a glance at the privacy side of phenomena such as **Bring Your Own Device** (**BYOD**) and remote working.

Appendix, explains how security, privacy and pandemic are changing our lives

To get the most out of this book

I recommend obtaining a copy of the following standards/frameworks/privacy laws:

- ISO 27001 standard: `https://www.iso.org/standard/54534.html`
- NIST Framework: `https://www.nist.gov/cyberframework`
- GDPR: `https://gdpr.eu/`
- **Lei Geral de Proteção de Dados** (**LGPD**), Brasilian data protection law: `https://www.gov.br/cidadania/pt-br/acesso-a-informacao/lgpd`
- CCPA: `https://oag.ca.gov/privacy/ccpa`
- CPRA: `https://thecpra.org/`

Download the color images

We also provide a PDF file that has color images of the screenshots and diagrams used in this book. You can download it here: `https://packt.link/elBjz`.

Conventions used

There are a number of text conventions used throughout this book.

> **Tips or important notes**
> Appear like this.

Get in touch

Feedback from our readers is always welcome.

General feedback: If you have questions about any aspect of this book, email us at `customercare@packtpub.com` and mention the book title in the subject of your message.

Errata: Although we have taken every care to ensure the accuracy of our content, mistakes do happen. If you have found a mistake in this book, we would be grateful if you would report this to us. Please visit `www.packtpub.com/support/errata` and fill in the form.

Piracy: If you come across any illegal copies of our works in any form on the internet, we would be grateful if you would provide us with the location address or website name. Please contact us at `copyright@packt.com` with a link to the material.

If you are interested in becoming an author: If there is a topic that you have expertise in and you are interested in either writing or contributing to a book, please visit `authors.packtpub.com`.

Share Your Thoughts

Once you've read *Cybersecurity and Privacy Law Handbook*, we'd love to hear your thoughts! Scan the QR code below to go straight to the Amazon review page for this book and share your feedback.

`https://packt.link/r/1-803-24241-8`

Your review is important to us and the tech community and will help us make sure we're delivering excellent quality content.

Download a free PDF copy of this book

Thanks for purchasing this book!

Do you like to read on the go but are unable to carry your print books everywhere? Is your eBook purchase not compatible with the device of your choice?

Don't worry, now with every Packt book you get a DRM-free PDF version of that book at no cost.

Read anywhere, any place, on any device. Search, copy, and paste code from your favorite technical books directly into your application.

The perks don't stop there, you can get exclusive access to discounts, newsletters, and great free content in your inbox daily

Follow these simple steps to get the benefits:

1. Scan the QR code or visit the link below

   `https://packt.link/free-ebook/9781803242415`

2. Submit your proof of purchase
3. That's it! We'll send your free PDF and other benefits to your email directly

Part 1: Start From the Basics

In this section of the book, you will come to understand how the company perimeter has changed and how it is important that security and privacy reflect those changes.

This part of the book comprises the following chapter:

- *Chapter 1, ISO27001 – Definitions and Security Concepts*

1

ISO27001 – Definitions and Security Concepts

My aim in writing this book is providing you a comfortable way to understand and enhance the cybersecurity and privacy within your entity. Of course this book is not targeted at seasoned experts in ISO27001 implementation; moreover, when I planned it, my *targets* were managers that know almost nothing about cybersecurity and privacy but want to improve company security, even using third-party consulting (and therefore wanting to know whether the external service is wasting internal budget), or novices that, for some reason, have to deal with IT security in a smoooth way.

It's a long trip, although I will try my best to help you digest an enormous amount of information in a short, agile book. I hope you find it interesting and forgive those mistakes that, unfortunately, will appear no matter how many corrections I make.

Since it's a long trip, I suggest you prepare by putting on a pair of comfortable slippers and making a huge cup of coffee (or tea, as you wish), and sit down and relax.

In this chapter, we will cover the following topics:

- The 27k family of standards
- Confidentiality, integrity, and availability
- Information security concepts and definitions
- Governance, policies, and incident management
- Differences of NIST

The 27k family of standards

There's more than walls and fences, if any, to protect in your company. Let's suppose your company has developed a new product. This product can guarantee a nine-figure income for at least the next decade. So, what's the most important asset of your company?

One of your company's most significant assets is information.

As you continue to read this book, this sentence will soon become your mantra. Ensuring the confidentiality, integrity, and availability of information is the goal of information security. These fundamental information security factors aid in ensuring that an entity's data is secure. So, getting back to your product, what does your company need to defend itself from?

The main pain points are the following:

- The leakage or disclosure of sensitive or confidential information, exposed either by accident or design
- The compromise of personally identifiable information
- Critical information being tampered with, either by mistake or on purpose, without the knowledge of the entity
- Critical corporate data disappearing without a trace or the possibility of recovery
- The unavailability of critical business information when it is required

The preceding statements lead us to a couple of valuable mantras about information:

Everyone within the company should be responsible for the information system, and they must do their best to ensure that their information is secure.

A human being is always the weakest link of the security chain.

Let's put it simply: everyone within the company needs to understand and help out to improve the security posture, and often, just following the company policies and procedures (or even using common sense) will vastly improve the standard security. For instance, just adopting and respecting a *clean desk policy* may prevent the cleaning staff from viewing unauthorized documents (and we don't know whether the cleaning staff is somehow ready to sell our company and/or private information – insiders can wear any kind of hat).

Let's see another example: your company spends thousands of dollars on implementing privacy screens (privacy filters designed for computer users to keep their private and confidential information safe). But if you leave your laptop unattended, then they are completely useless.

Information is adequately maintained and safeguarded against several threats.

Every entity can be at risk of data leakage by different means, and if a company wants to improve its security standards, it feels the need to improve those. The vast majority of companies (at least in Europe) use so-called frameworks (such as ISO 27001/27002, NIST, etc.) simply because they're ready to apply and use. More specifically, in regard to European entities, by implementing ISO 27001, you are also implementing things such as **General Data Protection Regulation** (**GDPR**, aka the European privacy law) and security over the cloud. Basically, you're killing three birds with one stone.

The following ISOs give us a foundation to establish an effective information management system:

- Information security management systems – ISO/IEC 27001:2017
- Security approaches – Requirements and ISO/IEC 27002:2022

While ISO 27001 has been prepared to provide requirements for establishing, implementing, maintaining, and continually improving an information security management system, ISO27002 is designed for organizations of all types and sizes. It is to be used as a reference for determining and implementing controls for information security risk treatment in an **information security management system (ISMS)** based on ISO/IEC 27001

Born as an independent, non-governmental entity, the **International Organization for Standardization (ISO)** comprises the national standards bodies from the 165 countries that make up its membership. There are more than 1,500 voluntary international standards developed by ISO.

According to Wikipedia:

> *More than 20,000 standards have been established, encompassing everything from manufactured goods and technology to food safety, agriculture, and healthcare services. ISO is a voluntary entity whose members are recognized authorities on standards, each one representing one country. Members meet annually at a General Assembly to discuss the strategic objectives of ISO. The entity is coordinated by a central secretariat based in Geneva.*
>
> *A council with a rotating membership of 20 member bodies provides guidance and governance, including setting the annual budget of the central secretariat.*
>
> *The technical management board is responsible for more than 250 technical committees, who develop the ISO standards.*

Products and services of high quality can be produced by adhering to the standards. Using the standards, businesses can boost productivity while reducing waste and errors. Comparing products from different markets makes it easier for businesses to expand into new markets and helps global trade develop on an equal footing. The standards also protect consumers and end users of products and services by ensuring that certified products meet international minimum standards.

Since we are interested in the information security side of ISO, let's set aside what's irrelevant to our scope.

The ISO/IEC 27001 requirements for approved third-party **Information Security Management System (ISMS)** certifications can be applied to third-party accreditations of ISMSs. ISMS audits are conducted by accredited certification bodies as part of the accreditation process. With the help of ISO/IEC 27001, they can be confident that their management systems and procedures comply.

ISO/IEC 27002, a guidance document, provides information security best practices and implementation guidance. As part of the risk management process, ISO/IEC 27001-compliant entities can use these controls to protect their information assets.

Confidentiality, integrity, and availability

One of the main components of ISO 27k is something called the CIA triad (of course, this has nothing to do with either the Mafia and/or the US Central Intelligence Agency).

In information security, the CIA triad is widely accepted as a model. It's not a single doctrine, and there is no single author of it either. On the contrary, the model seems to have evolved over time, with roots that go back as far as modern computing. It appears that Ben Miller, vice president of Dragos, is the only one who has done any research into the triad's origins. When he went looking for the origins of this model, more than a decade ago, he couldn't find anything. Concepts appear to have been pulled from a variety of sources, including a 1976 Air Force report and a paper from the 1980s comparing commercial and military computer systems.

It's mostly based on a triangle made of confidentiality, integrity, and availability, which are the main pillars of IT security.

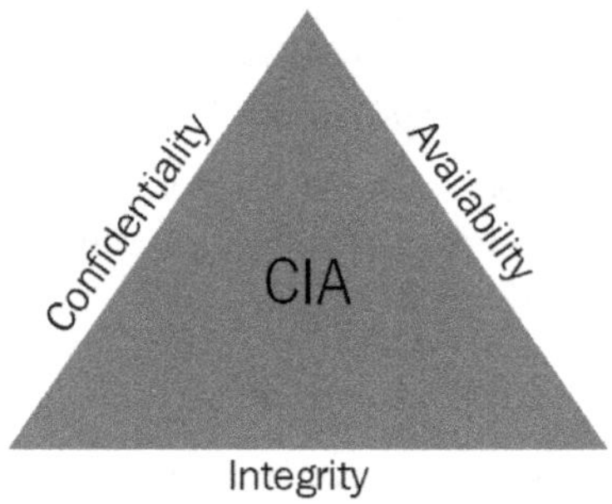

Figure 1.1 – CIA triad

Whatever the case may be, the CIA triad includes the following three elements:

- A company's data must be kept private to maintain **confidentiality**. This usually means that data should only be accessed or modified by processes and users who have been granted permission to do so.
- **Integrity** is the quality of being able to have confidence in one's data. An accurate and authentic record should be kept in a safe place where it cannot be changed or tampered with.
- Authorized users should be able to access data **at any time (availability)**, just as it is critical to keep unauthorized users out of an entity's data in the first place. Maintaining a stable network of computers, servers, and other devices is to be considered an integral part of availability.

Let's see an example to better understand these concepts.

You are sending an email to me because you'd like me to clarify some concepts you don't understand (probably because they were badly explained by me – who knows). While preparing the email, you also attach a document in which there's the part you don't understand. Finally, you send the email.

In this case, *confidentiality* means that you sent this email to me and to me only. Unless a third party was involved in our email exchange, this email is sent exclusively to me.

If you send me a message with a few words, including *Dear Mr.*, some sort of body text, some salutation at the end, and an attachment, I will receive exactly that message body and that attachment (this is *integrity*; if we want, we can measure the number of kilobytes used to send that message and you can bet that the body text and attachment are the same size).

Finally, we can log in to an email server at any time, 24/7, using our email client, and check whether there are new messages: that's *availability*.

But, of course, this is just an example of how to adopt the CIA triad.

Access control methods such as two-factor authentication and passwordless sign-on are examples of confidentiality. However, it's not just about allowing authorized users access; it's also about preventing certain files from being accessed. Both accidental disclosure and malicious attacks can be prevented by using encryption.

Access control and encryption can help maintain data integrity, but there are many other ways to protect data integrity, both from attacks and corruption. It can be as simple as making a file read-only at times. In some cases, data can be audited using hashing or data checksums, which ensure the integrity of the data. In some cases, the integrity of a system may be shielded from external influences.

Availability refers to the ability of your systems to remain operational in the event of an attack. **Distributed Denial of Service** (**DDoS**) attacks, for example, are based on a lack of resources. You can ensure uptime by building redundancy into your systems to combat DDoS attacks. In the absence of an attack, systems can still fail and become unavailable, so load balancing and fault tolerance can be used to prevent systems from failing.

It is important for security professionals of all kinds to understand these concepts. For information security professionals, the triad of these three concepts makes it easier to think about the interrelationships, overlaps, and conflicts between them. Security professionals can use the tension between the triad's three legs to determine their information security priorities and procedures.

Information security concepts and definitions

Other best practices to remember are as follows:

- *Know thy system.*

  Knowing the system is perhaps the most critical factor when attempting to defend it. It makes no difference whether you're protecting a castle or a Linux server if you don't understand the intricacies of what you're defending.

  Knowledge of what software is running on your systems is an excellent illustration of this in the area of information security. What daemons do you have running? What kind of exposure do they generate? A decent self-test for someone in a small- to medium-sized environment would be to choose an IP address at random from a list of your systems and see whether you can recall the precise list of ports that are open on the computers.

  "*It's a web server, therefore everything's just running on ports 80, 443, and 22 for remote management; that's it,*" a skilled administrator should be able to say—and so on for each sort of server in the ecosystem. When seeing port scan findings, there should be no surprises.

  In this kind of test, you don't want to hear, "*Wow, what's that port?*" Having to ask that question indicates that the system administrator is not entirely aware of everything operating on the computer in question, which is exactly what we want to prevent.

- *The least privilege*

  The next crucial principle is that of least privilege. Least privilege simply states that people and objects should be able to do only what they need to do their tasks. I include these kind of examples because administrators frequently configure automatic processes that must be able to perform specific activities, such as backups. What usually occurs is that the administrator adds the user performing the backup to the domain admins group, even if they could get it to function in another way. Why? Because it is less difficult.

  Finally, this is a philosophy that is intended to directly contradict human nature, namely laziness. It is always more difficult to grant granular access that allows only specified tasks than it is to grant a higher level of access that covers everything that needs to be done.

  This rule of least privilege just reminds us not to succumb to this temptation. Don't back down. Take the time to make all access as granular and as minimal as feasible.

- *Defense in depth*

  Defense in depth is likely the least understood of the four concepts. Many people believe that it is as simple as stacking three firewalls instead of one or running two antivirus applications instead of one. This is technically correct, but it is not the fundamental nature of defense in depth.

The true concept is to build various types of protection between an attacker and an asset. These layers don't even have to be products; they might be applications of other notions, such as least privilege.

Consider an attacker on the internet attempting to breach a web server in the **Demilitarized Zone** (**DMZ**; basically a physical or logical subnetwork that contains and exposes an entity's external-facing services). Given a huge vulnerability, this may be quite simple, but with an infrastructure utilizing defense in depth, it may be substantially more difficult.

We need to take into consideration activities such as hardening (appliances such as routers, firewalls, IPDs/IDSs, and target hosts) and widely implementing antivirus and antimalware—any of these procedures can potentially prevent an attack from being totally or partially successful. The notion is that instead of thinking about what has to be put in place to stop an attack, we should think about what needs to happen for it to be successful. Perhaps an assault had to pass via network infrastructures to get to the host, execute, build an outbound connection to a host outside, download stuff, run it, and so on.

What if any of those steps were to fail? The key to defense in depth is to place barriers at as many sites as possible. Our aim is to try to make it so that it's hard for potential intruders to get into our network. By using this kind of approach, it will be difficult for hostile code to run on your systems, run your daemons and/or services as the least-privileged user, and so forth.

The advantage is straightforward: you have more chances to prevent an attack from succeeding. Someone may go all the way in, all the way to the box in question, and be stopped by the fact that the malicious code would not run on the host. However, once that code is modified so that it may run, it may be detected by an upgraded IPS or a more stringent firewall ACL. The goal is to secure whatever you can at every stage. Secure everything—file permissions, stack protection, ACLs, host IPSs, limiting admin access, running as limited users; the list is endless.

The core premise is also straightforward: don't rely on a single solution to protect your assets. Consider each layer of your defense as though it were the only one. When you follow this method, you have a better chance of stopping attacks before they reach their aim.

Also, in IT security (and ISO 27001 itself, which is a framework that is continuously improving), new concepts are arising on almost a yearly basis, and one of the most interesting concepts around is called zero trust.

Conventional security models are based on perimeter security. In practice, the protection of the corporate ecosystem trusts all traffic and action flowing within the perimeter.

The zero trust approach, on the other hand, is designed to address even all those so-called lateral threats that move through networks. How? By exploiting an approach linked to microsegmentation and the definition of granular perimeters, based on users, data, and their location.

- *Prevention is preferable, but detection is required.*

  This is a basic concept, yet it is incredibly significant. The concept is that while it is preferable to stop an attack before it is successful, if it is, it is critical that you are aware that it occurred. For example, you may have safeguards in place to prevent code from being executed on your system, but if code is executed and something is done, it is vital that you are notified and can act immediately.

  The difference between learning about a successful attack within 5 or 10 minutes and learning about it weeks later is enormous. Having the knowledge early enough can often result in the attack not being successful at all; for example, the attacker may get on your box and add a user account, but you get to the machine and take it offline before they can do anything with it.

  Regardless of the situation, detection is critical because there is no guarantee that your prevention actions will be effective.

Other remarkable best practices are as follows:

- *Protection and utility must be balanced.*

  Computers in a workplace could be entirely safeguarded if all networks were destroyed and everyone was thrown out—but then they would be of no use to anyone.

- *Determine your vulnerabilities and make a plan.*

  Not all of your resources are equally valuable. Some data is more vital than others, such as a database holding all accounting information on your clients, such as bank IDs, social security numbers, addresses, and other personal information (we'll talk about privacy later). Identifying what data is more sensitive and/or significant will assist you in determining the level of protection required to safeguard it and designing your security tactics accordingly.

- *Use uncorrelated defenses.*

  Using a single strong protection mechanism, such as authentication protocols, is only effective until it is breached. When numerous layers of separate defenses are used, an attacker must apply a variety of tactics to get past them.

  Because the causes of breaches aren't always obvious after the fact, it's critical to have data to track backward. Even if it doesn't make sense at first, data from breaches will eventually help to improve the system and prevent future attacks.

- *Run frequent tests.*

  Hackers are constantly honing their skills, so information security must evolve to keep up. IT professionals should run tests, conduct risk assessments, reread the disaster recovery plan, double-check the business continuity plan in the event of an attack, and then repeat the process.

- *The bottom line.*

  IT security is a difficult job that requires both attention to detail and a high level of awareness. However, like many seemingly complex tasks, IT security can be broken down into basic steps that can simplify the process. That's not to say it's easy, but it keeps IT professionals on their toes.

So, while we have seen some ways to improve your security posture, I am afraid to tell you that we have only scratched the tip of a huge iceberg. Although hardening is a very important topic and everyone dealing with security should at least understand these basic concepts, an entity is a bit more than a document with a plethora of *how-tos*.

An entity is the sum of many elements: core values, community, respect and many more, but also ethics, risk management, compliance, and administration, which form the governance of a company.

Governance, policies, and incident management

We are going to talk about what makes an entity (or company, association, or whatever you want to call it).

Governance

We can define corporate governance as "*a toolkit that enables management and the board to deal more effectively with the challenges of running a company. Corporate governance ensures that businesses have appropriate decision-making processes and controls in place so that the interests of all stakeholders are balanced.*" (This definition is taken from `https://www.itgovernance.co.uk/`.)

A strong corporate governance framework can assist you in meeting the requirements of laws and regulations such as GDPR, that is, the European privacy law.

GDPR, for example, requires data controllers and processors to verify compliance with its standards through specific documentation, such as applicable logs, rules, and procedures.

Throughout this book, I will use examples from GDPR, although there are several other legislations around, such as LGPD (the Brazilian privacy law) or CCPA from California, and many more about to come. But GDPR is, with the *UK variant*, an umbrella for roughly 400 million people in 28 countries and therefore, the most popular.

Using IT governance aspects will assist you in creating and maintaining proper policies and procedures to help satisfy your data privacy obligations.

IT governance is a component of corporate governance that aims to improve overall IT management and get more value from investments in information and technology.

IT governance frameworks have the following functions:

- Assisting entities in efficiently managing their IT risks and ensuring that information and technology operations are aligned with their overall business objectives
- Showing demonstrable achievements in relation to broader business plans and goals
- Complying with applicable legal and regulatory duties, such as those outlined in GDPR
- Assuring stakeholders that your entity's IT services are trustworthy
- Facilitating a higher return on IT investment
- Following any business governance or public listing guidelines or procedures

According to ISACA (`https://www.isaca.org`), we can break IT governance (ISO 38500) into five different domains:

- Value delivery
- Strategic alignment
- Performance management
- Resource management
- Risk management

Consider that there are several frameworks and methodologies to comply with IT governance, such as ISO 27001, NIST, ISO 27000 (aka ITIL), COBIT, ISO 31000, ISO 38500, and ISO 22301. Since we are dealing with a security compliance framework, it would be better to stick to the most popular, that is, ISO27001 and NIST, alongside ISO 27701 (privacy framework).

Policies and procedures

Policies and procedures are the documents that describe how your business is run in the information security industry.

A policy is a set of rules or guidelines that your entity and its employees must follow in order to comply:

- Policies provide answers to the questions of what employees do and why they do it
- A procedure is a set of instructions for implementing a policy

So, what exactly is a policy?

A policy is defined as a set of rules or guidelines that your entity and employees must follow in order to achieve a specific goal (i.e., compliance).

What is the function of a policy?

An effective policy should outline what employees must and must not do, as well as directions, principles, and decision-making guidance. It should answer the questions *What?* and *Why?*. Both are related to the meaning of a policy and it's important to understand what a policy is and why it is needed.

What exactly is a procedure?

A procedure is the inverse of a policy; it is the instructions on how to implement a policy:

- It is the step-by-step guide for implementing policies, outlined previously
- A policy defines a rule and a procedure defines who is expected to do what and how
- Procedures provide answers to questions such as *how*, *when*, and *where*

What is the importance of documented policies, procedures, and protocols?

Too many businesses regard policies and procedures as a necessary evil, failing to consider their purpose. It's not about following best practices or becoming a soulless corporate entity; the goal of policies and procedures is to explain what management wants to happen and how it will happen.

I've come to believe that the primary difference between a small and medium business is not found in quantifying a company's maturity by revenue or employee count, but rather in whether or not management has taken the time to develop, implement, and maintain policies and procedures.

So far, this definition has not disappointed me; companies with mature policies, procedures, and systems are easier to audit, have a better understanding of their security posture and risk, and appear to be operating far more sustainably than those that haven't paid much attention to governance.

Objections about policies and procedures

Once management understands the definitions of policies and procedures, they will no longer ask, "*What are policies and procedures?*" or "*What is the purpose of a policy?*" and instead proceed to ask, "*Why do I have to write policies and procedures?*"

Management in small businesses generally has the same set of objections to writing down a set of policies and procedures, all of which are related to difficulty, company culture, and time constraints. But keep in mind that the benefits outweigh the inconvenience of policies and procedures. The goal of policies and procedures is much more than simply writing down some rules.

It's difficult to create policies and procedures.

But it's extremely difficult! Yes, but also no. Most businesses that do not have mature policies and procedures are doing fairly well; otherwise, they would not be in business. It's certainly easier to define security from the start, but that doesn't mean it can't be simple to start with what you're doing now and refine it later.

Sometimes, the real objection isn't how difficult it is to write down policies and procedures, but how afraid most people are of writing down how they're doing things incorrectly. Begin with where you are, and then be realistic about where you want to go. You may not be keeping up with best practices in some areas, but if you let embarrassment keep you from putting policies in writing, you're missing the point. Knowing exactly what you're doing now allows you to determine what you should be doing tomorrow. It's how you can create a real budget, identify real enterprise risks, and respond effectively when something goes wrong.

But no worries, we'll deep dive into these things later.

Incident management

The goal of the incident management procedure is to restore normal service operation as soon as possible and to minimize the negative effect on business activities while maintaining agreed-upon standards of service quality. The incident management process's goals are to do the following:

- Ensure that standardized processes and procedures are utilized for effective and timely incident response, analysis, recording, continuous improvement and reporting
- Increase incident visibility and communication to business and IT support personnel
- Improve the business view of IT by taking a professional approach to addressing and communicating problems as they might arise
- Align incident management efforts and priorities with business priorities
- Maintain satisfaction among users with IT service quality

So, we conclude a very rapid journey on the essential topics concerning governance. Let's move on to an interesting topic, differences of NIST.

Differences between ISO 27001 and NIST

As it has fewer controls to implement, and since there's no control over it (NIST doesn't have a certification scheme), NIST is considered somewhat less mature; also, as it is backed by the US government and not an international committee, it is not considered much outside the US. But if you like plain instructions and don't want to spend a fortune, at least in the beginning, it can be a good idea to use NIST. Finally, it is possible to get *the best of both worlds* by implementing both at the same time.

What's NIST?

The **National Institute of Standards and Technology** (NIST) is a non-regulatory US government agency founded in 1901 that develops technology, standards, and metrics to drive innovation in the US science and technology sectors. NIST is headquartered in Gaithersburg, Maryland.

NIST publishes the Special Publication 800 series, which contains guidance documents and recommendations. As part of the previous series, they released Special Publication 800-53, which catalogs 20 security and privacy control groups. NIST recommends that entities implement these security and privacy controls as part of their risk management strategies. These controls cover access control, security awareness training, incident response plans, risk assessments, and continuous monitoring.

The NIST compliance framework was developed to provide a customizable guide for entities on how to manage and reduce cybersecurity-related risks. In its guide, NIST combines existing standards, guidelines, and best practices. However, it is critical to understand that simply adhering to NIST guidelines will not make your entity 100% secure, which is why the NIST guidelines begin by instructing entities to use a value-based approach to protect their assets.

The NIST **Cybersecurity Framework** (**CSF**) is a voluntary (recommended by the Department of Commerce) cybersecurity framework that allows businesses to develop information security, risk management, and control programs. NIST standards are now used in fields ranging from nanotechnology to cybersecurity. Through an executive order in 2013, NIST was tasked with developing a cybersecurity framework, and in February 2014, it published version 1.0 of the Framework for Improving Critical Infrastructure Cybersecurity. Version 1.1 was released to the public in April 2018.

The CSF is one of NIST's voluntary programs that is based on existing standards and guidelines and is designed to assist entities in better managing and reducing cybersecurity risk. The CSF is presented in a 48-page document that details various cybersecurity activities and desired outcomes that entities can use to assess their cybersecurity risk, risk maturity, and information security infrastructure.

What is the purpose of the NIST CSF?

The CSF has three major components, the framework core, implementation tiers, and profiles, all of which are designed to help you benchmark your entity's risk maturity and prioritize actions to improve it.

At its *core*, it has five functions: identify, protect, detect, respond, and recover.

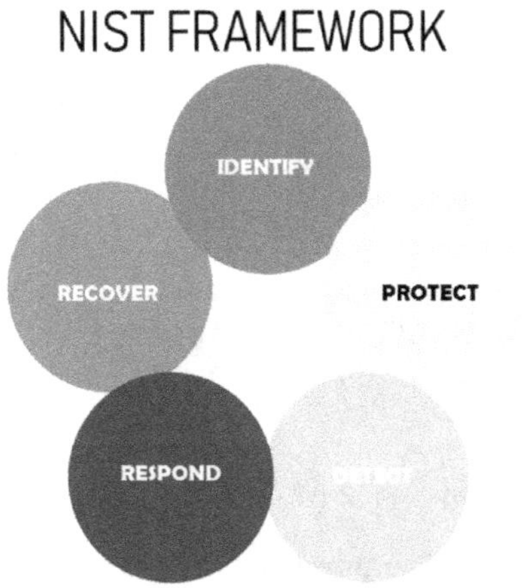

Figure 1.2 – The five functions, NIST

While the CSF focuses on cybersecurity issues, these activities are common in most risk management systems. The functions are further subdivided into 23 categories that cover the fundamentals of putting together a cybersecurity program.

The CSF has implementation tiers. For each of these five functions, the NIST CSF employs a ranking system on a scale of 0-4 to generate a final number that can be used to benchmark an entity's level of risk maturity.

A profile, which is based on a tier, allows an entity to pinpoint its current level of risk tolerance and prioritize security controls and risk mitigation tactics. This section is intended to assist an entity in growing by comparing its current profile to target profiles, thereby assisting you in determining how to allocate budget and employee resources to improve cybersecurity practices over time.

What are the parallels between ISO and NIST?

When comparing NIST CSF and ISO 27001, both provide strong frameworks for cybersecurity risk management. It would be simple to integrate ISO 27001 standards and NIST CSF into a company that wants to become ISO 27001 compliant. Their control measures are comparable, and their definitions and code are fairly interchangeable across frameworks. Both frameworks provide simple vocabulary, which enables clear communication about cybersecurity issues across multidisciplinary teams and with external stakeholders.

What's the distinction between ISO and NIST?

There are a few key differences between NIST CSF and ISO 27001, including risk maturity, certification, and cost.

Risk maturity

ISO 27001 is a good choice for operationally mature entities seeking certification, whereas the NIST CSF may be best for entities in the early stages of developing a cybersecurity risk management plan or attempting to mitigate previous failures or data breaches.

ISO 27001 certification provides globally recognized certification through third-party auditing, which can be costly but can improve your entity's reputation as a business that stakeholders can rely on. The NIST CSF does not provide such certification.

Cost

The NIST CSF is free to use, whereas ISO 27001 requires a fee to access the documentation—another reason why a start-up might want to start with the NIST CSF and then make a larger investment in the process as it scales with ISO 27001.

NIST versus ISO – which is better for my company?

Finally, what is best for your company is determined by its maturity, goals, and specific risk management requirements. ISO 27001 is an excellent choice for operationally mature entities that are under external certification pressure. However, you may not be ready to embark on an ISO 27001 certification journey just yet, or your entity may be at a stage where it would benefit from the NIST CSF's clear assessment framework. A NIST audit can provide you with an idea of where your entity stands before developing and implementing more stringent cybersecurity measures and controls.

As your entity matures, the two frameworks can be integrated—following the NIST CSF can be a useful precursor to your ISO 27001 certification journey. The NIST CSF provides a framework for growing entities to structure their **Information Security** (**IS**) risk assessments. If you already have these structures in place, you may want to pursue ISO security and compliance certifications. A proactive and efficient ISMS benefits from the right software, whether you're starting with NIST CSF or growing with ISO 27001.

Summary

In this chapter, we spent some (hopefully useful) time understanding the basics of cybersecurity. We had a walk-through of ISO 27001 and 27002, then we discussed the definition of the CIA triad, alongside the definition of confidentiality, integrity, and availability, using some examples to better understand these concepts. Then, we had a look at information security concepts and definitions. We had a glance at governance, policies, and incident management. Then, we moved on to the NIST CSF and how ISO 27001 and NIST can be used at once.

In the next chapter, we will talk about ISMS, commitment, project management, context, scope policy, and objectives. We will look at how to identify, protect, detect, respond, and recover and ponder the question can ISO27001nd NIST coexist?

Part 2: Into the Wild

In this part, you will come to understand ISO 27001 and data protection.

This part of the book comprises the following chapters:

- *Chapter 2, Mandatory Requirements*
- *Chapter 3, Data Protection*
- *Chapter 4, Data Processing*
- *Chapter 5, Security Planning and Risk Management*

2

Mandatory Requirements

In the previous chapter, we spent some time learning what frameworks are and how we can use them to populate these frames (ISO 27001, NIST and so on)

In this chapter, if you were brave enough to follow me through all those acronyms and *uncommon* wording, you are probably eager to find out what's next. We will spend the next pages learning how ISO 27001 works in the real world, then we will do the same for the NIST framework, and finally, we will see whether ISO 27001 and NIST can coexist.

In this chapter, we will cover the following topics:

- iSMS, controls, commitment, context, scope policy, and objectives
- Identify, Protect, Detect, Respond, and Recover
- Can ISO 27001 and NIST coexist?

iSMS, controls, commitment, context, scope policy, and objectives

Let's try to understand what an iSMS is and how to deal with it.

iSMS

You might not have heard the word iSMS.

It isn't very common outside of **Governance, Risk management, Compliance** (**GRC**) nerd slang, but if you want to be part of the club, you should refer to the **information Security Management System,** or, for short, the iSMS. If your company has implemented (or is on its way to implementing) a risk-based information security management policy, be sure that it was (or it will be) done by using an iSMS, to ensure things are standardized.

The main advantage is that such a system facilitates compliance with several regulations, including the **General Data Protection Regulation** (**GDPR**), and focuses on the three critical components we have already seen: *confidentiality*, *integrity*, and *availability*. For the sake of correctness, we should add *non-repudiation* (you cannot pretend you haven't received an email, for instance) and *reliability* (the system, being healthy, has to be reliable too). At some point, NIST introduced the concept of *authenticity*, which is the property of being genuine and being able to be verified and trusted; but, although correct, it introduces a highly debated topic. I am referring to the *old* problem of digital copies, where the main question is: can a digital copy (for instance, a PDF file) be considered the original one or a *real copy*? When you and another person fill in a form either in a private or public environment, which one is seen as the original one? Is any of them to be seen as the original one? Is the *master*, the file originating all the copies, to be seen as authentic, even though the *copies* are 100% the same? This has been an ongoing debate within the IT security community for ages, and there is no *final answer*.

The proliferation of increasingly complex, sophisticated, and global threats to this information and its systems, combined with the compliance requirements of a flood of computer- and privacy-related regulations around the world, is compelling organizations to take a more integrated approach to information security. Individual information security concerns no longer require hardware-, software-, or vendor-driven solutions.

They are, in fact, catastrophically insufficient on their own.

News headlines about hackers, malware, and online fraud are only the tip of the iceberg when it comes to data security. Corporate losses caused by computer breakdown, large interruptions to their data and operating systems, or theft or loss of intellectual property or vital business data are more significant and costly.

The practical upshot of the previously mentioned strategy is an iSMS. Smaller businesses are unlikely to refer to it as such, but it is still an iSMS. At its core, this is nothing more than a collection of controls that minimize the risks that an organization has opted to *accept but control* to a level compatible with its control standard or risk acceptance criteria, as well as the framework within which those controls function. Every information management system for example, is an iSMS, but not one meant to be ISO27001 certified.

My suggestion is to post your iSMS documentation online, perhaps on the business intranet or a comparable common directory/shared location. This technique has various advantages:

- Anyone with access to a PC on the corporate LAN will be able to access the intranet and hence the iSMS documentation across the enterprise. Other departments can then not only read and refer to your resources but also hyperlink directly to them in their own rules, procedures, and so on. Basically, the idea is to integrate policies, procedures, and standards in a formal methodology, including those, if any, related to secure software development.
- The material may be nicely formatted and presented (for example, brief, easy-to-read summary/ intro pages hyperlinked to more thorough supporting pages providing the nitty gritty; embedded images such as process flow charts, mind maps... yeah, and security awareness stuff).

- Controlling the iSMS website is simpler than controlling printed/hardcopy iSMS papers, as long as someone has authority over what is put in the intranet iSMS section (implying some sort of change management process to review and publish stuff). Everyone should understand that the iSMS resources available on the intranet are the most recent, active versions. (You may want to create a distinct "trial" or "draft" section to expose suggested policy modifications for input, but make that area immediately identifiable as such, for example, with a different colored page backdrop and an obvious declaration that these are drafts, not the actual, live versions of your policies.)

However, there are two drawbacks:

- You must have the ability and tools necessary to create, produce, publish, and manage the website, or have easy access to someone who does.
- Because online pages don't normally print well, you may need to provide printable copies (e.g., PDFs) to download and print from the same websites that cover the format and kind of communication for items that people want to print and refer to, comment on, or whatever. You'll have to work on developing your writing style. While certain aspects of the iSMS must be defined (e.g., rules), others may be made more user-friendly (e.g., guidelines). It's totally OK to have some fun with security awareness items that are more creative, such as quizzes, crossword puzzles, seminars/workshops, and prize drawings. The goal is to pull people in and engage them by providing helpful, digestible material, rather than scaring them away with miles of impenetrable red tape.

Implementation tip

Having a uniform style/format for each sort of information, and even better, consistent components across all of them, helps to connect them into a cohesive, professional suite. Do you have an iSMS logo that you could use to "brand" your paperwork and other security awareness materials? Do you hire professional writers? Do they employ templates and styles on a regular basis?

Of course, you're not obliged to use them, but these kinds of actions can be easily recognized as part of a whole, in terms of management's commitment.

Statement of applicability, risk treatment plan, and action plan

Another list of acronyms? Yes, but these are really important.

A **Statement of Applicability** (**SoA**) is a document that states why you aren't compliant with all 18 annexes of ISO 27001. It is basically your formal specification of the ISO/IEC 27002 controls that are applicable to your iSMS. There must be some logic to your thinking in order to convince the auditors that significant choices were not taken randomly. Prepare for heated debate with them if you opt not to apply common controls or accept major risks.

It's very difficult to explain it without an example. Let's suppose your entity is within the retail industry. In this case, requirement A.15 (concerning supplier relationships) *must* be your top priority, as shown in the following table:

A.15		
Supplier relationships		
A.15.1 Information security in supplier relationships		
Objective: To ensure the protection of the organization's assets that are accessible by suppliers		
A.15.1.1	Information security policy for supplier relationships	Control
	Information security requirements for mitigating the risks associated with the supplier's access to the organization's assets shall be agreed upon with the supplier and documented.	
	Addressing security within supplier agreements	Control
A.15.1.2	All relevant information security requirements shall be established and agreed upon with each supplier that may access, process, store, communicate, or provide IT infrastructure components for the organization's information.	
	Information and communication technology supply chain	Control
A.15.1.3	Agreements with suppliers shall include requirements to address the information security risks associated with information and communications technology services and product supply chain.	

Table 2.1 – Example of control in supplier relationship (source: ISO 27001)

In the preceding example, we need to identify the *side* of security protection to implement when dealing with suppliers, either internal (I mean, part of the same company) or third party.

Don't worry about the jargon or the kind of generic information given; this is ISO, they would, of course, need to include as much information as possible. Remember, this is a framework and you are an individual deciding what you need into this framework, and you will decide on the subject and the author. But then don't complain if you aren't satisfied with your framework: it will be entirely your fault. The frame isn't the content. Therefore, if the framework chosen is not working somehow, it is not the framework to be blamed, but who decided to use it. So, furnish your frame in the best possible way, which doesn't mean using something more expensive or whatever: just in a more consistent way. It has to be reliable and ready to be used in many different ways, according to your needs and your environment. I'll get back to the framework later; the table was just meant to give you an idea of what to expect.

The **Action Plan** (**AP**) and **Risk Treatment Plan** (**RTP**) seem to be synonymous at first look; however, the AP is often a development or reduction of the RTP. The RTP methodically defines the controls required to handle each of the hazards identified in your risk assessment, while the AP (or program or project plans) states what you want to accomplish – who will do it, when, and how. A single control, particularly a baseline control such as physically guarding the organization's perimeter, may handle several risks and hence appear multiple times in the RTP but presumably just once in the AP when it is created, implemented, validated, and "operationalized" (a dreadful term!).

ISO/IEC 27000 should help clear up any residual ambiguity.

Don't get too caught up on document abbreviations and titles. Concentrate on their core goal of documenting the relationships between information risks, control goals, and controls.

From an *operational* point of view, the first thing we need to understand is the importance of an inventory of assets. In a few words, it's imperative to know and understand what is in our inventory to protect the assets from hostile activity, and they can be protected either manually or using software (needless to say in case of automatic software would avoid us forgetting things).

Controls

Controls are a combination of technological, procedural, and behavioral components that work together to achieve a specified, recognized, and recorded control goal. For example, your desktop user systems are under attack from a harmful combination of viruses, worms, Trojans, and spam, which will jeopardize the availability, confidentiality, and integrity of the data on your desktop. Email, online browsing, and instant messaging are the attack vectors. Among the controls would be the following:

- Anti-virus and anti-spyware software, anti-spam filters, firewalls, and automated updating are examples of technical advances
- Processes including software and firewall configuration, upgrading procedures, incident management procedures, and acceptable usage policies
- Behavioral – user awareness and training in dealing with these risks and techniques of reaction, such as identifying when malicious software attempts to download into a PC

This three-pronged approach is typical of all successful controls; implementing merely two of them exposes a substantial vulnerability that can reverse all that has been put in place. The false sense of security that most businesses gain from having only a partial solution in place may be very damaging.

Of course, this is something we will deep dive into later.

Commitment and project management

To have a decent implementation, there are several requirements, usually, but not only, recorded on paper. One of those *not on paper*, and arguably the most important of them, is the management commitment. The entity has to believe in what they are willing to do, and C-levels have to show all their support and commitment, agree on finding a team (or a representative to follow the works of the external company), and also show some support on internal and external social media (from the intranet up to social platforms). Also, external commitment can be seen, from a company perspective, as a way to advertise their services throughout the web, aside from, of course, justifying the important investment the company made.

> **Tip**
> Management commitment is something really important and has to be seen as a formal act, as well as the request for support from the implementation team, in order not to waste money and engagement.

It's important to note how project management is important in these cases. If we want to approach the company's security posture, we need to get through 18 annexes and, therefore, a great planning capacity is needed; moreover, if we want to get a holistic including NIST and other frameworks such as CIS Controls (`https://cisecurity.org`), the battleplan becomes really interesting. Scope policy and objectives

Although one or more standards can lead to a certification, in our case, as already explained, it helps us to establish objectives and priorities, and in this context, we need to verify what is needed by our company. As you can imagine, some controls count more than others depending on the kind of industry we want to improve the security posture of, and, incidentally, some standards are to be meant for specific industries (for instance, ISO 27011 is specific for telecoms); but this is something that goes beyond the scope of the book and, therefore, has to be taken as a fact only.

Identify, Protect, Detect, Respond, and Recover

In the previous chapter, we had an important (and hopefully good) introduction to the NIST Framework. Let's talk more about the most important points.

Remember from the previous chapter the most important points related to NIST?

Identify

NIST describes the Identify function as "*developing the corporate knowledge to manage cybersecurity risk to systems, assets, data, and capabilities.*" As a cybersecurity stakeholder, you may utilize this function to work on creating the groundwork in your business for future successful usage of the framework. The emphasis of Identify is on the company and how it relates to cybersecurity risk, particularly when resources are limited. Some of the result categories linked with this function are as follows:

- Asset Management
- Business Environment

- Governance
- Risk Management
- Strategy for Risk Management

The significance of the Identify function is obvious: it establishes the framework for future cybersecurity-related activities that your firm will take. Identifying what exists, what risks are connected with those settings, and how it connects to your company objectives is critical to the framework's success.

The successful execution of the Identify function might result in a variety of results, such as the following:

- All assets and environments must be defined
- Identifying the existing and desired states of controls
- Making a strategy to close such gaps
- Prioritizing mitigation approaches in a commercial environment
- Putting all stakeholders' and business leaders' needs first, determining how to convey cybersecurity concerns to all parties

Organizations must adapt their cybersecurity processes and put in place the necessary protections to control and mitigate the effects of future cybersecurity events. All digital and physical assets must be tracked, and responsibilities must be specified along with clear communication processes for incidents and risks. The rules and procedures you put in place will offer the stability your cybersecurity program needs as it progresses through all five functions and develops.

Protect

According to NIST, the framework's purpose is to "*assist an organization in expressing its cybersecurity risk management by organizing information, allowing risk management choices, managing risks, and improving by learning from prior operations.*"

The Protect function is vital because its goal is to *create and execute necessary safeguards to assure the delivery of critical infrastructure services*. The Protect function assists in limiting or containing the effect of a possible cybersecurity incident. Identity Management and Access Control; Awareness and Training; Data Security; Information Protection Processes and Procedures; Maintenance; and Protective Technology are examples of result categories under this function, according to NIST.

Protect covers the following categories:

- Access control entails confirming identities and granting access to various systems, facilities, and so on
- Education and training provide workers and others with the capacity to participate in your cybersecurity strategy

- Data security includes managing your data in accordance with corporate standards to reduce cybersecurity risks and secure its availability, integrity, and confidentiality
- Processes and procedures for information protection are for establishing the policies, processes, and procedures required to oversee the protection of your assets
- Maintenance helps to repair and mitigate your information system components on a regular basis
- Protective technology helps to implement the security solutions required to keep companies safe in accordance with business regulations

Organizations must adjust as data breaches become increasingly widespread. By concentrating on the Protect function, you can establish the rules and procedures that will serve as a solid basis for your cybersecurity program as it evolves across all five functions.

Detect

The Detect function necessitates the development and implementation of relevant operations to detect the presence of a cybersecurity incident.

The detect feature allows for the prompt detection of cybersecurity occurrences. Anomalies and Events, Security Continuous Monitoring, and Detection Processes are examples of result Categories under this Function.

Clearly, the Detect function is one of the most critical, since identifying a breach or occurrence might be the difference between life and death for your company. There is no question that using these solutions and adhering to these best practices will assist you in scaling your program and mitigating cybersecurity risk.

Respond

NIST defines Respond as *developing and implementing suitable actions to take action in response to an identified cybersecurity event.*

The Respond Function helps to limit the effect of a possible cybersecurity event. Response Planning, Communications, Analysis, Mitigation, and Improvements are some examples of result Categories within this Function.

The following are the components of the Respond function and their significance:

- **Response planning**: To guarantee a prompt response to suspected cybersecurity incidents, response processes and procedures are implemented and maintained.

  Analysis is carried out to guarantee a sufficient reaction and assist with recovery actions.
- **Mitigation**: Activities that are carried out to prevent the spread of an occurrence, minimize its impacts, and eliminate the incident.

- **Communications**: As needed, response operations are coordinated with internal and external parties, including law enforcement authorities.

Improvements are made to organizational response activities by applying lessons gained from current and prior detection and response operations.

When breaches occur in businesses, an incident response strategy is essential for dealing with the immediate aftermath. Surprisingly, many firms do not have an incident response plan or have not tested the plan that they do have.

Recover

NIST defines the Recover function as the necessity to *create and perform the relevant operations to maintain resilience strategies and to restore any capabilities or services that were affected due to a cybersecurity incident.*

The Recover function enables the quick return to regular activities in order to mitigate the consequences of a cybersecurity occurrence. Recovery planning, improvements, and communications are some examples of outcomes of this function.

Recovery planning includes testing, executing, and maintaining recovery processes so that your program can lessen the impacts of an incident as quickly as possible.

When events occur, opportunities for improvement are discovered, solutions are developed, and recovery planning and procedures are enhanced. In this case, it's important to coordinate both internally and externally to improve the structure, detailed preparation steps, and execution.

The Recover function is critical not only for your company or organization in recovering from an assault but also for your consumers or market. A quick recovery managed with elegance and tact will put you in a much better position internally and publicly than you would have otherwise.

Can ISO 27001 and NIST coexist?

Yes, of course. There are many points in common between those frameworks.

As an example of common things between frameworks, here's a mapping between ISO 27001 and NIST SP 800:

ISO/IEC 27001 (Annex A) CONTROLS	NIST SP 800-53 controls
A.5 Security policy	
A.5.1 Information security policy	
A.5.1.1 Information security policy document	XX-1 controls

ISO/IEC 27001 (Annex A) CONTROLS	NIST SP 800-53 controls
A.5.1.2 Review of the information security policy	XX-1 controls
A.6 Organization of information security	
A.6.1 Internal	
A.6.1.1 Management commitment to information security	XX-1 controls, PM-2; SP 800-39, SP 800-37
A.6.1.2 Information security coordination	CP-2, CP-4, IR-4, PL-1, PL-6, PM-2, SA-2; SP 800-39, SP 800-37
A.6.1.3 Allocation of information security responsibilities	XX-1 controls, AC-5, AC-6, CM-9. PM-2; SP 800-39, SP 800-37
A.6.1.4 Authorization process for information processing facilities	CA-1, CA-6, PM-10; SP 800-37
A.6.1.5 Confidentiality agreements	PL-4, PS-6, SA-9
A.6.1.6 Contact with authorities	Multiple controls with contact reference (e.g., IR-6, SI-5); SP 800-39; SP 800-37
A.6.1.7 Contact with special interest groups	AT-5
A.6.1.8 Independent review of information security	CA-2, CA-7; SP 800-39, SP 800-37
A.6.2 External parties	
A.6.2.1 Identification of risks related to external parties	CA-3, PM-9, RA-3, SA-1, SA-9, SC-7
A.6.2.2 Addressing security when dealing with customers	AC-8, AT-2, PL-4
A.6.2.3 Addressing security in third-party agreements	CA-3, PS-7, SA-9
A.7 Asset management	
A.7.1 Responsibility for assets	
A.7.1.1 Inventory of assets	CM-8, CM-9, PM-5
A.7.1.2 Ownership of assets	CM-8, CM-9, PM-5
A.7.1.3 Acceptable use of assets	AC-20, PL-4
A.7.2 Information classification	
A.7.2.1 Classification guidelines	RA-2

ISO/IEC 27001 (Annex A) CONTROLS	NIST SP 800-53 controls
A.7.2.2 Information labeling and handling	AC-16, MP-2, MP-3, SC-16
A.8 Human resources security	
A.8.1 Prior to employment	
A.8.1.1 Roles and responsibilities	XX-1 controls, AC-5, AC-6, AC-8, AC-20, AT-2, AT-3, CM-9, PL-4, PS-2, PS-6, PS-7, SA-9
A.8.1.2 Screening	PS-3
A.8.1.3 Terms and conditions of employment	AC-20, PL-4, PS-6, PS-7
A.8.2 During employment	
A.8.2.1 Management responsibilities	PL-4, PS-6, PS-7, SA-9
A.8.2.2 Awareness, education, and training	AT-2, AT-3, IR-2
A.8.2.3 Disciplinary process	PS-8
A.8.3 Termination or change of employment	
A.8.3.1 Termination responsibilities	PS-4, PS-5
A.8.3.2 Return of assets	PS-4, PS-5
A.8.3.3 Removal of access rights	AC-2, PS-4, PS-5
A.9 Physical and environmental security	
A.9.1 Secure areas	
A.9.1.1 Physical security perimeter	PE-3
A.9.1.2 Physical entry controls	PE-3, PE-5, PE-6, PE-7
A.9.1.3 Securing offices, rooms, and facilities	PE-3, PE-4, PE-5
A.9.1.4 Protecting against external and environmental threats	CP Family; PE-1, PE-9, PE-10, PE-11, PE-13, PE-15
A.9.1.5 Working in secure areas	AT-2, AT-3 , PL-4, PS-6, PE-2, PE-3, PE-4, PE-6, PE-7, PE-8
A.9.1.6 Public access, delivery and loading areas	PE-3 , PE-7, PE-16
A.9.2 Equipment security	

ISO/IEC 27001 (Annex A) CONTROLS	NIST SP 800-53 controls
A.9.2.1 Equipment siting and protection	PE-1, PE-18
A.9.2.2 Supporting utilities	PE-1, PE-9, PE-11, PE-12, PE-14
A.9.2.3 Cabling security	PE-4, PE-9
A.9.2.4 Equipment maintenance	MA Family
ISO/IEC 27001 (Annex A) CONTROLS	NIST SP 800-53 CONTROLS
A.9.2.5 Security of equipment off-premises	MP-5, PE-17
A.9.2.6 Secure disposal or reuse of equipment	MP-6
A.9.2.7 Removal of property	MP-5, PE-16
A.10 Communications and operations management	
A.10.1 Operational procedures and responsibilities	
A.10.1.1 Documented operating procedures	XX-1 controls, CM-9
A.10.1.2 Change management	CM-1, CM-3, CM-4, CM-5, CM-9
A.10.1.3 Segregation of duties	AC-5
A.10.1.4 Separation of development, test, and operational facilities	CM-2
A.10.2 Third-party service delivery management	
A.10.2.1 Service delivery	SA-9
A.10.2.2 Monitoring and review of third-party services	SA-9
A.10.2.3 Managing changes to third-party services	RA-3, SA-9
A.10.3 System planning and acceptance	
A.10.3.1 Capacity management	AU-4, AU-5, CP-2, SA-2, SC-5
A.10.3.2 System acceptance	CA-2, CA-6, CM-3, CM-4, CM-9, SA-11
A.10.4 Protection against malicious and mobile code	
A.10.4.1 Controls against malicious code	AC-19, AT-2, SA-8, SC-2, SC-3, SC-7, SC-14, SI-3, SI-7
A.10.4.2 Controls against mobile code	SA-8, SC-2, SC-3, SC-7, SC-14, SC-8, SC-18

ISO/IEC 27001 (Annex A) CONTROLS	NIST SP 800-53 controls
A.10.5 Backup	
A.10.5.1 Information backup	CP-9
A.10.6 Network security management	
A.10.6.1 Network controls	AC-4, AC-17, AC-18, AC-20, CA-3, CP-8, PE-5, SC-7, SC-8, SC-9, SC-10, SC-19, SC-20, SC-21, SC-22, SC-23
A.10.6.2 Security of network services	SA-9, SC-8, SC-9
A.10.7 Media handling	
A.10.7.1 Management of removable media	MP Family, PE-16
A.10.7.2 Disposal of media	MP-6
A.10.7.3 Information handling procedures	MP Family, SI-12
A.10.7.4 Security of system documentation	MP-4, SA-5
A.10.8 Exchange of information	
A.10.8.1 Information exchange policies and procedures	AC-1, AC-3, AC-4, AC-17, AC-18, AC-20, CA-3, PL-4, PS-6, SC-7, SC-16, SI-9
A.10.8.2 Exchange agreements	CA-3, SA-9
A.10.8.3 Physical media in transit	MP-5
A.10.8.4 Electronic messaging	Multiple controls; electronic messaging not addressed separately in SP 800-53
A.10.8.5 Business information systems	CA-1, CA-3
A.10.9 Electronic commerce services	
A.10.9.1 Electronic commerce	AU-10, IA-8, SC-7, SC-8, SC-9, SC-3, SC-14
A.10.9.2 Online transactions	SC-3, SC-7, SC-8, SC-9, SC-14
A.10.9.3 Publicly available information	SC-14
A.10.10 Monitoring	

ISO/IEC 27001 (Annex A) CONTROLS	NIST SP 800-53 controls
A.10.10.1 Audit logging	AU-1, AU-2, AU-3, AU-4, AU-5, AU-8, AU-11, AU-12
A.10.10.2 Monitoring system use	AU-1, AU-6, AU-7, PE-6, PE-8, SC-7, SI-4
A.10.10.3 Protection of log information	AU-9
A.10.10.4 Administrator and operator logs	AU-2, AU-12
A.10.10.5 Fault logging	AU-2, AU-6, AU-12, SI-2
A.10.10.6 Clock synchronization	AU-8
A.11 Access control	
A.11.1 Business requirement for access control	
A.11.1.1 Access control policy	AC-1, AC-5, AC-6, AC-17, AC-18, AC-19, CM-5, MP-1, SI-9
A.11.2 User access management	
A.11.2.1 User registration	AC-1, AC-2, AC-21, IA-5, PE-1, PE-2
A.11.2.2 Privilege management	AC-1, AC-2, AC-6, AC-21, PE-1, PE-2, SI-9
A.11.2.3 User password management	IA-5

It's important to note that, as stated on their website, this document from NIST is available for free at `https://doi.org/10.6028/NIST.SP.800-53r5`.

However, while NIST is free, ISO 27001 is not. I strongly suggest you buy a copy of ISO 27001 standard once you finish reading the book, to better understand both the controls and the jargon.

As you may see, general rules between ISO and NIST are somewhat interchangeable and that's why it is not only possible but also desirable, at least in some cases, to use the NIST ones. When it comes to asset disposal, for instance (see the highlighted ISO 27001 annex), ISO refers to media only (i.e., USB and hard disk drives), while NIST throws out an impressive number of network devices with a very detailed plan on how to safely dispose of them (considering that they can retain network configurations and a malicious actor can easily copy and use them against our company). The real benefit of using ISO instead of NIST, as mentioned elsewhere in the book, is that you can *prove* that you are following a standard and this would be highly beneficial for your entity.

Summary

Do you remember *The Hitchhiker's Guide to the Galaxy*, one of the funniest sci-fi books of all time? Well, we can imagine ISO 27001 as the famous towel from The Hitchhiker's Guide to the Galaxy: we can use both the towel and ISO 27001 in several ways, alongside other frameworks, both reassure us, and from time to time we need to clean them to avoid issues.

So, the chapter is over. We covered how to formally (although this is not strictly necessary if your company doesn't require a certification) write an iSMS with all the bells and whistles, and then moved on to look at how ISO 27001 works in the real world. Then, we did the same for the NIST framework and saw whether ISO 27001 and NIST can coexist.

In the next chapter, we will be covering data protection, with a big focus on GDPR and some mapping with other privacy laws around the globe.

3

Data Protection

In the previous chapter, we were talking about how to build our framework according to our needs, by using one or more frameworks; even better, at a certain point, we got the assumption that we could get the best of both worlds, or several, since we can, in fact, even use four or five different frameworks. What is fundamental, at the end of the day, is that you implement a Fort Knox-like infrastructure.

Specifically, in the following pages, we will try to understand some data protection-related topics, some of them beginning with a question mark, such as, for instance, *What is privacy (and why do we desperately need it)?* Then, we can try to get an idea of the reason why the word *privacy* is such an important part of our lives nowadays (and why it's misused from time to time). Then, we will dive into the surface of the most famous privacy laws, such as GDPR, CCPA, and LGPD. Following this, we will analyze the common points of these different laws and how these laws (and other laws) can give us a reasonable degree of safety when a company uses our data. The last topic of the chapter is about the *mechanisms* that allow entities to use our data safely.

> Tip
>
> If you want to become a privacy expert, this is not the right book for you – but if you want to understand what's under the privacy hood or try to implement it alongside cybersecurity, or even better, your business from outside the EU has suddenly become important within the EU, I'll try to do my best to help you understand privacy issues and even somehow make them fascinating.
>
> For sake of clarity (and I am referring to the European side here), the difference between a law and a directive must be pointed out.

While a law, or bill, is something that comes from Europe and applies without any difference among the EU member states, a directive is something that the member states have a reasonable amount of time to apply (usually 2 years) and can apply differently locally, among other distinctive pain points.

In this chapter, we will cover the following topics:

- What is privacy (and why do we desperately need it)?
- GDPR and his brothers
- Why deal with data protection?
- The six principles of the GDPR

What is privacy (and why do we desperately need it)?

How were the GDPR and the other privacy laws born? It's not as if people who write European standards decided to govern the subject of personal data processing in this way just to make life tough for all European businesses, organizations, and experts. No, the history of the protection of personal information begins far before the EU, long before the privacy code, and most importantly, begins in the late nineteenth century in the United States, when privacy was discussed for the first time.

> **Caution – spoiler**
>
> Personal data protection and privacy are not identical. They are commonly thought to be essentially equal, but as we will show, this is not the case.

I am referring to the late 1800s in the US, when two attorneys, Warren and Brandeis, wrote the first essay on the right to privacy in the Harvard Law Review.

Consider Boston at the turn of the century. Carriages can still be found. The radio is basically non-existent (Marconi et al. are still working on it). No TV. Photography is the most advanced technology in the media industry. The press is the most widely used medium of communication.

Are you imagining it? Good. Newspapers began to publish images of high-society women wearing skirts and hats while attending social functions. Is it a coincidence that individuals start talking about personal information in this scenario? No, because if we look at it from the perspective of data protection, we can see that the technical infrastructure and equipment – the press and cameras – existed to disseminate photos of individuals through newspapers en masse. Large-scale data processing and distribution are what we would call it now.

Don't get me wrong – personal data isn't created by technology. Mankind has been generating data since its arrival on the planet. Even cave paintings are personal data that we can't connect to the individuals who created them – there's no signature, at least to our understanding – yet are provided anyhow (anonymously). As a result, we create personal data regardless of the circumstances and ensure that it is constantly protected.

What has changed in Boston since the mid-nineteenth century?

Technological progress. The diffusion of information is no longer restricted to town square, cafes, or gentlemen's clubs. The photographs of the lovely, stunning women are published in the newspaper for everybody to see. Individuals have an issue with technology not because of the technology itself, but because of how it is used.

Problems of this kind have arisen as a result of information technology's ability to disseminate data far and wide. Another is the snapshot of the paparazzo who exposes the actress's affair in the press and yet another is the photograph posted on social media, which is accessible to millions of people.

But let us return to Warren and Brandeis.

As a result of this intrusion into people's lives, Warren and Brandeis create an essay called *The Right to Privacy*, in which they effectively state that everyone has the right to their private life and that everyone should respect that right. It is an autonomous zone, a closed sphere, that must be defended from outsiders, whether they be third parties or the government.

Based on the preceding assumptions, privacy is linked to confidentiality. There is a boundary beyond which you are not permitted to travel and only approved people are granted access. Do you wish to come into my garden? You will not be able to do this without my permission. It's a concept that's comparable to, but not identical to, personal data protection.

Privacy and data protection are not synonymous, since when we speak of privacy and confidentiality, we are referring to the preservation of privacy in accordance with American tradition, whereas data protection encompasses all the information about an individual.

If Mark goes around his house in his (or someone else's, for what it's worth) underpants, with a pink shower cap on his head, a baseball bat, and a garter, that is his choice and constitutes his privacy. If David purchases a plane ticket from Paris to Marseille for work that includes his name, departure time, and seat, this is the processing of his personal data.

As you may imagine, this is a slight but significant distinction, since privacy is never mentioned in the text of the GDPR.

This notion of privacy and the preservation of our personal, private realm eventually reaches Europe. However, this scenario is completely different. If in the United States the aim is to guard against the encroachment of private persons – media, businesses, and other people – in Europe, the objective is to defend against the intervention of the state or private industry.

It is crucial to stress that the right to privacy is not directly addressed in the US Constitution, yet this does not prohibit the contention that privacy is legally guaranteed. It is equally essential to understand that there is a clear separation between the Constitution, which controls the sectors in which the Government is permitted to intervene, and the Bill of Rights, which was intended to restrict the instances in which such action is permissible. The relationship between different needs, such as the power of the democratically elected political majority to dictate rules that affect the entire community, and that of the individual to self-determine and establish a boundary against the intrusions of public power into his private life, is the oldest and most complex relationship between freedom and democracy.

It has been suggested in the past that an explicit guarantee of privacy was not included in the United States Constitution for two primary reasons: first, the notion of privacy was so ingrained into the American spirit that its formal inclusion was unnecessary.

But secondly, because (and this is a more persuasive argument than the first) the true threat to privacy emerged when the growth of media and telecommunications made the violation of this right tangible, as we pointed out previously. Consequently, the notion of privacy as an asset deserving of protection has always been an integral part of the pursuit of pleasure, to which the Declaration of Independence speaks.

In conclusion, we need privacy *because* we are using technology.

GDPR and his brothers

The first *real* privacy law was the **General Data Protection Regulation** (**GDPR**), which came into the light in 2016 and was enforced in 2018, after an attempt made in 1995, known as *Directive 95/46/ec of the European Parliament and of the Council of 24 October 1995*, where the Directive wasn't adopted by member states in the same way.

The GDPR unites data privacy regulations across Europe while preserving and empowering the data privacy of the people of the EU. It also affects any organization that handles or manages the data of the people of the EU, regardless of location, making the GDPR legally obligatory for US corporations with worldwide operations, overseas locations, and even remote employees.

Individual rights are bolstered and new ones are established under the GDPR. These include the following (but there are also many more):

- *The right to data portability*: You have the right to get your personal information from a company in a frequently used format, allowing you to readily share it with another entity
- *The right to not be profiled*: Unless required by law or contract, decisions affecting you cannot be based only on automated processing unless it is essential to do so
- *The right to erasure (the right to be forgotten)*: You may request that an organization removes your personal data – for example, if it is no longer required for the reasons for which it was gathered or if you have withdrawn your permission

Although the GDPR is the most important privacy law in the world, it isn't the only one around. Other examples are the **California Consumer Privacy Act** (**CCPA**, limited to California), and **Lei Geral de Proteção de Dados Pessoais** (**LGPD**) in Brazil.

Let's examine the fundamental parallels between these three sets of legislation. It is crucial to note that while the CCPA is sectoral legislation, the sheer size of California's customer base essentially makes it an omnibus statute.

Territorial scope

In terms of geographical coverage, the GDPR and LGPD have several parallels. However, the CCPA has a far narrower reach and a more nuanced definition of the regulated parties.

The GDPR applies to any entity that handles the personal data of EU data subjects, regardless of their location. The LGPD also applies to any firm that handles data in Brazil, regardless of whether it has a physical presence there. In other words, these restrictions apply whether you handle client data in either the EU or Brazil.

The **CCPA** applies to any for-profit company that operates in California and handles the personal information of California citizens. Additionally, covered parties must satisfy *one* or more of the following requirements:

- Minimum yearly gross sales of $25 million
- Processes the personal information of at least 50,000 users
- 50 percent or more of its earnings are derived from the sale of the personal information of Californian citizens

This implies that practically all enterprises with gross revenues over $25 million must comply with the CCPA if they have at least one Californian consumer. However, this exception exempts several smaller enterprises from the legislation.

Let's look at a few examples:

- *The Daily Bugle* is a huge company with operations across the United States. They must comply with CCPA since they do business with Californian citizens and are a significant organization with annual revenue of at least $25 million.
- *The Neighbor Post* has less than 50,000 customers in the United States. They earn around $18 million every year but do not benefit from selling personal information. Smaller entities are exempt from CCPA compliance.
- Both *The Daily Bugle* and *The Neighbor Post* are required to comply with the GDPR and LGPD since their websites get visitors from the EU and Brazil.

There are a few other minor issues, as the CCPA applies only to Californian citizens, while the GDPR applies to everyone in the EU, regardless of citizenship status.

Here are a few tips for you to keep in mind:

- The GDPR and LGPD both have an extraterritorial reach
- The CCPA applies exclusively to entities that either:
    - Have minimum yearly gross sales of $25 million

    - Process the personal information of at least 50,000 customers
    - Receive 50 percent or more of their income from selling information on California residents

- Almost all firms must comply with the GDPR and LGPD – however, some may not be required to comply with the CCPA

The GDPR applies to organizations with a presence in the EU, namely those with an *establishment* there. Consequently, the GDPR applies to the processing of personal data by EU-based organizations, regardless of whether the processing occurs in the EU or not. In terms of its extraterritorial applicability, the GDPR applies to the processing operations of non-EU-based organizations that sell products or services to EU-based persons. Regarding the concept of establishment, the LGPD has no corresponding clause defining it. Nonetheless, the LGPD applies to data processing activities conducted in Brazil. Regardless of the location of an entity's headquarters or the location of the data being processed, the LGPD applies if the data being processed pertains to Brazilian citizens or if the personal data being processed was obtained in Brazil. The definition of data gathered in Brazil is data relating to a person who was in Brazil at the time of collection. The LGPD also applies, regardless of the location of an entity's headquarters or the location of the data being processed, if an entity's processing activity is intended to provide or supply products or services to Brazilian residents.

The GDPR, CCPA, and LGPD each define personal data differently

As we are getting into privacy, let's get into on how the different laws behave:

- The GDPR defines personal data as information that may be reasonably attributed (directly or indirectly) to an identifiable or identified data subject. This includes direct data such as names, social security numbers, and addresses, as well as indirect data such as behavioral data and preferences. The GDPR also has specific exclusions, such as the use of personal data for certain research purposes.
- The CCPA defines personal data as any information that may be used to identify an individual, including social security numbers, residences, and names. Moreover, the CCPA includes data that may be used to identify a home or device.
- The LGPD defines personal data as information relating (directly or indirectly) to a natural person who is identified or identifiable. However, it provides no more information about what constitutes this sort of data. In addition, the LGPD considers any behavioral profiling data to be *personal data* if it may be used to identify a real person.

  There are significant variances here. Firstly, the GDPR defines personal data solely at the individual level, but the CCPA also includes household data. In addition to excluding some *publicly accessible* data, the CCPA does not necessarily encompass behavioral or demographic data.
- The LGPD is straightforward and very inclusive since it contains all sorts of data that may be directly or indirectly related to a person or household due to the absence of any defining data categories.

Here are some of the key points to take away:

- The definitions of personal data under the GDPR and LGPD are unsurprisingly similar. Nevertheless, the LGPD's reach is greater owing to its technological simplicity.
- The CCPA is less stringent than both the GDPR and the LGPD since it only applies to specific categories of data and only examines data that directly identifies a person.

The importance of anonymous, pseudonymous, de-identified, and aggregated information

Let's give some definitions here to better understand the rest of the text:

- **Anonymization**: The dataset does not contain any identifiable information and there is no way to link the information back to any identifiable information.
- **De-identification**: The dataset does not contain any identifiable information, but there is a way to link the information back to identifiable information.
- **Pseudonymization**: The dataset cannot be attributed to a specific data subject without the use of separately kept *additional information*.
- **Non-identifiable**: The dataset has been compiled, extracted, modified, anonymized, or aggregated in such a manner that the individual source of the data cannot reasonably be identified.
- **Aggregate data**: The dataset has been removed from any identifying information so that the individual data or information of a customer cannot be associated with that customer without extraordinary effort. Many datasets of de-identified or pseudonymized data streams form an aggregation.

Numerous businesses acquire, store, and sell data that has been anonymized by de-identification algorithms or aggregation. Under the CCPA, corporations are permitted to continue using this information without disclosing it. Businesses are permitted to utilize anonymous data under the GDPR, but not pseudonymous data.

There are some more key points to cover here:

- The CCPA permits firms to store, acquire, and sell de-identified, aggregated, and anonymous data without disclosing it
- The GDPR only permits organizations to store, gather, and sell non-identifiable data
- These forms of data are required to be published since the LGPD has no corresponding wording

Legal bases for data processing

There are significant distinctions between how each of these laws permits data processing. The GDPR and LGPD both have sections on the *legal basis for processing*. This implies that firms may only process data for specified purposes.

Specifically, the GDPR covers the following:

- Explicit consent
- Legal responsibility
- Legitimate interest
- Public duty
- Vital interest
- Contractual performance

This is a total of six data processing justifications, while the LGPD consists of ten:

- Consent
- Legal duty
- Protection of life
- Utilization of privileges in court proceedings
- Legitimate interest
- Security for credit (likely related to recent reforms to the Positive Credit Registry Law)
- Health security
- Public duty
- Investigation by public study agencies
- Contractual performance

The CCPA lacks any basis for processing data. In other words, the CCPA allows firms to handle data of Californian citizens as they see fit. Residents may, of course, opt out but there are no constraints on *the reason* why corporations handle data.

Let's recap the following:

- The GDPR offers six legal justifications for the handling of personal data
- There are ten legal bases for data processing under the LGPA
- The CCPA has no limits on the legal bases for data processing

Data access privileges

The GDPR, CCPA, and LGPD all provide natural persons with data privacy rights. Under the CCPA, customers have the right to seek disclosure of their personal information in order to find out what information companies hold about them. In addition, consumers have the right to obtain information on how companies gather and use their data, including how it utilizes third parties with whom it shares data.

Under both the GDPR and the LGPD, consumers are granted comparable but more expansive rights. Under the GDPR, for instance, people may seek written or portable disclosure, a right that is not inherent to the CCPA.

The periods for providing this information to consumers also vary across these statutes:

- The CCPA permits firms 45 days to respond to access requests for personal data
- The GDPR allows firms 30 days to respond to access requests for personal data
- The LGPD permits firms 15 days to respond to access requests for personal data

The CCPA grants customers the ability to opt out of the collection of data for sale, mandating that websites provide the possibility to opt-out. The GDPR provides a *right to object* that encompasses the ability to object to the consumption of data that falls within particular parameters. All three laws provide customers with the *right to erase* or *right to be forgotten*.

Overall, the GDPR and LGPD provide consumers with more rights. The LGPD has nine basic rights:

- The right to access data
- The right to rectify incorrect information
- The right to data portability
- The right to remove personal data
- The right to knowledge about the sharing of your data
- The right to withdraw consent
- The right to certify data processing presence (process shall be lawful only)
- The right to have access to processed data
- The right to knowledge about rejected consent and its repercussions

These rights are virtually identical to the eight granted by the GDPR.

Let's touch upon some more crucial differentiations:

- The GDPR, CCPA, and LGPD provide consumers with transparency and access rights
- The GDPR, CCPA, and LGPD provide consumers with deletion rights
- The CCPA only permits opt-outs for data intended for sale
- Each bill provides organizations with varying periods of time to respond to access requests
- Under some conditions, the GDPR and LGPD provide the right to correction and the right to prohibit processing

> **Tip**
>
> Regarding consumers within EEC boundaries, it must be pointed out that the *Directive 2002/58/EC of the European Parliament and of the Council of 12 July 2002* concerning the processing of personal data and the protection of privacy in the electronic communications sector (a directive on privacy and electronic communications) is still *alive and kicking*. As already mentioned at the beginning of this chapter, because of their nature, directives cannot be taken as laws. Therefore, I am just referring to it for the sake of completeness. The entire text can be found here: `https://eur-lex.europa.eu/legal-content/EN/ALL/?uri=CELEX%3A32002L0058`.

Fines and penalties

Rules change a lot in relation to fines.

GDPR penalties are by far the most severe of the three. The maximum GDPR penalty is €20 million or 4% of an entity's worldwide annual turnover, whichever is greater. The LGPD sanctions are 2% of an entity's worldwide annual sales or 50 million reals (about $12 million). The maximum CCPA sanctions are $7,500.

In the case of security issues, the LGPD does not specify a timetable for informing local authorities. Nevertheless, according to the instructions provided by the National Authority on 22 February 2021, the notification must be made within 2 working days of learning of the incident.

The CCPA, the GDPR, and the LGPD have commonalities, but they also have substantial distinctions. These privacy regulations will continue to be implemented in other jurisdictions. In the US, the majority of states are developing their own versions of the CCPA, and several European nations are complementing the GDPR with their own laws. Of course, other countries will enable similar bills too according to their needs.

Why deal with data protection?

Data becomes more valuable, as you can imagine, due to technological advances. In addition, the ability and opportunity to access various types of personal data are rapidly developing. Unauthorized, negligent, or uneducated handling of personal information may cause significant damage to individuals and businesses.

First and foremost, the goal of personal data protection is to safeguard the basic rights and liberties of the individuals whose data is being protected. It is feasible to secure personal data without violating the rights and liberties of individuals. For instance, improper processing of personal data might result in a person being ignored for a job opportunity or, even worse, losing their existing employment.

Second, noncompliance with personal data protection standards may lead to far more severe consequences, such as the theft of an individual's whole bank account balance or the manipulation of health information that poses a life-threatening risk.

Third, data protection measures are required to ensure fair and consumer-friendly commerce and service delivery. Personal data protection legislation results in a system in which, for instance, personal data cannot be sold freely, which gives individuals more control over who sends them offers and the nature of those offers.

Personal data leaks may do substantial harm to a company's image and incur fines, which is why it is essential to adhere to the legislation governing the security of personal information.

To protect the security of personal data, it is essential to understand what data is being processed, why it is being handled, and on what legal grounds. Additionally, it is essential to determine the safety and security measures in place. All of this is feasible via a comprehensive data protection audit that monitors data flows and their compliance with data protection standards. It is possible to conduct an audit by responding to a series of prepared, audit-specific questions. The findings will provide a comprehensive picture of the processes and any data breaches, which may then be halted.

Any company that gathers, processes, or keeps sensitive data must have a data protection plan. An effective plan can aid in preventing data loss, theft, or corruption, as well as lessening the impact of a security breach or natural catastrophe.

Data protection principles aid in safeguarding information and making it accessible under all conditions. This entails adopting components of data management and data availability, as well as operational data backup and **business continuity and disaster recovery** (**BC/DR**).

Data availability entails ensuring that users have access to and can use the data necessary to do business, even if this data is lost or corrupted.

Data life cycle management is the automated transportation of vital data to offline and online storage.

Information life cycle management entails the valuation, categorization, and protection of information assets against a variety of threats, such as facility failures and disturbances, application and user mistakes, equipment failures, and malware and virus assaults.

Data privacy is a guideline for how sensitive and important data should be acquired and managed. Typically, data privacy is applied to **protected health information** (**PHI**) and **personally identifiable**

information (PII). This includes financial data, medical records, social security or identification numbers, names, dates of birth, and contact information.

Concerns over data privacy apply to any sensitive information handled by a firm, including that of customers, shareholders, and workers. Frequently, this information is crucial to corporate operations, their growth, and finances.

Data privacy ensures that only authorized parties have access to sensitive data. It stops criminals from using data maliciously and aids enterprises in meeting the regulatory obligations.

Certain data types are governed by legislation regarding their collection, transmission, and usage. Personal information comprises names, photographs, email addresses, bank account information, IP addresses of personal computers, and biometric data, among other things.

Compliance with one set of rules does not ensure adherence to all laws. In addition, each legislation has various phrases that may apply in one circumstance but not in another, and all laws are susceptible to modification. This amount of complexity makes it challenging to execute compliance correctly and consistently.

As already mentioned both data protection and privacy are essential and are sometimes used interchangeably, but they do not refer to the same concept; one deals with policy and the other with mechanisms.

Data privacy is concerned with determining who has access to data, while data protection is concerned with enforcing these limitations. Data privacy outlines the rules used by data protection instruments and procedures.

Developing data privacy policies does not guarantee that unauthorized users will not gain access. Similarly, it is possible to limit access using data safeguards while leaving sensitive data accessible. Both are required to maintain data security; users manage its privacy and firms guarantee its protection.

Another significant difference between privacy and protection is who normally exercises control. Typically, consumers may select how much and with whom their data is shared. It is the responsibility of firms managing data to preserve its confidentiality. This distinction is reflected in the existence of compliance standards, which are designed to guarantee that corporations honor the privacy concerns of consumers.

The six principles of the GDPR

Data controller: purpose and means of processing data

Article 5 of the EU GDPR stipulates that the controller is accountable for the legality, fairness, and openness of information. Data controllers are also expected to ensure the accuracy of personal data, storage limits, and confidentiality. To avoid fines and penalties, data controllers should only choose data processors that comply with the GDPR.

In certain instances, a data controller may collaborate with a third party or another service to do data analysis, even if it can handle the data using its own methods. For instance, a payroll service provider is a third-party data controller since it determines how payrolls should be handled.

Data processor: maintain a record of activity

It is not always straightforward to determine what constitutes a data processor. Typical data processors include legal businesses, medical offices, and accounting firms. A processor must keep a record of all data processing actions. A reasonable rule of thumb is that an organization is a data processor if it must adhere to data and privacy orders and directions. Organizations that destroy or store data may also function as processors.

Generally, processors can and should strive to move data risk duties to third-party suppliers. The primary manner in which the GDPR has altered the responsibilities of data processors is by specifying their obligations inside the GDPR's laws and regulations so that they must be severely enforced.

The Gray Area

In the wake of the GDPR, it has also become obvious that certain businesses do not fit well into either category. Companies such as courier services exist in a gray area since they do not analyze individual-specific data.

If many organizations share responsibility for the processing of personal information, then joint controllers may be appropriate. These responsibilities would need to be clearly defined, and processors would serve as the primary contact point.

According to the regulations, the criteria of lawfulness are only met if at least one of the six legal reasons for processing specified in Article 6 is met:

- **Consent**: The data subject has agreed to the processing of their personal data for one or more specified purposes
- **Performance of a contract**: The processing is required for the performance of a contract to which the data subject is a party or to take action at the data subject's request prior to entering a contract
- **Legal requirement**: The processing is required for the controller to comply with a legal obligation to which the controller is subject
- **Vital interests**: The processing is required to safeguard the vital interests of the data subject or another natural person
- **Necessity**: It is needed for the fulfillment of a job in the public interest or an exercise of official power conferred to the controller

- **Legitimate interests**: The processing is necessary for the purposes of the controller's or a third party's legitimate interests, except where such interests are overridden by the interests or fundamental rights and freedoms of the data subject that require the protection of personal data, in particular where the data subject is a child

Except for the processing of certain categories of data (as in, sensitive data), which enjoys extra, special standards, all processing of personal data must be based on one of these six reasons.

It is essential to remember that there is no hierarchy between the permissible processing justifications.

Article 9 of the GDPR specifies the legitimate bases for processing special categories of data, meaning that anytime one of the special categories of data is handled, the Article 9 regulations on authorized uses of sensitive data apply. The Article 29 Working Party clarified that a controller processing particular categories of data can never rely merely on the broad reasons for processing listed in Article 6 of the existing GDPR. These rules "*will never be overridden, but will always apply with the guidelines for processing certain types of data in a cumulative manner.*"

Article 9 of the GDPR contains a comprehensive overview of the specific categories of data:

- Information exposing race or ethnicity
- Information exposing political viewpoints
- Information exposing religious beliefs
- Information exposing philosophical convictions
- Information concerning membership in a labor organization
- Genomic data
- Biometric data (for the purpose of uniquely identifying a natural person)
- Information on health
- Information pertaining to sexual activity or orientation

Article 9, Paragraph 1 of the GDPR prohibits, as a general rule, the processing of certain specific categories of data. Their processing is permitted under one of the exceptions specified in Article 9's second paragraph:

- **Consent**: The expressed consent of the data subject is given.
- **Employment and social security legislation**: It fulfills some duties under employment and social security protection law (if permitted by law or collective agreement).
- **Vital interests**: There is a need to safeguard the vital interests of the data subject or another person.

- **Political or religious non-profits**: It is carried out with appropriate safeguards by a foundation, association, or any other non-profit body with a political, philosophical, religious, or trade union purpose and on the condition that the processing relates solely to the members or former members of the body or to persons who have regular contact with the body and that the personal data is not disclosed outside of this body without consent.
- **Data demonstrably made public**: The processing pertains to personal data that the data subject has plainly made public.
- **Rights**: It is required for establishing, exercising, or defending legal claims.
- **Substantial public interest**: There is a necessity on the grounds of substantial public interest, based on EU or member state legislation.
- **Medical purposes**: There is a necessity for preventative or occupational medicine, for the evaluation of an employee's working capability, medical diagnosis, or the provision of medical treatment. The provision of health or social care or treatment, or the administration of health or social care systems and services, on the basis of Union or Member State legislation or by contract with a health professional.
- **Public health**: There is a necessity on the grounds of public interest in the domain of public health, such as defending against major cross-border dangers to health or guaranteeing high standards of quality and safety in health services, pharmaceutical goods, and medical equipment, based on EU or member state legislation.
- **Archiving, scientific or historical research**: There is a necessity for reasons of public interest, scientific or historical research purposes, or statistical purposes according to Article 89 of the GDPR on the basis of EU or member state legislation.

In addition, member states may establish additional requirements, including restrictions, if they pertain to the processing of genetic data, biometric data, or health-related data.

I hope everything is clear, up until now at least. I did my best to avoid *legalese* jargon!

Summary

So, we have discussed the basics (a definition of privacy, why privacy laws are important, how the bills assume we can protect data, and the legal principles around processing data). You will (or should) now have a good understanding of topics such as the differences between data processors and data controllers, which data can be set as special or sensitive, how different laws behave differently in terms of data protection, extraterritoriality, and many other aspects. We recapped a quick history of privacy and set a lot of useful definitions to better understand it, while in the next chapter, we'll get our teeth into the matter a bit more while still trying to be as clear as we can.

4
Data Processing

In the previous chapter, we looked at privacy, why it is important, the main modern privacy bills, and the rights of the data subject.

We will continue from there, specifically talking about accountability, tools, instruments, measures, and **Schrems** (Max Schrems is an Austrian lawyer; we'll get into the details later in this chapter). Getting a bit more specific, we will be going deep into data processing. Although somewhat complex, these topics help us to decipher the weak points of GDPR and the ongoing discussions on how to improve it. I'd like to point out that this discussion isn't merely academic; since it involves people, goods, and companies, it is something that we have to deal with.

The accountability principle requires you to take responsibility for what you do with personal data and how you comply with the other principles. You must have appropriate measures and records in place to be able to demonstrate your compliance. When processing data, it is necessary to produce, update, and keep adequate documentation. But before that, we should introduce some definitions to better understand the matter.

In this chapter, we will cover the following topics:

- The data controller
- The data processor
- Accountability
- EU–US Privacy Shield

The data controller

The data controller has the greatest duty under GDPR and other privacy regulations for preserving the privacy and rights of the data subject, such as a website user. Simply expressed, the data controller is in charge of data utilization methods and objectives.

In brief, the data controller is responsible for dictating how and why the business will utilize data.

A data controller may use its own methods to process gathered data. In some circumstances, however, a data controller must collaborate with a third party or external service in order to process the collected data.

The data controller will not cede custody of the data to the third-party provider, even in this circumstance. The data controller will maintain authority by dictating how the data will be used and processed by the external service.

The data processor

The data processor processes any data provided by the data controller. The data processor is usually the third-party organization selected by the data controller to utilize and process the data.

The third-party data processor neither owns nor controls the data that it processes. This means that the data processor will be unable to alter the data's purpose and method of use. Moreover, data processors must adhere to the directives provided by the data controller.

For instance, The Daily Bugle's website gathers information on the pages its visitors see. This includes the page they entered the site on, the subsequent sites they viewed, and the amount of time they spent on each page. In this example, The Daily Bugle is the data controller since they choose how and why this information will be used and processed.

Google Analytics is used by The Daily Bugle to determine which pages on their website are the most popular and which pages cause visitors to quit. This enables businesses to better design their content by revealing the precise amount of time each visitor spends on each page. In addition to knowing which themes to write about, The Daily Bugle also discovers new topics that may be of interest to their clients. Additionally, it helps them enhance the existing material.

To get the desired insights from Google Analytics, The Daily Bugle must provide Google with the data they collect. Google Analytics is the data processor in this instance.

Accountability

The GDPR establishes the general level of responsibility that data controllers, such as entities and public administrations, have for any processing of personal data that data controller carry out directly, or that others have carried out on their behalf.

In particular, the data controllers are not only required to put adequate and effective measures in place but must also be able to demonstrate the compliance of their processing activities with the GDPR itself.

In practice, in the application of the principle of subsidiarity, each owner is called to set, within their organization, the rules (both technical and organizational) to integrate the general principles of the GDPR into business processes. For example, they must adopt internal processing policies and demonstrate the implementation of these policies.

Both entities and PAs perform this delicate function through the people who naturally exercise the function of the owner, that is, through the C-LEVEL or senior public managers to whom the decision-making power is attributed as regards the purposes and means of the processing of personal data.

These people, with the constant support of the **Data Protection Officer** (**DPO**), starting from the full awareness of the importance of this sector, must build a vision to be transformed into a mission that is expressed in the aforementioned processing policies.

In concrete terms, this mission must be transfused into a **Privacy Management System** (**PMS**), that is, a system of documents, rules, training, and control procedures that is homogeneous, integrated, and harmonious. A PMS should be constantly updated in relation to the evolution of the context, while guaranteeing the effectiveness and efficiency of company processes.

In any event, all personal data processing actions must be shown via the creation, maintenance, and preservation of suitable documentation, beginning with the design phase.

First, it should be noted that by document, we mean any graphic, computerized, photographic, electromagnetic, or other type of representation of the content of legally relevant deeds, facts, or data. This also includes internal or external documents relating to a specific business process, policy and/or administrative procedure.

Recommended documents

It's important to evaluate which documentation should be available in public and private entities, identifying who should generate it, how it should be updated, and how it should be preserved. We will also indicate which documents are mandated by the GDPR and which are suggested as valuable governance tools.

The privacy dashboard

This is a document that is not required by the GDPR, despite the fact that its utility makes it highly recommended. Many refer to it as the **privacy manual**, but I've dubbed it the **privacy dashboard** to convey the nature and purpose of this document, which is a true control instrument and an operational dashboard accessible to C-Levels and senior public managers who exercise the tasks of the owner.

It is a synoptic document that provides a comprehensive perspective of *who* must do *what* with the protection of personal data inside an entity.

Consequently, this document must report the privacy organization chart with a general description of the tasks, sub-divided between company functions/homogeneous organizational areas, and with the indication of only the managers/officers who direct them, including their primary tasks.

The designated managers must take care to produce, maintain, and update the privacy function charts, (i.e, the papers that correctly outline the roles and duties of all the entities, such as the people who make up the different organizational units, under their management authority). All actions of designation of appointees/permitted by the operator holding the powers of the owner and all papers pertaining to the training of appointees may be linked to the functional chart.

Thus, the so-called waterfall model is created, which makes the correct implementation of the organizational model prescribed by the GDPR easily demonstrable. At the same time, this document upholds the principle that any activity that takes place within an organization must be returned to the sphere of responsibility of a company (i.e., an identifiable person).

Still on the privacy dashboard, beyond the organization chart scope, the document is required to provide proper monitoring of the company's data processing (such as documents relating to training, information, forms for the exercise of rights, plans, treatment registers, and specific procedures).

> **Important clarification**
>
> The manager/official who is responsible for monitoring the stated activity must be identified in communication with each document shown on the privacy dashboard.

Now, let's analyze in detail the privacy dashboard part that each company and function within the organizational chart is responsible for generating.

Training materials

Training is the first and most essential organizational measure since it fosters general knowledge and sensitivity and ensures the system's stability. It is specified in both *Article 29* and *Article 32, Section 4*, of the GDPR, which, unsurprisingly, addresses the security of processing. Any technological or organizational measure is doomed to fail in the absence of sufficient training for the operational staff.

Training is vital in the strictest meaning of the word: training activities form the basis of the data protection system.

The privacy dashboard must identify the physical person responsible for training. The DPO will need the highest care and attention for training that must be taken seriously, (i.e., it must be assessed and quantifiable). Therefore, assessments must be administered at the conclusion of training activities to determine whether, and to what degree, the training message has been received.

The aforementioned training manager is obliged to keep all paperwork that is created.

Mandatory documents

Now, we will consider all the relevant documentation for data processing.

Information and legal bases

Each time personal data is processed, there is information that must be given to the interested party to implement the principle of correctness and transparency.

For this reason, each company process manager, administrative procedure, or so-called process owner's duty is to prepare specific information and adapt it to the concrete processing activities, taking care to insert the minimum contents prescribed by *Article 13* and *Article 14* of the GDPR. The information must contain a description of the *life cycle* of the data, and therefore also any recipients or categories of recipients, the owner's intention to transfer the collected data to a third country or an international organization, and the existence or absence of a commission adequacy decision. In the absence of an adequacy decision, the appropriate or opportune guarantees, the means of obtaining a copy of such guarantees, or the place where they have been made available must always be specified. It is also essential to always specify the data retention period. If this is not possible, then you should use another criterion. For instance, in some EU countries, if there's no mandatory retention period, this has been set to two years. In other countries, is *de facto* used the same lapse of time in which other documentation must be kept (tax receipts or similar documentation)

The legal bases that justify the processing must also be indicated. In particular, if the processing is based on consent or legitimate interest, it is mandatory to prepare further specific documentation. In fact, *Article 7, paragraph 1* of the GDPR prescribes that if the processing is based on consent, the data controller must be able to demonstrate that the data subject has given their consent to the processing of their personal data.

Therefore, the process owner will have to design a procedure to collect the consent of the data subject and keep their related records stored in a secure way.

In order to base the processing on legitimate interest, however, the same process owner will need to prepare a specific procedure to carry out the so-called *balancing test* or a comparative test between the legitimate interest of the owner, and the interests or fundamental rights and freedoms of the data subjects. Very useful in this regard is this guide, to which you are referred: `https://www.hldataprotection.com/2013/04/articles/international-eu-privacy/article-29-working-party-gives-new-guidance-on-purpose-limitation/`.

Procedure and forms for the exercise of rights

The data controller must facilitate the exercising of the rights of the data subjects regarding the protection of personal data and carry out specific procedural obligations within the time constraints established by *Article 12* of the GDPR.

It is, therefore, necessary to define a specific procedure, while at the same time setting up individually written designations/authorizations for each entity called upon to apply the identified procedure or appropriate forms.

Documentation relating to data processors

According to *Article 28* of the GDPR, the following is required:

- The treatments by a data controller must be governed by a contract, or other legal act, that binds the manager to the owner

- The data controller must make available to the owner all the information necessary to guarantee compliance with the GDPR, and allow the same owner to perform audits to verify the correct execution of the instructions

Therefore, during the implementation of these provisions, the person exercising the functions of the owner must prepare and keep the contract and all the documents drawn up during the contractual relationship with the manager.

Treatment register

The register, prescribed by *Article 30* of the GDPR, is a mandatory document for business owners and managers. The treatment register is one of the most important accountability tools, as it is a precious information resource for the privacy authority during the control phase. Moreover, if the owner does not equip themselves with general system governance tools, such as the aforementioned privacy dashboard, the register becomes an essential monitoring tool for the owner/manager.

The register must contain a census of all the treatments performed. It may happen that the manager does not adopt it, so for safety, the owner must always expect the manager to send them a copy.

Preparation and management of the register is a task assigned to the owner, who can also delegate this task to a manager/official of the organization. However, it is important that they have the awareness that the responsibility for this task remains anchored to their sphere of competence.

The register must make it possible to identify the subjects involved in the processing of data and their purposes, the categories of data subjects and the data processed, who can access the data, to whom the data is communicated, how long it is kept, and how safe it is.

Although not required by the GDPR, I suggest inserting other items to indicate the information of each treatment, such as the legal bases and the level of risk for the fundamental rights and freedoms of the data subjects. In this way, it is possible to highlight the *high-risk* treatments on which the impact assessment (or data protection impact assessment) will be carried out.

It should be noted that the register should not be seen as a merely bureaucratic task but as a real operational tool, similar to the mandatory warehouse registers of medium-sized and large companies. This is the reason for the register's usefulness in carrying out internal audits and inspections by the control authority.

Documentation regarding security measures

The measures that ensure data security within the organization are divided into two categories: organizational measures and technical measures. The latter must be identified while taking into account the state of the article and the costs of implementation, as well as the nature, object, context, and purposes of the processing. *Article 32* of the GDPR recommends pseudonymization and data encryption as minimum technical measures.

The concerns of provability, in this area, are mainly to do with both physical and logical organizational measures. These are aimed at ensuring the confidentiality, integrity, availability, and resilience of the processing systems and services permanently. They are also used to promptly restore the availability and access of personal data in the event of a physical or technical accident.

To achieve this purpose, the head of the IT function must prepare an IT security policy, which is an organic set of formal rules that define the methods for managing the IT tools and data of the company or body in question. The components of the policy are the following:

- Authentication
- Internal and external data integrity
- Data backup
- Host security
- Network security
- Physical security
- The safety of operations
- Configuration management (minimum security profile)
- Alert mechanisms activated on systems (SIEM and similar)
- The operating procedures for changing the policy in the event of unforeseen external events

Tip

Similar requirements are requested by the ISO 27001. Therefore, you can incorporate all of the documentation in one place.

To apply the security policy to the entities, each process owner must, on the basis of a specific delegation issued by the owner on the privacy dashboard, make personal designations in writing.

These designations must reflect the main contents of the individual tasks assigned to each collaborator.

They should strictly regulate, at least, the matters referred to in *paragraph 3* of *Article 28* of the GDPR, or those that the designated/authorized person is in possession of and provides sufficient guarantees on, such as the nature, purpose, duration, and methods of processing.

The process owner should administer and verify the acts of designation at the beginning of the activities, and periodically (at least once a year), the designations are subject to a process of analysis and possible revision. The system administrator must be designated by an individually written document, containing an analytical list of the areas of operation allowed on the basis of the assigned authorization profile. The identification details of the persons designated as system administrators, with a list of the functions assigned to them, must be reported in an internal document to be kept updated and available in the event of an investigation by the privacy authority. If the activity of system administrators also indirectly concerns services or systems that process or allow the processing of personal information of workers, the public and private owners are required to make the identity of the system administrators publicly available in the scope of their organizations, according to the characteristics of the company or service, in relation to the various IT services for which they are responsible, making use of the information provided to the interested parties pursuant to *Article 13* of the GDPR.

After implementing the organizational security measures, to meet *Article 32, paragraph 1, letter d)* of the GDPR, the operator of the functions of the owner or a suitable delegate must prepare a procedure to test, verify, and regularly evaluate the effectiveness of technical and organizational measures in order to guarantee the security of the processing.

This is the well-known penetration test (or pen test) performed by white hat hackers to analyze and evaluate the robustness of a computer system.

Data Protection Impact Assessment (DPIA)

While, as we have seen, safety assessments must be performed on all treatments, impact assessments should only be carried out when the treatment involves the use of new technologies and can present a high risk to the rights and freedoms of individuals.

Therefore, the merchant, or a suitable delegate specifically indicated on the privacy dashboard, will have to execute and document the process developed, following the WP 248 rev.01 guidelines adopted by WP29 on October 4, 2017.

Documents concerning the management of any data breach

The security measures described previously, however accurate they may be, can never eliminate the likelihood of a data or security breach.

When a data breach occurs, the owner must do the following:

- Notify the authority within 72 hours, pursuant to *Article 33* of the GDPR, of the violation if it presents a risk to the rights and freedoms of individuals
- Communicate the violation to the interested parties when it is likely to present a high risk to the rights and freedoms of individuals
- Document any violations of personal data (even those not relayed to the guarantor and not communicated to the interested parties) including the circumstances relating to it, its consequences, and the measures taken to remedy it

Therefore, the owner is obliged to keep a register of security breaches, which must be kept up to date.

Furthermore, since it is necessary to react to the data breach in a timely, structured, and effective manner, it seems appropriate to prepare a procedure for managing the violation by identifying the entities involved in the particular process and entrusting them with specific tasks in writing.

For this task, it is suggested to follow the *Guide to Personal Data Breach Management and Notification* published in May 2018 by the Spanish Authority (AEPD).

The data controller must ensure that the DPO is promptly and adequately involved in all matters concerning the protection of personal data in order to allow them to carry out the tasks of consulting the data controller and monitoring the compliance of the treatments, which are attributed to the DPO by the GDPR. In case of doubts, please remember that data controller will control how data is collected from data subjects, ensuring that the required consent is obtained from the users. In addition, they will appoint a DPO to ensure that all information remains confidential as governed by the GDPR. So, to cut it short, DPO and data controller are not the same function.

It is important to specify that the owner, in cases in which they decide not to follow the indications offered by the DPO, must draw up and keep the document in which they indicate the reasons why they intended to make a decision that differed from the indications and suggestions received.

So, in this particular case, the communication of data to third parties and the export of data outside the EEA must be adequately documented, perhaps even by structuring specific procedures in which the conditions, contexts, and methods of communicating with third parties and exporting data are specified. As mentioned, this type of documentation must be reflected in the information provided to the interested parties pursuant to *Articles 13* and *14* of the GDPR.

Data protection – the last warning

All of the requirements discussed so far represent a difficult organizational burden that must be met to effectively defend the basic rights and freedoms of people and to foster the confidence essential for the free flow of personal data and corresponding economic growth.

Consider the probability of harsh and dissuasive sanctions in the case of noncompliance if these lofty goals do not provide adequate incentives for the owners.

**As a warning, consider the financial sanction of 300,000 Euros that was imposed on a significant public body at the beginning of 2021, after the authority found insufficient documentation to demonstrate which decision-making levels were involved, the assessments made, and the reasons underlying the decisions made.*

The personal body also failed to provide adequate documentation of the measures adopted in relation to their processing of personal data.

Moreover, the DPO was not promptly involved even though according to the regulation, the DPO should have been quickly and properly engaged in all data protection-related problems.

EU–US Privacy Shield

One of the most controversial parts of the GDPR is the so-called Privacy Shield, which followed the Safe Harbor, and has since been invalidated by the Schrems II judgments.

Brief summary

Following Edward Snowden's 2013 revelations of Facebook and other US service providers' participation in the US government's **PRISM** mass surveillance program, Austrian activist Maximillian Schrems filed a complaint with the Irish Data Protection Commissioner (the complaint was filed in Ireland because it is Facebook's European headquarters) arguing the unlawful processing of your personal data, which would have been transferred to the United States and subjected to the massive control of the US government authorities, along with the data of millions of other individuals. This would have been eased by the 2000 EU Commission-approved **Safe Harbor** agreement, which permitted the unfettered flow of personal data between the EU and the US, under specific circumstances.

After the matter was referred to the Court of Justice of the European Union, it accepted Schrems' complaints with judgment C-362/14 of October 6, 2015 (the *Schrems I* judgment), invalidating Decision 2000/520 / EC, in which the EU Commission had deemed the level of protection provided by the Safe Harbor Privacy Principles to be adequate and referred the matter to the Irish Guarantor for a new ruling.

In the meantime, also at the invitation of the Working Party pursuant to *Article 29* (today known as the **European Data Protection Board (EDPB**)), which brings together all the privacy authorities of the Member States, the EU Commission and the US Department of Commerce reached an agreement called the **Privacy Shield** in February 2016. This was intended to resolve the inadequacy concerns raised by the Court of Justice in relation to the Safe Harbor agreement. The Privacy Shield, which was approved by the EU Commission with Decision 2016/1250 on July 16, 2016, stipulated stricter obligations for US companies that import the personal data of European citizens, including the periodic monitoring of compliance with these obligations, the application of sanctions, and the provision of guarantees and transparency obligations for the access of the US government and public authorities to the personal data transferred for law enforcement purposes.

Following the advent of *Regulation (EU) No. 679/16* of the GDPR (which replaced *Directive 95/46/EC* and all local transposition regulations), it was inevitable that the referral proceedings pending before the Irish Data Protection Commissioner would necessitate a new assessment of the adequacy of the protection provided by the Privacy Shield and, more generally, of the so-called **standard contractual clauses** (**SCCs**)

In May 2018, the Irish High Court, which had jurisdiction over the case, referred a number of questions to the European Court of Justice concerning the legality of the SCCs and the Privacy Shield's data transfers, highlighting the potential violation of *Articles 7, 8, 47,* and *52* of the *EU Charter of Fundamental Rights.*

Schrems II ruling

With the judgment of July 16, 2020 (the *Schrems II* ruling), the Court of Justice found the 2016/1250 Decision by which the EU Commission approved the Privacy Shield's adequate protection of personal data for EU-US data transfers, to be incorrect.

To be more precise, the **Court of Justice of the European Union** (**CJEU**) investigated the EU-US Privacy Shield's legality in light of the GDPR's requirements during the proceedings. The CJEU determined that there were restrictions on the protection of personal data because of domestic law in the US as well as the access to and use of personal data obtained from the EU by US public bodies. It was decided that US legal provisions do not satisfy standards that are almost identical to those set forth by EU law.

The CJEU noted the following in its ruling:

- The proportionality principle did not place limitations on how the US governmental authorities used or had access to EU data
- The Ombudsperson mechanism does not give data subjects any recourse against a body that provides protections that are at least somewhat comparable to those demanded by EU legislation

In contrast, the ruling does not directly affect the validity of the SCCs approved by the EU Commission for the transfer of data to non-EU countries. However, the Court has clarified that, unless there is a valid decision on the adequacy of the country's privacy law data importer adopted by the EU Commission, the supervisory authority of each Member State is required to suspend or prohibit a transfer of personal data to a non-EU country when it believes, in light of the specific circumstances, that the transfer cannot be guaranteed by other means.

Nonetheless, several supervisory authorities, such as the Irish one, intervened with an official remark on the Schrems II judgment, questioning the validity of transfers made on the basis of SCCs to the United States and urging the other authorities to adopt a unified stance on the issue. The Italian Authority for Data Protection did not comment on this issue.

The frequently asked questions issued by the EDPB

In response to a request from the Irish Supervisor, the EDPB prepared a **Frequently Asked Questions** (**FAQs**), where, in essence, the EDPB emphasizes that parties, meaning EU exporters and extra-EU importers of personal data, are required to conduct their own assessments of existing transfers within the SCCs (the FAQs document also includes the **Binding Corporate Rules** (**BCRs**) that typically regulate intra-group transfers) in light of the Court's concerns.

The FAQs mean that the ability to transfer personal data on the basis of the SCCs would rely on the outcome of the data exporter's assessment of the assurances supplied in the importing nation (namely the United States) in terms of adequate protection. The evaluation must take into consideration the circumstances surrounding the transfer and any further contractual steps taken to alleviate the Court's concerns. These procedures should guarantee that the transfer of personal data outside of the EU does not compromise the degree of protection required by the GDPR and relevant European laws.

In addition to the comments on individual assessments, the most important comment is related to the validity of SSCs and BCRs.

The FAQs specifically recognize that the SCCs and BCRs may still be regarded as appropriate instruments if additional measures are introduced that are capable of addressing the Court of Justice's concerns. Specifically, after reiterating that the parties are responsible for evaluating the transfers, they stated: *The EDPB is currently analyzing the Court's ruling to determine the type of additional measures that could be provided in addition to the SCCs and BCRs, such as legal, technical, or organizational measures, in order to transfer data to third countries where the SCCs or BCRs alone do not provide an adequate level of protection. The EDPB is studying further what these new steps could entail and will offer further direction.* In this context, informal talks with various European authorities show that the EDPB is contemplating potential measures, and some proposals involving technological precautions, such as encryption, have already surfaced. In reality, technicians and engineers are expected to analyze the technological consequences and alternative solutions.

What occurs next? Vade mecum for entities

The EDPB has not formally declared a moratorium on inquiries into the legality of personal data transfers to countries outside the EU, particularly the United States. Despite what transpired following the first judgment of the Court of Justice in the Schrems case, which deemed Safe Harbor illegal, avoiding a moratorium seems to be the course chosen. In fact, it is impossible to take action against corporations who have commenced renegotiation of their contracts based on the Court of Justice's ruling. In the FAQs, the data protection authorities urge enterprises to take urgent steps to comply with the ruling, including doing a study of their data transfers overseas and initiating an adequacy evaluation of the SCCs.

These are, in short, the recommendation from EDPB:

- To avoid potential sanctions and, above all, to avoid measures to block the transfer of personal data by the supervisory authority, companies should take appropriate measures to demonstrate that data transfers outside the EU comply with the GDPR and take into account the concerns expressed by the Court of Justice in the Schrems II decision. To this end, it is preferable that enterprises exporting personal data undertake specific virtuous behaviors that the regulatory authorities would definitely value. For instance, where the Privacy Shield has been used as the legal basis for the transfer of personal data to the United States, they should assess whether it is permissible to alter the legal basis of the transfer, taking into account, for instance, the hypotheses stated in Article 49 of the GDPR, such as the following:
    - Consent of the interested person (considering the preceding EDPB standards about the validity of consent).
    - Transfer (essential) for the performance of a contract between the data subject and the data controller or for the performance of pre-contractual measures at the request of the data subject.
    - Transfer required for the conclusion or performance of a contract between the data controller and another natural or legal entity in favor of the interested party (such as a contract in favor of a third party.

  - Transfer required for significant public interest considerations. This exception has a wide scope. Typically, the public interest is determined by statute or administrative regulation and not by the judgment of the person. However, the existence of public interest must be evaluated periodically.
  - Transfer required to establish, exercise, or defend a legal claim. It is the case in which the European owner must defend themselves or assert their own right before the courts of a third country, in which case the transfer of personal data (possibly to a consultant, to a defender, and then to the judicial authority of the third country) is required to allow the defense activities to be carried out. In any instance, the proportionality limitation applies to both the substance of the transmitted data and the duration of its storage.
  - Transfer required to safeguard the vital interests of the data subject or of another person if the data subject is physically or legally incapable of providing permission. It is the standard case of a patient receiving medical care overseas.
- If the preceding hypotheses cannot be adopted as a valid legal basis for the transfer, it is necessary to first check the decisions of the EU Commission on the adequacy of the personal data protection laws of certain third countries. More important, is necessary to check any statements by the EDPB relating to the legality of data transfers to certain countries on the basis of the SCCs, with specific attention to data transfers to the United States. In fact, it is conceivable (and probably desirable) that the supervisory authorities will issue a vade mecum or recommendations on the use of SCCs and any other contractual protections applicable to certain nations. Moreover, it is probable that the EU Commission anticipates any potential EDPB ruling.
- In the near term, however, where no alternative legal foundation is possible (i.e, the SCCs have already been stated between the parties), it is preferable to discuss with the data importer the inclusion of additional security measures to the SCCs assurance for the parties engaged in the transfer in the manner indicated by the European Court of Justice in the Schrems II decision. This action must be preceded by a kind of due diligence about the assurances provided by the importing country:
  - Identify the flows of personal data transmitted and the degree of risk for the persons concerned in the event of subsequent transfer to the supervisory authorities.
  - Analyze the local laws of the recipient country and the obligations contained therein for the transmission of data to public authorities. In this regard, for data transfers to the United States, it will be especially pertinent to determine the extent to which the recipient of the data is subject to Section 702 FISA and EO 12333.
- Process and negotiate with the data importer, based on the findings of the verification, a series of extra-contractual measures to be included in the SCCs in order to improve the assurances for the data subjects in the case of the transfer of their personal data. Until the EDPB publishes recommendations or provides clarifications on the most appropriate extra steps to safeguard

the rights of data subjects in the case of the transfer of personal data via the SCCs, there are a number of technological and organizational measures to take:

- Preventive examination of which data must be sent based on the proportionality and privacy by design principles
- Application of cryptographic methods
- Data pseudonymization
- Modification of access methods: instead of providing the data to the importer, give restricted access importer personnel with remote access credentials to the exporter's systems and databases
- Access documentation
- Additional provisions mandating the exporter's prior notice and authorization in the case of a disclosure request by a foreign public body, or the exporter's power to restrict the flow of data and effectively prohibit further transfer
- The provision of forms of cooperation between exporter and importer to enable the interested party, in addition to transparency with respect to subsequent transfers of his data, to use, without incurring economic or legal costs, the procedural tools and rights of action required by the legislation of the importing country to oppose the disclosure

Conclusions

Beyond the proposed solutions, there is a serious danger of generating actual *blacklists* of non-EU governments that do not guarantee the protection of the privacy of European residents, with obvious implications for international commerce and geopolitics. The review of the "countries at risk" might have significant effects on international transactions and the worldwide supply of services, including cloud computing, banking, and insurance. The majority of transactions and commerce rely on the transfer of data to non-EU nations, including the United Kingdom. If it is true that personal data is the new *black gold* and that the accumulation of enormous masses of data (so-called big data), and its study and use for commercial and market purposes, is the foundation of the fortunes of big players (online service providers, cloud computing, social media, big tech), then it is also true that the majority (if not all) of them are located in the United States or other non-EU, countries such as China and South Korea.

One, therefore, wonders if the judgment in question is not the result of a political will to redesign future relations in the context of a European *neo-sovereignism* vis-à-vis the excessive power of non-EU suppliers; if you want to force the retention of data within European borders by making it more difficult to transfer data outside the EU in order to entice stakeholders to choose European suppliers, as opposed to US operations, then Europeans need to create a whole technological ecosystem, starting from cloud operations, but the technological gap will increase.

Moreover, the large players themselves may be compelled by this decision to explore a *Europeanization* of their services, bringing them inside the EU, as many of them had already done before the Schrems II ruling, and resolving the issue of the transmission of personal data upstream.

In a sense, the principle affirmed by the European Court of Justice is unavoidable, according to which, going forward, the effective sovereignty of European citizens' data will always be safeguarded against mass data collection by foreign government authorities under the guise of security surveillance. Could this be the conclusion of Orwell's 1984?

Summary

In this chapter, I was trying to help you understand the laws around data protection and that, even though the GDPR is a good bill, it is quite far from perfection. Always remember that bills, laws, frameworks, and so on are made by humans, and, therefore, are not perfect. But there is time to get them closer to perfection. We have now finished exploring data protection. In the next chapter, we will dive into risk management.

5
Security Planning and Risk Management

After the last few chapters in which we spent lots of time and effort dealing with the issue of privacy, it's time to get back to cybersecurity. This time, we are going to move to something called **risk management**. But, before moving into risk management, we need to understand the basics by learning a bit of the jargon as well as considering what the real menaces to security in an entity can be.

In the next few pages, we will cover topics such as security threats, challenges, and risk management in depth. If you want to know more about the subject, I strongly suggest you obtain a book specifically focusing on the topic.

In this chapter, we will explore the following topics:

- Security threats and challenges
- Implementing a risk management program

Security threats and challenges

Information security risk management is the continuous process of identifying, resolving, and preventing security problems. Risk assessment is a fundamental component of an organization's risk management method, meant to ensure adequate data system and data security levels.

We can define risk as anything that threatens or restricts an organization's capacity to carry out its objective. Risk management should be a collection of ongoing and evolving procedures employed across an organization's strategies and should systematically manage hazards surrounding past, current, and future endeavors.

The information security threats that a business faces will vary based on the characteristics of the processing employed and the sensitivity of the data handled. To create a safe computing environment quickly and effectively, it is necessary to comprehend risks and the software of risk assessment techniques.

Risk assessment is the process of identifying vulnerabilities and threats to the data resources used by an organization to achieve its business objectives and determining what countermeasures, if any, should be taken to reduce the risk to an acceptable level. The value of the data resource to the organization determines which countermeasures should be taken. Successful risk management requires the effort of all levels of an organization's management

What are the different types of security threats?

There are several cyber threats that may result in assaults. Malware is among the most significant danger vectors. It has drastically developed over the last several years, compromising both endpoint and server systems. In addition to giving an attacker complete control over a computer, ransomware may encrypt data and only unlock it upon payment of a ransom.

Malware is often a component of an additional prevalent security threat: hacking. Hackers obtain access to the internal systems of a corporation, either for a one-time assault or for a prolonged campaign in which they lurk for an extended period and collect information at their leisure. The latter is regarded as an **Advanced Persistent Threat** (**APT**).

Other assaults, such as a **Distributed Denial of Service** (**DDoS**), hinder an organization's online operations by sabotaging its resources. As botnets, these assaults often originate from millions of hacked machines.

What is risk and what is a threat?

What is the difference between a risk and a threat?

Risk management is the process of guarding against risks. Risks and threats are intertwined, yet it is essential to recognize their major distinctions.

A threat is simpler to define since it pertains to the negative event that might occur inside an organization. A *risk*, on the other hand, may be a difficult notion to understand; *it is the probability that something will occur*, together with its potential consequences. It does not necessarily indicate that the event will occur.

It is advantageous for administrators and **managed security service providers** (**MSSPs**) to be able to quantify the amount and location of a company's risk. Understanding this degree of risk can help you prioritize what to protect inside the business and choose how to allocate security expenditures.

Some security experts utilize a security risk calculation to assist arrive at a precise number:

Risk = Threat x Vulnerability x Consequence

This definitely wouldn't hold up in a math class, but it provides you with a general understanding of how people assess the probability and effect of risks.

In this method of calculating a security risk, the vulnerability is the organizational flaw that enables an attacker launch an attack on the company. A company's failure to correctly install a firewall, for instance, might make it simpler for a hacking attack to succeed. Operating a business on Windows XP, which is no longer supported and consequently impossible to patch, might make it simpler for an adversary to undertake a malware-related assault.

Certain vulnerabilities are more susceptible to assault than others. Some vulnerabilities may be simpler to find and exploit than others, reducing the barrier for attackers.

Some vulnerabilities may be less detrimental to the company if exploited than others. Each exploit may have a technical effect on the availability, confidentiality, and integrity of data. These three elements are referred to as the CIA triad.

For instance, a DDoS assault may temporarily render data inaccessible, but an attacker would likely be unable to modify or take that data. Malware, though, may enable an attacker to do all three.

In turn, the technological impact affects the company. Depending on the nature of the vulnerability and the threat, the effect on the company might vary from negligible to catastrophic.

For instance, an assault that temporarily blocks service to a seldom-used and isolated portion of a system may go unnoticed. In contrast, an assault that successfully steals sensitive customer data might have severe legal, financial, and reputational ramifications for a firm. If clients' social security numbers and health information appear on websites similar to Pastebin, regulators and class action attorneys will take a keen interest.

Sometimes, substantial repercussions are far from evident. What damage, for instance, might an attacker do by eavesdropping on obscure robotic process data at a manufacturing facility? Quite a bit, if they can modify that data to cause robots to generate faulty goods.

The process of determining the degree of risk a business confronts may also be automated; some software allows you to assign a monetary value to this risk. It does this by scanning for unprotected data throughout a network, including persistent storage, and estimating an organization's potential financial exposure in the case of a data breach.

Companies must take these threats seriously, which necessitates refining their IT risk management approach.

Looking at the multitude of cybersecurity risks without any context may be both confusing and intimidating. Instead, businesses may analyze risk probability and effect by categorizing and evaluating risks. This entails instituting an IT risk management procedure to assist you in assessing cybersecurity threats across the whole firm.

Administrators and MSSPs should begin their study by focusing on high-impact factors, such as ransomware, when conducting this kind of evaluation. You must examine what would occur if the organization's security were broken by using ransomware; would it be only a little nuisance while they restored everything from a backup or a massive catastrophe? Considering attack scenarios in this manner gives a potent point of reference, enables the creation of a risk threat vulnerability matrix based on this assessment, and helps in the prioritization of investments.

Dealing with cybersecurity risks may be difficult, but it does not have to be as expensive as you might think. By carefully considering the impact of various threats on your risk, you can prioritize the protection of your organization's most vital assets and stay one step ahead of attackers.

This has important ramifications for MSSPs, as it provides them with an important starting point for security conversations with prospective clients by examining the real business impact of having systems go down or data stolen—and even considers whether the business could be used as a conduit to gain access to other partners' systems.

By moving the dialog in this manner from security to risk, MSSPs position themselves to have a far more useful and effective conversation with their prospects.

Implementing a risk management program

An effective risk management program assists a business in evaluating the whole spectrum of threats it confronts. Risk management also identifies the link between risks and the cascading effects they might have on the strategic goals of a company.

This comprehensive approach to risk management is known as **enterprise risk management** (**ERM**) since it focuses on predicting and comprehending risk throughout a business. In addition to a focus on internal and external risks, ERM highlights the need to manage positive risks.

Positive risks are opportunities that, if seized, may increase the value of a corporation or, if ignored, can harm it. In fact, the goal of a risk management program is not to eliminate all risk, but rather to protect and increase corporate value by making prudent risk choices.

The following categories are the three forms of risk management:

- **Project risks**: Multiple types of financial, scheduling, human, resource, and user-related issues constitute project risks. Schedule slippage is a primary project risk. Because software is intangible, monitoring and controlling a software project is difficult. It is difficult to govern something that cannot be identified. For some manufacturing programs, such as the production of automobiles, the plan executive may identify the product taking form.
- **Technical risks**: This includes possible difficulties, installation, interface, testing, and upkeep challenges. It also consists of a vague specification, an incomplete specification, a specification that is constantly changing, technological ambiguity, and technical obsolescence. Due to the development team's lack of project expertise, there are a number of technical dangers.
- **Business risks**: This includes the possibility of creating an exceptional product that no one wants, failing to meet financial or personnel obligations.

Why is risk management so important?

Possibly, risk management has never been more crucial than it is today. Due to the fast speed of globalization, the risks faced by contemporary enterprises have become increasingly complicated. Constantly, new threats emerge, often resulting from the extensive use of digital technology. Climate change has been termed by risk specialists as a *danger multiplier*.

The coronavirus pandemic, a recent external risk that manifested as a supply chain issue at many companies, rapidly evolved into an existential threat, impacting the health and safety of their employees, the means of conducting business, the ability to interact with customers, and corporate reputations.

Businesses made swift adaptations in response to the pandemic's risks. In the future, however, they face additional risks, such as whether or not to bring staff back to the office and how to make their supply networks less sensitive to disasters.

As the globe continues to grapple with COVID-19, corporations and their boards are reevaluating their risk management systems. They are reevaluating their risk exposure and analyzing their risk management methods. They are also reevaluating who should participate in risk management. Companies that now use a reactive approach to risk management—protecting against previous dangers and modifying processes when a new risk causes damage—are evaluating the competitive benefits of a more proactive strategy. Supporting sustainability, resilience, and corporate agility is gaining popularity. Companies are also investigating how advanced **governance, risk, and compliance** (**GRC**) systems and artificial intelligence technology may enhance risk management.

In financial institutions, for instance, there is the role of the **chief risk officer** (**CRO**), despite the fact that banks and insurance corporations have maintained huge risk departments for decades. In addition, the risks faced by financial services organizations tend to be anchored in statistics and can thus be quantified and successfully examined using established technology and procedures. Risk situations in financial institutions may be accurately predicted.

The need for a thoughtful, rigorous, and consistent approach to risk management increases as qualitative risk becomes more difficult to manage in other sectors. Enterprise risk management strategies are designed to assist firms to manage risk as intelligently as possible.

Of course, this is still a preamble. But now we can continue with more exciting discussions around risk management, starting with the difference between traditional risk management and enterprise risk management.

Traditional risk management versus enterprise risk management

Enterprise risk management has a reputation for being superior to traditional risk management. Both techniques seek to reduce potential threats to companies. Both purchase insurance to protect against a variety of dangers, from fire and theft losses to cyber liability. Finally, both correspond to the recommendations of the main standards organizations. Experts say that conventional risk management lacks the attitude and processes necessary to comprehend risk as an inherent component of corporate strategy and performance.

In conventional risk management programs, risk has traditionally been the responsibility of the company executives in charge of the risk-bearing divisions. For instance, the CIO or CTO is accountable for IT risk, the CFO for financial risk, the COO for operational risk, and so on. Even if the business divisions have sophisticated procedures in place to manage their different sorts of risks, the organization might run into difficulties if it fails to see the links between risks or their cumulative influence on operations. Traditional risk management is generally reactive as opposed to proactive.

The pandemic is a perfect example of a risk that is simple to overlook if you do not have a comprehensive, long-term strategic perspective of the kind of risks that might harm your firm. Many businesses will look back and say, "You know, we should have known about this or at least considered the financial consequences of such an event before it occurred."

Risk management in enterprise risk management is a collaborative, cross-functional, and holistic endeavor. An ERM team, which may consist of as few as five individuals, collaborates with business unit executives and employees to debrief them, assist them in using the appropriate tools to evaluate risks, compile the data, and deliver it to the organization's senior leadership and board. Risk leaders of this type must have credibility with executives across the organization.

Increasingly, these sorts of professionals come from consulting experience or have a *consulting mentality*, and possess a profound grasp of the mechanics of business. In contrast to traditional risk management, in which the head of risk typically reports to the CFO, the heads of enterprise risk management teams—whether they hold the title of chief risk officer or another title—report to their CEOs, indicating that risk is an integral component of business strategy.

Another characteristic of conventional risk management groups is an aversion to risk. However, businesses that self-identify as risk-averse and have a low-risk tolerance are not always accurate in their risk assessment.

In the following figure, you can see the most important factors related to risk exposure:

What is risk exposure?	Risk exposure is the quantified potential loss from business activities currently underway or planned
How is calculated?	The level of risk exposure is calculated by multiplying the probability of a risk incident occurring by the amount of its potential losses: risk exposure = risk impact x probability
Why is risk exposure important?	Risk Exposure in business is used to rank the probability of different types of losses and to determine which losses are acceptable or unacceptable
What are the most common types of risk exposure?	Brand damage, compliance failures, security breaches and liability issues

Figure 5.1 – Factors related to risk exposure

Until now, we have explored just the surface of the topic. Let's go deeper and analyze the whole process.

What are the steps involved in risk management for information security?

Risk management is the examination of hazards associated with a certain activity or occurrence. Information technology, projects, security issues, and other activities where risks may be analyzed quantitatively and qualitatively all use risk management.

Risks are a component of any IT project and corporate enterprise. The management of risk should be updated often in order to identify new possible risks. Strategic risk management minimizes the possibility and impact of future risks.

Although many bodies of knowledge prepared a framework to manage risk, we will be sticking to *ISO 31000 standard, Risk management – Guidelines*, developed by the already-known ISO.

ISO's five-step *risk management process* comprises the following and can be used by any type of entity:

1. **Identify the risk** – The first stage is to identify the risks that the organization is exposed to in its operational environment. There are several forms of risks, such as legal risks, environmental risks, industrial risks, and regulatory risks, among others. It is crucial to identify as many potential risk factors as possible.

   In a manual setting, these hazards may be mitigated manually. If the firm utilizes a risk management solution, some data is immediately entered into the system.

   This strategy has the benefit that these risks are apparent to all organization stakeholders with system access. Anyone who needs to know which risks have been identified may access the data in the risk management system, as opposed to this information being locked away in a paper that must be requested by email.

2. **Analyze the likelihood and impact of each risk** – Once the risks have been calculated and recognized, the process of risk analysis should analyze each risk that will manifest, and determine the repercussions associated with each risk. It also determines how they may influence the IT project's objectives.

   When implementing a risk management system, mapping risks to numerous documents, rules, procedures, and business processes is one of the most fundamental phases. This specifies that the system will have a mapped risk structure that computes risks and comprehends the far-reaching consequences of each risk.

3. **Evaluating the risk** – Following an analysis of the risk that supports a concept about which IT assets are valuable and which threats may have a negative impact on them, it is possible to develop a plan for risk management that generates control recommendations that can be used to mitigate, transfer, accept, or prevent the risk.

4. **Treating the risk** – The purpose of this stage is to implement the steps necessary to eliminate or decrease the risks identified in the analysis. It can resolve or at least lessen each risk such that it no longer poses a danger, starting with the risk with the highest priority.
5. **Monitoring and reviewing the risk** – This stage is responsible for monitoring the security risk on a regular basis in order to identify, evaluate, and manage hazards, which should be an integral element of any risk analysis procedure.

In the following figure, you can see the risk management steps:

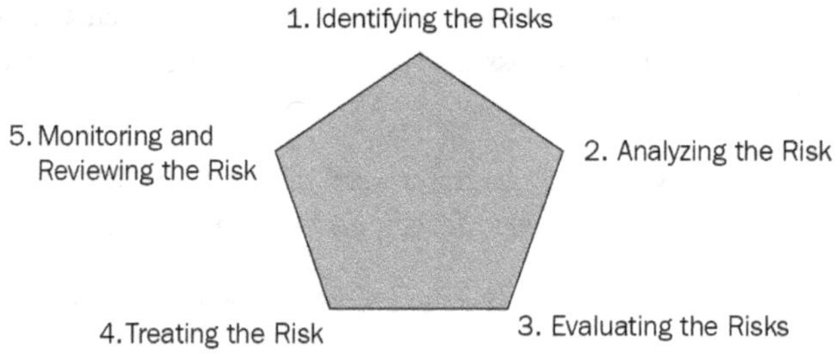

Figure 5.2 – Risk management steps

In the last phase of risk identification, companies document their results in a risk registry. It facilitates the tracking of risks across the next four phases of the risk management process.

The ideal status is to implement any framework or program in a top-down approach, including a risk management framework, of course.

From the top-down to the bottom-up

Many risk committees find it advantageous to employ a top-down, bottom-up strategy when considering risk scenarios that might hinder or advance an organization's goals. In the top-down effort, the leadership identifies the organization's mission-critical processes and collaborates with internal and external stakeholders to identify the situations that potentially hamper these activities. The bottom-up view evaluates the possible effect of threat sources (earthquakes, economic downturns, cyber-attacks, etc.) on important assets.

Benefits and challenges of risk management

There are several advantages to effectively managing risks that might have a negative or positive effect on capital and profitability. Even for firms with sophisticated governance, risk, and compliance procedures, it creates obstacles.

Among the advantages of risk management are the following:

- Enhanced risk awareness within the company
- Increased confidence in corporate aims and goals as a result of incorporating risk into strategy
- Compliance coordination results in greater and more efficient compliance with regulatory and internal compliance regulations
- Enhanced operational efficiency via the implementation of risk protocols and control more consistently
- Increased employee and consumer workplace safety and security
- A distinct competitive advantage in the market

The following are some of the obstacles that risk management teams are likely to face:

- Initially, costs increase because risk management strategies often need costly software and services
- To comply with the growing focus on governance, business units must also devote time and money
- Reaching an agreement on the severity of a danger and how to address it may be a tough and controversial task that can lead to analytical paralysis in certain cases
- It is difficult to demonstrate the benefit of risk management to executives without concrete figures

Building and implementing a risk management plan

A risk management strategy outlines how a company will manage risk. It outlines components such as the organization's risk strategy, the roles and duties of the risk management teams, the resources it will employ to manage risk, and the rules and procedures for risk management.

Let's use the ISO 31000 standard (there are many around, from **Committee of Sponsoring Organization, COSO** (`https://www.coso.org/`), to eBIOS (`https://www.enisa.europa.eu/topics/threat-risk-management/risk-management/current-risk/risk-management-inventory/rm-ra-methods/m_ebios.html`, a similar framework sponsored by the European Community) but, for sake of simplicity, we are going to utilize something that you have already heard of:

- **Consultation and communication** – Since increasing risk awareness is a crucial component of risk management, risk leaders must also design a communication strategy to disseminate the organization's risk policies and procedures to workers and other relevant parties. This stage sets the tone for all risk-related choices. The audience consists of anybody interested in how the company capitalizes on favorable risks and mitigates negative ones.

- **Providing the context** – This phase entails determining the organization's specific risk appetite and risk tolerance (i.e., the extent by which risk may deviate from risk appetite). Included in these considerations are corporate goals, company culture, regulatory laws, and the political climate.
- **Risk identification** – This stage identifies the risk scenarios that may have a favorable or negative effect on the organization's capacity to do business. As stated before, the resultant list should be entered into an up-to-date risk registry.
- **Risk analysis** – The probability and severity of each risk are examined in order to classify them. The creation of a risk heatmap, which gives a visual picture of the nature and effect of a company's risks, might be beneficial in this situation. A worker calling in sick is a high-probability occurrence that has little or no influence on the majority of businesses. Depending on its location, an earthquake is an example of a low-probability but high-impact danger.
- **Risk assessment** – Here, companies consider how to address the threats they confront. Techniques consist of at least one of the following:
    - **Risk Avoidance** – The objective of risk avoidance is to remove, withdraw from, or avoid possible danger
    - **Risk Mitigation** – The process through which an organization minimizes or optimizes a risk
    - **Risk Sharing** (or **Risk Transfer**) – The organization contracts with a third party (e.g., an insurer) to shoulder some or all of the expenses associated with a risk that may or may not arise
    - **Risk Acceptance** – A risk that fits within the risk appetite and tolerance of the company is accepted without action
- **Risk Treatment** – This phase involves implementing the agreed-upon controls and procedures and verifying that they function as intended.
- **Monitoring and evaluation** – Are the controls operating properly? Can they be made better? Monitoring operations should monitor **key performance indicators** (**KPIs**) and search for **key risk indicators** (**KRIs**) that might prompt a strategy adjustment.

In the following figure, you can see an example of a risk management heatmap:

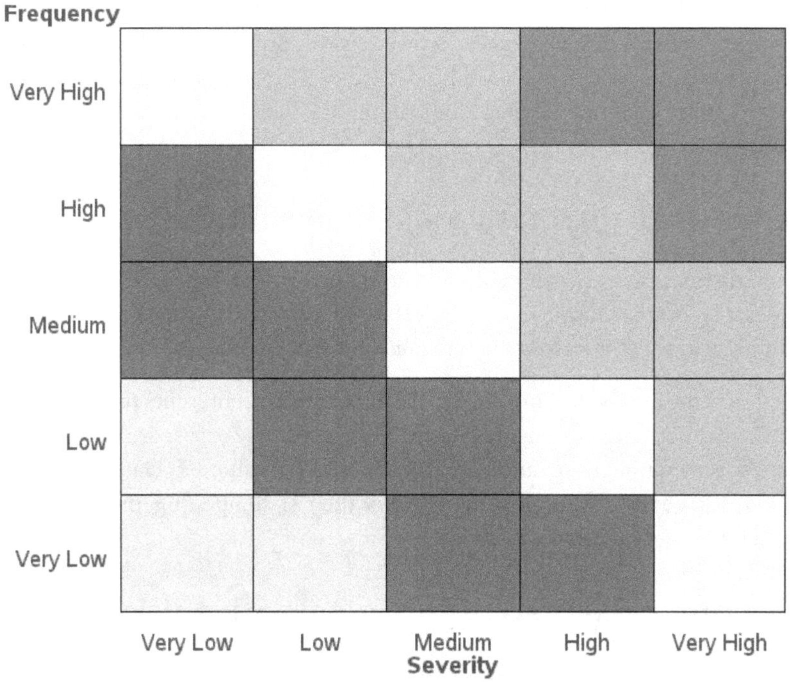

Figure 5.3 – A risk management heatmap

Now that we have explained a bit of jargon related to risk management, let's add something on top of it.

Qualitative risk analysis

Analyzing risk based on an individual's perceptions of its severity and probability is qualitative risk analysis. The objective of qualitative risk analysis is to provide a list of risks that must be prioritized above others.

Qualitative risk analysis is the first line of defense against risks for a project manager. It helps eliminate possible obstacles to the project's success, such as risks that are unlikely to cause major damage. By focusing on the most serious risks first, project managers can allocate time and resources more efficiently.

Quantitative risk analysis

Quantitative risk analysis is the calculation of risk based on collected data. The objective of quantitative risk analysis is to identify how much the effect of the risk will cost the company. This is accomplished by leveraging existing knowledge to forecast or estimate a result.

For data to be appropriate for quantitative risk analysis, it must have been analyzed over an extended period of time or seen in many circumstances. In five previous experiments, equipment type A failed after seven hours of usage, for instance. With this knowledge, it is reasonable to predict that if a project needs employees to utilize equipment type A for eight hours, then it has a one hundred percent risk of malfunctioning.

Difference between qualitative and quantitative risk analysis

The fundamental distinction between qualitative and quantitative risk analysis is the evaluation foundation. As stated before, qualitative risk analysis is based on an individual's impression or judgment, while quantitative risk analysis is based on confirmed and specified facts.

Another distinction is the corresponding risk levels. This number represents the risk rating or score in qualitative risk analysis. A danger may be given a rating of *Low* or a score of 1 to signify that it does not demand urgent action. In quantitative risk analysis, the value associated with a risk is often expressed as a percentage indicating the likelihood of the risk happening, or of the risk having a particularly negative impact on project goals.

When to perform a qualitative and quantitative risk analysis

When the perception of a risk changes and when a new danger is found, a qualitative risk analysis should be conducted. Every project should start with a qualitative risk assessment, as a general rule. In addition, qualitative risk analysis may be performed at any point throughout the project, or whenever the project manager feels it is required due to its simplicity, speed, and cheap cost.

Quantitative risk analysis should be conducted when there is an abundance of data on the risk and its effect, and when qualitative risk analysis must be confirmed. Since quantitative risk analysis may be complex and time-consuming, most project managers do not endorse it until the project's safety depends on exact risk estimates. In such circumstances, a quantitative risk analysis may be mandated by legislation or by project stakeholders.

Summary

Well, if you arrived here, you deserve a round of applause. This was a really dense chapter, with a lot of new things to explain. Just to let you know, by talking about risk management, ISO 31000, and quantitative versus qualitative risk analysis, we just landed on the surface of the iceberg. But, considering that risk management is an incredibly difficult topic including math, statistics, and so on, I thought it was only fitting to give you a longer chapter!

In the upcoming chapter, our attention will be devoted to *our beloved* ISO 27001: we will be going into great depth and it will be really exciting.

Part 3: Escape from Chaos

In this section, you will gain a clear view of what is needed, in terms of the general principles, to get the work done.

This part of the book comprises the following chapters:

- *Chapter 6, Define ISO 27001 Mandatory Requirements*
- *Chapter 7, Risk Management, Controls, and Policies*
- *Chapter 8, Preparing Policies and Procedures to Avoid Internal Risk*
- *Chapter 9, Social Engineering, Password Guidance, and Policy*
- *Chapter 10, The Cloud*
- *Chapter 11, What about the US?*

6

Define ISO 27001 Mandatory Requirements

After spending some time on data protection, we are back to our beloved ISO 27001. This time, we'll go past the tip of the iceberg to see what's hidden, and we'll spend some time (the whole chapter) better understanding ISO 27001 requirements

The main topics here will be related to iSMS: the meaning of PDCA, project objectives and estimates, team building, project development and selections of controls to be used, and many more.

We will cover the following topics in this chapter:

- ISO 27001 operations
- ISO 27001 support requirements (or Clause 7)

ISO 27001 operations

The iSMS constitutes a benchmark in the implementation of a corporate security controls framework and can become one of the fundamental pillars in guaranteeing a structured, continuous, and risk-oriented approach across the entire entity

Correctly weighing the perimeter of applicability, the necessary resources and skills, and strong support from senior management are the key elements for the success of the iSMS.

The most obvious benefits of an iSMS model are the following:

- It allows you to have an overall vision of corporate security that goes beyond the perimeter of IT security, also including people and processes
- It is an adaptive model that adapts to the temporal evolution of threats and therefore to the rapid changes typical of today's information systems

- It returns a correct view of the state of security and thus becomes the fundamental tool for optimizing the allocation of budget, directing it toward initiatives that give a greater return in terms of risk reduction
- Implementing this control model allows us, in many cases, to also respond to external regulatory constraints that normally require a series of measures that are nothing more than a subset of the possible controls of the framework
- In fact, the application of controls allows an effective tool for corporate security governance, and ISO/IEC 27001 is undoubtedly one of the most complete standards, consisting of an innumerable collection of indications and controls that must be carefully selected or declined by choosing the relevant and feasible measures for the organization

The ISO 27001 standard – what it is and what requirements it establishes

Annex A of ISO/IEC 27001 contains the objectives and controls, or the thematic areas considered and the controls to be applied (the 14 thematic areas are then broken down into lower-level controls, more details of which are provided in ISO/IEC27002). The areas, or domains, of the whole ISO/IEC 27001 are broken up into the following 14 controls:

- A.5: Information security policy
- A.6: Organization of information security
- A.7: Human resource security
- A.8: Asset management
- A.9: Access control
- A.10: Cryptography
- A.11: Physical and environmental security
- A.12: Operation security
- A.13: Communications security
- A.14: System acquisition, development, and maintenance
- A.15: Supplier relationships
- A.16: Information security incident management
- A.17: Information security aspects of business continuity management
- A.18: Compliance

Each of these sections then contains subareas that provide directives without, however, providing stringent specifications on the security measures that must be chosen and used in a specific case.

How to structure an iSMS

With regard to what has been said previously, the impact of iSMS crosses widespread across the entire organization, so top management support is a fundamental prerequisite to starting the project.

Having said that, it is possible to break down the project into different phases. Let's analyze them in detail.

Structuring an iSMS – project objective and estimate

This is the first step of the project in which it is necessary to estimate the scope of the project and calculate the construction and maintenance costs.

The size and maturity of the company determine very different approaches: we could consider the basic perimeter at the beginning of the implementation, thus including only the network equipment related to the company (of course including devices in use by remote workers, if any), systems at greatest risk, and consider gradually enlarging in subsequent project waves, including social accounts, cloud computing and remote repositories

Other variables to consider are support from other structures and offices of the company, aside from the security offices, touching many areas of the company, including the human resources office, legal, and purchases.

Having the right commitment from all the actors involved and from management will be essential to the success of the project.

ISO 27001 relies on continuous improvement and, even if not directly explained in the standard. It will therefore be possible to choose **Plan-Do-Check-Act** (**PDCA, known also as Deming Cycle**) as the best iterative methodology.

Figure 6.1 – Plan-Do-Check-Act

PDCA consists of a continuous implementation aimed at constant improvement for effective and adaptive management that follows the evolution of the information system. The four phases of PDCA are described as follows:

- **Plan**: Establish the iSMS plan by defining its perimeter and objectives, carry out the risk assessment, and establish the plan and procedures for risk management.
- **Do**: Implement the iSMS plan. The procedure becomes operational.

- **Check**: This is the monitoring and correction phase of the iSMS plan, which is carried out through internal audits, and the results are reported to top management.
- **Act**: Maintain and improve the plan through corrective actions.

PCDA is adopting the aforementioned cycle because it reflects the evolutionary nature of threats. As threats and risks change they require continuous re-evaluation and adaptation, in order to reach the ultimate company goal: Ensure the adequate containment of the overall risk, below an established threshold. We cannot set an arbitrary risk threshold, as company risk appetites may differ.

Structuring an iSMS – team building

This is the project phase in which the team responsible for managing the project estimates the necessary effort.

An iSMS requires strong knowledge and experience of the ISO 27001 and its implementation should be followed by professionals who have a background of working on projects of this type and at the same time will need senior managers with sufficient authority to orchestrate all the resources and structures involved.

Structuring an iSMS – project development and selection of controls

First of all, it is necessary to identify controls, processes, and procedures that already regulate the scope within which ISO 27001 is to be implemented and all the assets and actors involved: customers, data, partners, offices, and so on.

Once these entities have been identified, it will be necessary to select the controls to be implemented and all the necessary metrics that will serve monitoring purposes.

As ISO 27001 is devoted to any kind of company, the selection of controls and how to interpret and implement them cannot be specific because they depend on the sector in which the company operates, its size, the technologies it uses, and the resources that the company has to implement and manage these controls.

In fact, it is necessary to pay close attention to how many controls to use to ensure you do not jeopardize the *psychological acceptability* of users and not overload the operational processes. Remember that implementing controls can affecting a company at all levels, at every department. Therefore, it is imperative to work on a few controls at a time.

Structuring an iSMS – project development and documentation system

Once the scope and controls have been established, the management of the iSMS will have to be included in the business processes, and then the PDCA quality management process should be tailored accordingly, formalizing it by following a fairly lean document system that includes at least one policy, a standard, and an operational guide.

Structuring an iSMS – project development and risk analysis

At the heart of the iSMS is the risk analysis and assessment process, which allows you to assess the riskiness of threats and therefore establish possible countermeasures.

In this case, the suggestion is to adopt an approach already used in the company, if present, or to create a new one that is simple enough so as not to make the project excessively complicated.

Being able to identify relevant threats and weigh them accurately is a very difficult aspect and typically requires coordinated work between security specialists.

Without going into excessive detail, the risk analysis phases must be as follows:

- **Risk identification**: This is the phase in which the possible risks must emerge, which, if they materialize, would lead to a compromise in terms of the integrity, confidentiality, or availability of data.
- **Risk measurement**: Once the possible risks have been identified, they must be weighed according to the impact they would have on the organization. They can be both quantifiable, such as monetary impacts (usually in the case of material losses), and immaterial, as in the case of damage to reputation.
- **Risk weighting**: In this step, the results of the previous phase are compared with the risk criteria to establish the priorities and methods of risk treatment.

Ultimately, therefore, it is decided how to intervene when risk is encountered and how to proceed. The options are as follows:

- Accept the risk if it is not believed to substantially affect the overall risk
- Transfer the risk, where possible, if, for example, it is easier than having to compensate for it with mitigation actions
- Cancel the risk, for example, by decommissioning a service if the cost of correcting the risk is excessive compared to the actual benefit that this service entails
- Mitigate the risk or implement one or more controls in order to bring the risk back to a value that is considered acceptable

Structuring an iSMS – assessment

Periodically, it is important to schedule iSMS review and monitoring phases to evaluate its effectiveness and adherence to controls with respect to the context of current threats that could be significantly modified over time.

From this point of view, the quality of the audit and the metrics chosen become the key points for evaluating the project. In particular, the more the metrics are an objective and significant measure of the control in question, the more truthful and simple the analysis will be to carry out.

One of the most important clauses of ISO 27001 is Clause 7 because it sets the standards for implementation (related to training, the implementation team (if internal), and so on). Let's see the requirements in detail.

ISO 27001 support requirements (or Clause 7)

In this part, we will focus in depth on Clause 7, which is fundamental because it deals with training and resources. It applies to people, infrastructure, and the environment just as much as it does to physical resources, materials, and equipment. This clause focuses on acquiring the necessary resources, personnel, and infrastructure to build, deploy, maintain, and continuously enhance the iSMS. It addresses the need for competence, awareness, and communication to support the iSMS, and might involve, for instance, providing training and access to staff. This article also stipulates that all individuals working for a company must be aware of its information security policy, how they contribute to its success, and the consequences of failing to comply. Additionally, the company must ensure that internal and external communications pertinent to information security and the iSMS are conveyed effectively. This entails determining what must be conveyed to whom, when, and how.

> **Tip**
>
> Please consider that, once implemented, ISO 27001 has to be maintained too. Therefore, your organization requires someone that is able to improve the value of the certification. Remember the PDCA or Deming cycle? Let's imagine this with the example of a bicycle: once you jump on and start to cycle, it (you complete the first PDCA cycle) is quite difficult to keep the bicycle steady and at a good speed. After a few meters, you will be pedaling at a faster pace and the handlebars will be more stable, and, in a perfect world, you will be steady forever. Of course, in real life, it works differently: there are traffic lights, pedestrians, cars, and so on that inhibit our progress, but our ride continues.

Organizations must assess the degree of recorded information required for iSMS control. Controlling access to recorded information is also emphasized, reflecting the significance of information security. In your company, there is also a renewed emphasis on knowledge as a vital resource. When designing your quality targets, the present capacity and capability of your resources, as well as those you may need to acquire from external suppliers/partners, will be a crucial concern. This section of the standard specifies the prerequisites for establishing and operating an iSMS. Included in Section 7 are the following:

- 7.1 – Resources required to establish and operate an iSMS
- 7.2 – Competency
- 7.3 – Awareness
- 7.4 – Communication
- 7.5 – Documented information

7.1 – Resources required to establish and operate an iSMS

The company must select and provide the necessary resources for establishing, implementing, maintaining, and continuously improving the information security management system.

Clause 7.1 includes information about the selection and allocation of resources to establish and manage an iSMS, as well as the requirements for ongoing awareness for all personnel executing work within the scope of the iSMS and under the authority of the organization. A sufficient amount of resources must be allocated to the creation, implementation, maintenance, and ongoing enhancement of the iSMS. It is sufficient that roles, duties, and authority be clearly defined and owned – assuming that the appropriate amount of resources will be deployed – but it does not demand that the iSMS be staffed with full-time personnel. Clause 7.1, which serves as an overview of the *resources* promise, is followed by more detailed criteria in the following clauses

- 7.2 – Competence of the support resources for ISO 27001
- 7.3 – Awareness of the people doing the work for the iSMS to meet ISO 27001
- 7.4 – Communication (this clause is about communicating the iSMS to the interested parties internally and externally)
- 7.5 – Documented information about the iSMS to demonstrate it conforms to the ISO 27001 standard

Having access to the necessary resources at the appropriate time is a crucial factor in the success of an iSMS deployment. Remember that each iSMS position holder needs to be competent in their function. Therefore, it is essential to recall the essential duties and resources you will need. This relates to the iSMS's installation and operations. Core roles will presumably include the following:

- The iSMS owner, typically a senior manager.
- Members of the governance forum, regardless of its titles.
- The individual responsible for managing information security inside the organization.
- Those accountable for diverse operational operations that influence information security. This covers operational support professionals, including server and network support teams, service desk workers, and human resources management people.
- The iSMS internal auditor.
- The person entrusted with ensuring that the iSMS complies with the standard.
- The person responsible for reporting iSMS performance to upper management.

During implementation planning, there are many questions that must be presented and answered, such as the following:

- What skills do we require?
- Do we have access to these capabilities? If not, can we recruit somebody who does? Can we hire them on a contract basis?
- What internal training and development is needed to retain the requisite competencies over the long term?

These issues are mostly concerned with verifying the availability of the requisite capabilities. Included are inquiries about recording the desired capabilities, determining the present competency set, and establishing potential methods to resolve any competency gaps. Typically, gaps are remedied as follows:

- By hiring – acquiring permanent resources with the appropriate skill set
- By acquiring temporary contract resources
- By developing *in-house* capabilities via training and mentorship

The decisions about these alternatives will rely on the magnitude of the skill gap and whether the competencies are necessary for the iSMS's adoption or continuous operation.

7.2 – Competency

The organization must identify the requisite competence of all individuals doing work under its control that impacts the performance of information security. It must also guarantee that these individuals are qualified based on their degree, training, or experience. Whenever relevant, it must carry out activities to acquire the required competence, assess the success of those efforts, and keep the requisite documentation as proof of competence. Examples of applicable activities include training, mentorship, or reassignment of present personnel, as well as the recruiting or contracting of competent individuals.

Clause 7.2 of ISO 27001 essentially states that the entity will guarantee it meets the following requirements:

- Assessed the ability of the iSMS personnel whose job might impact its performance
- Has people regarded as qualified based on their applicable education, training, or experience
- Whenever necessary, takes action to obtain the essential competency and assess the efficacy of their activities, and preserved proof for auditing

Clause 7.2 stipulates that all iSMS personnel must be competent in their respective tasks. The supply of training, education, experience, and skills leads to competence. All of these must be addressed while managing human resources. To effectively deploy and sustain an iSMS, supporting resources must be in place.

The organization must do the following:

- Decide who has to have the requisite skills to undertake tasks under its supervision that have an impact on information security performance
- Confirm that these individuals possess the necessary education, skill, or experience to be considered competent
- If necessary, take steps to develop the essential skills and assess their efficacy
- Save pertinent documentation as proof of competency

> **Tip**
>
> Be careful as requirements related to sensitive and private information could interfere with data protection.

Clause 7.2 outlines the requirements for individuals to be aware of their iSMS duties. The expertise and abilities of your workers, vendors, and contractors is crucial to the successful application of information security rules. To guarantee an adequate knowledge and skill basis, you must do the following:

- Specify the needed knowledge and abilities
- Identify who must possess the necessary knowledge and abilities
- Specify how you will evaluate or confirm that the appropriate individuals have the necessary knowledge and abilities

Beyond knowledge of physical security, cybersecurity, computer security, and other kinds of information security, a multitude of talents and experiences is necessary for the effective deployment and continuous administration of an iSMS that is certified to ISO 27001. These include commercial, legal, HR, IT, and goods and services expertise relevant to the scope of business. Developing and maintaining an iSMS is often a team effort. Your auditor will expect you to have documentation outlining your required knowledge and abilities. Where you feel the standards have been met, you must provide documentation such as training certificates, course attendance records, or internal competency evaluations. The majority of firms that currently utilize tools such as training/skills matrices, evaluations, or supplier assessments may meet the need for competence records by increasing the categories covered to include information security.

> **Tip**
>
> Of course, this has to be read differently in case you are using a third-party company to implement ISO 27001, but still, your entity should be able to maintain this certification.

Training

The iSMS mandates that all individuals be competent with regard to their iSMS-related roles. Any identified competence deficiencies must be remedied. However, there is limited iSMS-specific training for certain user groups. The following table lists some of these categories and the sort of training that may be necessary:

Audience	Type of Training
Users	User awareness training
iSMS governance	Those in charge of the implementation
Information security manager	The individual who supervises implementation
Service desk	• Normal user and access management • IT security employees in charge of event and incident management
Human resource	Responsibilities for employee recruiting, training, and termination
IT support personnel	• Incident response management • Secure operations
Executives	iSMS support

The following should be considered in the training plan:

- User awareness training
- Documentation for governance
- Specialized instructions for important *control owner* groups:
  - Network and server support
  - Service desk (user support, incident response)
  - Human resources
- Briefings for senior executives and line officers

When establishing a training plan, the following factors must be considered:

- Who is the intended audience?
- What messages are required?

- How will the training/message be delivered – in-person, online, via PowerPoint, or through team briefings?
- When will the training occur and how often it must occur?
- Who will be accountable for planning the training, maintaining the content, and distributing the materials?
- Are evaluations and effectiveness metrics necessary? How about quizzes or surveys?

This sort of data may be collected through a gap analysis. Once this sort of data has been collected, a training program may be designed.

The training program should include the following:

- Who the target demographic is
- Which messages they need
- How the information or instruction will be conveyed
- When the training will take place
- How often training must occur
- Who will be in charge of organizing/delivering the project
- Whether any evaluation methods are necessary and if so, what they would entail

7.3 – Awareness

People performing work under the control of the organization must be aware of its information security policy, their contribution to the effectiveness of the information security management system, including the benefits of improved information security performance, and the consequences of failing to comply with the information security management system requirements.

Clause 7.3 is a combination of Competency (Clause 7.2) and Communication (Clause 7.4).

The following information must be known by anybody working for the organization:

- The information security policy
- Their role in enhancing the efficiency of the information security management system, including better information security performance's advantages
- The effects of failing to adhere to the information security management system requirements

Typically, this will lead to the setup of training and awareness programs aimed at various groups. Awareness of non-compliance with iSMS rules must also be addressed. In addition to assuring the specialized information security competency of key persons, the broader group of workers, suppliers, and contractors must be aware of the fundamental parts of your iSMS. As part of the iSMS implementation, the organization's employees must collaborate on the design of an information security policy for approval by senior management. Their job should be well understood since it would have been agreed upon and recorded as part of Clause 7.1. This is essential for developing a supportive culture inside the business. All employees, vendors, and independent contractors should be aware of the following:

- That you have an iSMS and the reasons why
- That you have an information security policy and which portions are applicable to them
- What they must do to assist the company in achieving its information security goals and how they may help your firm safeguard its precious information
- Which policies, procedures, and controls are applicable to them and the repercussions of noncompliance
- Awareness and comprehension of the following clauses 6.1 – Risk management, 6.2 – iSMS goals, 9.1 – Wider measurement and evaluation, 9.2 – Internal audits, 9.3 – Management reviews, 10.1 – Non-conformities and remedial measures, as well as continuous improvements in accordance with 10.2. (Continual Improvement)
- This information may often be communicated using current procedures and documentation, such as orientations, employment contracts, toolbox discussions, supplier agreements, staff briefings, and updates

7.4 – Communication

The company must identify the necessity for internal and external information security management system-related communications. While determining the communication system, it must establish what is to be communicated, when it is to be communicated, with whom it is to be communicated, who will communicate, and how communication will be carried out.

Communications are crucial to the iSMS implementation process. By making the program and its benefits evident inside and beyond the company, they assist, gain, and sustain support for the program. Benefits of excellent communications programs include ensuring that information security is not regarded as a *side problem* and is rather *front and center*. Good communication tactics extend beyond the deployment phase and into the ongoing operations of the iSMS. Important security dashboards, briefings, and warnings are all components of a robust communications system.

Internal and external communication considered important to the iSMS must be decided, as well as the methods by which they must be carried out, taking into account what must be communicated, by whom, at what time, and to whom. To allow the operations of your iSMS to operate well, you must ensure that your communication activities are well planned and controlled. ISO 27001 specifies them in detail by mandating that you determine the following:

- What must be communicated
- When must it be communicated
- To whom must it be communicated
- Who is accountable for communication
- What the communication processes are

If your communication needs are clearly stated in your organization's policies, rules, and procedures, you do not need to take any further steps to meet this criterion. If they are not, you should consider documenting your important communication actions in the form of a table or method using the preceding headings. Remember that these papers' contents must also be transmitted. Similar to the realm of training, good communication involves the identification of target audiences, the methods that may be employed (existing or new), the content, and the frequency of messages. The preceding bullet points uncover these components and enable the construction of an all-encompassing communications strategy. The incorporation of resources from corporate communications departments adds substantial value to this arena. Communication techniques have a crucial role:

- Sustain a commitment to installation and operations in order to garner support for the iSMS
- Continue keeping information security *at the forefront*
- The creation of a communications strategy facilitates the dissemination of messages

Plans for communications must include the following:

- Which current communication channels may be utilized
- What participation may be expected from corporate communications and other agency groups
- The present levels of assistance within the agency's core areas and how they could be modified

Clause 7.4 mandates a definitive response to a number of security-related questions:

- Organizations should clearly express their priorities: the need for information security and the need to comply with laws and standards. Communication will handle risk management concerns, new or altered security goals, and vulnerabilities, events, or incidents in order to activate the appropriate response from all parties, most notably the trained individuals who execute the predetermined response. Celebrating accomplishments and commending exemplary security habits have very beneficial impacts. Including security provisions and requirements in the contract is also a method of communicating your needs to service and product suppliers.

- What should the message be like? To generate what is supposed to be communicated, the message should be clear and concise in both form and substance. This section considers the kind of communication channel to relay messages. You may use narration, visuals, metaphors, or cartoons. Messages must be concise and focused on their true objective. You can use any media or way to communicate, but it has to be comprehensive.
- Who is allowed to communicate? Organizations should make clear who is permitted to communicate, particularly with external parties. Top management, the CISO, and the support desk are excellent internal examples. Public relations officers are employed by large corporations to connect with external parties. The communicator should have the requisite authority to ensure that the message will be received with the proper attention and will elicit the desired action or response.
- Who is the recipient? Not all recipients should get every communication. Depending on the categorization of the information, the required technical competence, and the recipient's position within the company, messages should be tailored to a particular audience. The communication plan should be effective and exclusively target those who will benefit from it or must act based on it, such as users, partners, internal and external service providers, regulatory authorities, and shareholders.
- How should the communication process should be carried out? The first and easiest communication method is the security policy and all the papers that specify what to do (and how to do it) to achieve the policy's goals. Particularly in the event of accidents and emergencies, messages to any kind of audience (either internal or external) should be planned and authorized. Defined channels (and protocols) should be used to ensure that the message reaches the target audience at the optimal time and with the greatest potential efficacy. Examples include emails, pop-up windows, screensavers, posters, audio messages, meetings, regulations, and directives.
- When are we supposed to communicate? Continuous and event-based communication is required (in reaction to events). To ensure that the message, any message is not forgotten, you need to ensure that it is regularly and repeatedly delivered, for instance, to new starters in the organization as well as at regular intervals to existing staff. You should also be able to alter messages and add new messages, formats, and channels as the scenario demands. Compared to events or crises, communication in regular circumstances might be drastically different.

Plan for internal versus external communication

It is crucial to acknowledge that the communication plan comprises both internal and external components. They will require different considerations to the questions that follow.

The internal communication plan is used by upper management to communicate its aims and commitment to information security. The information security policy, the team within the organization with the essential roles and duties related to security, the awareness strategy, and the general and specialized requirements for responding to incidents are some examples of communication. The internal communication plan should not, however, be unidirectional. Mediums such as telephone and email, for instance, should also be recognized and used to communicate security breaches or emerging vulnerabilities in a bottom-up manner, that is, from on-the-ground users.

The majority of the preceding examples pertain to the internal communication plan, although they also apply to the external communication plan. You may need to communicate with regulatory authorities, public authorities, shareholders, customers, and partners to announce good (success) or bad (failure) occurrences (incidents, accidents, and crises). You will also need a communication plan that answers the answers listed previously in this section. You must be careful with this since you should not reveal or broadcast sensitive information that could worsen your condition.

Depending on the organization's size and security goals, the formality of the communication plan will vary, being either completely documented as a distinct document or simply expressed in a few phrases within other rules, processes, and plans. So, as long as the required information is communicated to the correct people your solution will be appropriate for your goals and available resources.

7.5 – Documented information

Clause 7.5 discusses the obligations for preserving the relevant papers and records that support the iSMS's activities. Formal documentation of when things have been approved demonstrates compliance with this provision. For the documented information used to develop and manage your iSMS to be useful, it must meet the following requirements:

- Be accurate
- Be intelligible to those who use it and assist you in complying with regulatory obligations, managing information security risks, and achieving your goals

Access to documented information is controlled so that it cannot be accidentally changed, corrupted, deleted, or accessed by individuals to whom it is not appropriate. Information is deleted in a safe way or returned to its owner when this is a requirement, and you can track changes to information to ensure that the process is in control.

Documentation is necessary to guarantee that procedures are executed in accordance with the management system's goals. Documentation defines what you will accomplish and gives proof that you have carried out your intentions. The ISO 27001 standard does not define the scope of documentation, which is influenced by a variety of variables. These consist of the following:

- The complexity and interplay of business processes
- The control environment, sometimes influenced by external duties
- The organization's size and core activities
- The qualifications of personnel
- Other legal or regulatory requirements

Always develop documents with the intended audience in mind. The documentation must be beneficial to the people who will use it. Organizations are required to define and record their procedures as needed. Afterward, they must adhere to their own documents. *Say what you do and do what you say.*

The following criteria apply to procedures that are not explicitly documented:

- The process is methodical
- Communicated
- Understood
- Applied
- Effective

Documentation, however, does need management. This management comprises document approvals, standards for accessibility and readability, and other specifications mentioned in Clause 7.5 of the standard.

Internal or external sources may be the origin of your documented information; thus, your control procedures must handle documented information from both sources. Companies with effective document control often have one or more of the following in place:

- A single individual or a small group responsible for ensuring that new/modified papers are examined prior to issuance, are kept in the correct place, and are removed from circulation when superseded, and that a record of charges is maintained
- Automated processes and controls included in an electronic document management system
- Effortless electronic data backup and paper file archiving/storage procedures
- Strong staff understanding of document management, record-keeping, and information access/retention regulations

As we have provided a summary of the clause, now we will detail every subclause.

7.5.1 – General

The term *documented information*, which will be used several times throughout this chapter, now encompasses both the *documents* and *records* definitions from the previous version of the ISO 27001 standard.

This modification was intended to assist with the administration of papers and records mandated by the standard, as well as those deemed vital to the iSMS's functioning by the organization. It should also be emphasized that the quantity and scope of recorded information required by an organization will vary based on its size, activities, goods, and services, the complexity of its processes and their interrelationships, and the expertise of its employees.

7.5.2 – Developing and revising

The standard stipulates that information generated or updated within the scope of the iSMS must be appropriately recognized and characterized, taking into consideration how the content is presented and the medium through which this is done. All recorded information must be subjected to appropriate review and approval processes to verify its suitability.

7.5.3 – Management of recorded data

The standard says that recorded information required by the iSMS, as well as the standard itself, must be accessible, usable, and sufficiently safeguarded against destruction or loss of integrity and identity, regardless of its internal or external origin. For the correct management of recorded information, the organization must provide distribution, retention, access, use, retrieval, preservation, and storage methods, as well as control and disposal procedures.

Documented information required by the information security management system and by ISO 27001 documentation must be appropriately checked to ensure (note: the originating clauses are in brackets):

- iSMS scope (documents) (**4.3**)
- High-level information security policy (documents) (**5.2**)
- Risk assessment methodology (documents) (**6.1.2**)
- Risk assessment report and risk treatments (record) (**6.1.2**, **6.13**, **8.2**, **8.3**)
- Statement of applicability (documents) (**6.1.3 d**)
- Information security objectives (documents)(**6.2**)
- Evidence of competencies (record) (**7.2**)
- Documented information as required by the iSMS (documents and record) (**7.5.1 b**)
- Documents and records required by ISO 27001 (documents and record)(**7.5.1 a**)
- Monitoring and measurement results (record)(**9.1**)
- Internal audit program aid results (record) (**9.2**)
- Results of management review (record) (**9.3**)
- Non-conformances and results and corrective action (record) (**10.1**)

> **Tip**
> The terms in **bold** are the respective clauses of Annex A of ISO 27001. Concerning non-conformance, ISO defines them as "the failure to meet one or more requirements that are outlined throughout the mandatory clauses."

The distinction between a document and a record is that records are time-stamped proof of activity. Periodically, documents are examined and updated. Typically, they are versioned. In addition to the records mentioned previously, other relevant documents may include the following:

- Evidence of the risk owner's consent for specified controls or risk acceptance
- Visitor records, including CCTV photos and access logs

- Security incident logs and root cause analysis
- Rectifications and enhancements

> **Tip**
>
> I think you imagine a truckload of documentation to be prepared and ready, but a high percentage of the companies I personally assessed needed "only" the paperwork required to fulfill the criteria of clauses 4 to 10 consisting of around 25 to 35 pages in total (excluding title pages and version control, I mean the version number). Among them are the outcomes of the management review, the internal audit report, the risk assessment, and the performance evaluations. This amount of pages for clauses 4 through 10 is generally intended to be independent of the organization's size; nonetheless, bigger organizations have additional paperwork related to, for example, performance management and internal auditing.

The second major sort of documentation is information security policies, which are more diverse. 20 to 40 pages of documentation have been required for the ISO 27001 implementations I've performed for smaller organizations (with maybe a few thousand users). Larger organizations need more policy-related paperwork, although it typically did not exceed 60 pages.

The third form of documentation is the documentation/records generated as a consequence of running the controls/procedures, such as visitor records, change control records, and penetration test reports, where the type of documentation generated is highly reliant on what is implemented.

If you have more than this, you may have made things more complicated than necessary. Or maybe you do need it all to effectively handle information security concerns. But I doubt it.

So, once everything is in place (policies, controls, procedures, and so on), you can have your audit and, if it's successful, you can obtain your ISO 27001 certification. But can you later lose it?

Yes. Auditors will periodically return on-site (or remotely) and request evidence that you are continuing to comply with all regulations. If you cannot provide evidence that you are, they will revoke your ISO 27001 certification. So, we must ensure that we continue to comply with all ISO 27001 requirements.

How can you ensure you do so?

- Be familiar with the primary tenets of your information security policy.
- Be familiar with the primary concepts of the content of the intranet's primary information security pages and complete the yearly training on information security.
- Know where to locate the organization's rules and procedures, especially those that pertain to information security and apply to you.
- You are not required to grasp every detail, but you should understand the fundamentals.

- Read, understand, and agree to the terms of the acceptable use policy annually.
- Understand your role in helping to secure the organization's information and the significance of that information. For instance, avoid revealing your password and handle sensitive information with extreme caution.

Be aware that if the organization has a policy or procedure that specifies how things should be done, it is crucial that the policy or process is accurate. For instance, if a policy or procedure states *All visitors must be accompanied by a relevant member of staff*, it is imperative that all visitors without exception. If a policy or procedure is not consistently adhered to in practice, either the policy or procedure must be revised, or individuals must ensure that they adhere to it.

It is vital to record instances of disparity between an organization's policies/processes and what is really in place in order to determine whether the policy/process should be amended. Remember that a policy or practice does not need to be recorded in order to be legitimate and adhered to.

Be cautious when adopting *improvements*, *shortcuts*, or *changes* that do not align with the organization's rules or processes. You should get formal approval for this action and, if required, modify the policies/processes properly.

You should also report anything that seems to have the potential to expose sensitive information to unauthorized parties, for instance, if you notice that a door lock is broken or that critical papers have been left on a desk overnight.

Remember the fundamentals of security , such as the following:

- Use extreme caution when links from people external to your organization emails
- Clear your desk papers with confidential information while you are not present
- Lock your workstation's display before leaving your desk
- Deposit all rubbish containing confidential information in the designated containers

In previous paragraphs, I translated the main requirements of Clause 7 to demonstrate how to use them more easily. Of course, as we have said many times, ISO 27001 is continuously evolving and improving. You can improve on the basic requirements proposed within the clause. For instance, you can require internal training every 3 months for all your employees and install document shredding machines to destroy documents. It's entirely up to you; there is always room for improvement. Just remember: don't excessively implement bureaucratic or unsustainable procedures; they can be a waste of time for your employees and your company.

Summary

Well, that's another chapter filled with a lot of information that we've completed. You've learned what the requirements, steps, and documentation to provide to fulfill ISO 27001 accomplishment are. At the same time, you should be aware that you can lose the status of ISO 27001 certified company just by non-completing the relevant information.

In the next chapter, we'll deep dive into risk management, policies, and controls.

7

Risk Management, Controls, and Policies

One of the most important things to sort out, aside from preparing all the documentation needed and confirming support from management, is to have a list of all the entity's assets. In this chapter, we will be covering risk management, data classification, and the controls defined within ISO 27001.

An asset is a resource having economic worth that a person, business, or nation owns or manages with the idea that it will produce future benefits. The balance sheet of a firm lists its assets. They are acquired or established to raise the value of a company or to boost its operations. In our context, an asset is defined as any goods or services, tangible or intangible, that are considered part of an entity.

So a firewall, for instance, is an asset; a pen is an asset; but also the documents on the local or online repository of the company are considered to be an asset, as well as that server that they were supposed to dismiss five years ago, but for some reasons as unknown as the Bermuda triangle, is still there.

Why in the world is a document (MS Word, Excel, PowerPoint, you name it) considered an asset? Well, of course it's not due to the document(s) themselves, but because of what those documents are worth: let's suppose that you are the King of Reign1 and your plans for invading Reign2 and therefore becoming Emperor of the Galaxy are in your safe waiting to be used – how much are they worth? Or let's suppose that you've got 50 kilos of bearer shares? What is their value? Or all the notebooks that you used while at primary school, how much are they worth, according to your parents?

You got the point: if the shape of water depends on the container that encloses it, the value of a document does not depend on the physical document but on the information it contains.

In this chapter, we will cover the following topics:

- Elements of project risk management
- Data classification
- ISO 27001 controls

Elements of project risk management

Project risk management is an essential project management strategy that aims to minimize the number of surprises that occur during a project's execution. Despite the fact that it is impossible to forecast the future with absolute certainty, a straightforward and simplified risk management method may be used to anticipate uncertainties and reduce their occurrence or effect. This raises the probability that the project will be completed successfully and decreases the implications of these risks.

The basic processes for project risk management are therefore the following:

- **Risk identification**, or the identification of risks or their sources.
- **Risk evaluation**, or the evaluation of risks in terms of probability and impact to establish an order of priority among the identified risks.
- **Risk handling**, which is the process that identifies, evaluates, selects, and implements various remediations in order to obtain an acceptable risk threshold in compliance with the constraints and objectives of the project. In particular, it includes what must be done, when, who is responsible for it, and the related cost and schedule.
- **Risk controlling**, meaning the continuous reporting and monitoring of both risks and their management mechanisms.

Risk reporting in particular has a dual purpose: in the immediate term, it enhances communication within the project, and in the long term, it generates historical precedents that may be utilized to produce more accurate risk forecasts in future projects.

The risk management plan

During my career, also as a risk manager, I learned some fundamentals of risk management:

Risk management is uninteresting to 99 percent of the population of the globe. They see no value in it.

I developed a risk register strategy that was as straightforward as I deemed it needed to be in order to assist conversations and decision-making. It worked well, and after a few years as a general risk manager, I transitioned into the information security field, carrying the strategy with me to the current day.

Fundamental notions

A few broad views on risk management

Risk management is a management method that helps your organization accomplish its goals by concentrating on helping you understand some of the undesirable events that might prevent you from reaching your goals. It then assists you in deciding what you might do to handle these negative events, and perhaps prevent them from occurring. It is a managerial approach designed to aid in decision-making; if it is not aiding in decision-making, then it is a waste of time. Risk management is a subpar method for managing hazards, but it is the best method available, and like other management method, it sometimes works and sometimes does not. Again, like any management strategy, it requires some talent to be effective, and the more you practice, the better you get at it. Like the finest management strategies, it is fundamentally straightforward.

Risk evaluation

To select the most effective risk reduction approach, it is necessary to analyze risks. There are three stages involved:

- **Identification**: Identifying and defining the kinds of risks your firm confronts is the first step. Both internal and external threats exist. Consider also whether the risks are avoidable, such as operational risks, or not, such as natural calamities, when recognizing them.
- **Impact assessment**: Once a risk has been identified, its effect may be assessed. This entails defining the likelihood of a risk's occurrence and its corresponding effect or outcome.
- **Develop strategies**: Finally, you may establish the required approach for risks with a medium or high likelihood of occurring. Despite the fact that you may still choose to monitor minor risks, they are less important when it comes to taking the next step and developing a strategy.

Risk characteristics

These are the 10 characteristics that each risk should be ascribed:

- **Risk ID** of some form, e.g., R0417. This can be anything that allows you to individually distinguish each risk.
- **Risk description**: What is *the undesirable event that might lead to the loss of confidentiality, availability, or integrity of information under your scope?* You should strive for clarity on the business repercussions of this negative event and its source or causes.
- **Risk owner**: There must be a designated risk owner. This individual must be able to make risk-related choices and is often a senior member of staff. Who will have to deal with the consequences if this unfortunate event occurs? What is sometimes advantageous is having a *delegated risk manager* who reports to the risk owner but can handle the risk on a continuing basis. Nonetheless, it is essential that the risk owner possess some degree of comprehension of and responsibility for the risk. It is uncommon for certification auditors, in my experience, to speak with risk owners to inquire about their awareness of the risks and the decisions they have made. But they must!
- **Existing essential controls**: What do you currently have in place that aids your risk management? You don't need to mention every control already in place to manage the risk, since the standard just asks you to describe the essential measures. Try to keep the number of items on this list modest. If there are controls that you believe should be in place but are not, you should explain them in your risk improvement actions.

- **Current likelihood**: How probable is it that something will occur during the next 12 months? People use many scales, but I propose a range from 1 (low) to 5 (high). I propose basing this probability assessment on your current awareness of how effectively the controls are working to manage the risk today – i.e., how effective they are today in light of any presently known deficiencies in the controls.
- **Current effects**: What is the single-number business effect of the loss of confidentiality, availability, and integrity of the impacted information? Typically, this is a single number from 1 (low) to 5 (high). Some individuals like to use three different numbers/evaluations – one for each of confidentiality, availability, and integrity – but to keep things simple, I suggest using a single value. The criterion does not require three separate evaluations. As with the probability, this should account for any information on the present efficacy and known current flaws of the controls managing the risk.
- **Current risk rating**: There are more intricate approaches but multiplying the numbers for probability and effect will suffice. This is also referred to as the *level of risk*, i.e., a value from 1 to 25.
- **Current risk assessment**: This indicates whether or not this risk is within your risk appetite, however that is defined. Typically, this is determined by the risk score. For example, *All hazards with a score over 12 exceed the risk appetite.* People often have two breaking points: one for risks that are far outside their risk appetite (e.g., with a score above 20) and one for risks that are above the risk appetite but not quite as far – e.g., between 12 and 21. This is represented by the colors red, amber, and green.

  (Optional) *Should you be pleased with this result?* Yes, if the current risk score is within the risk tolerance. Otherwise, the answer is no. This characteristic is optional, however it may facilitate thought.
- **Risk treatment determination**: If the risk is acceptable, *Accept* should be selected. This means we are satisfied with this risk and no more action is required. Depending on your risk assessment methodology and risk acceptance criteria, *Accept* might be selected if the risk exceeds your risk tolerance. Nonetheless, if it exceeds risk tolerance, the most probable response is *Treat*, i.e., take action. You might alternatively select *Avoid* or *Transfer* as the risk treatment choice, but these options are unlikely to be utilized much, if ever.
- **Risk improvement activities**: If you have selected the *Treat* option, you will add one or more new controls or enhance existing controls in the majority of situations. The expectation is that, after these steps have been implemented, they will have some influence on the probability or impact, which will ideally be sufficient to bring the risk below the established risk tolerance. Each activity should have a designated owner and a deadline for completion.

Hopefully, this was clear enough to let you understand the list of characteristics that a risk should have. Next stop, heatmaps.

Risk heatmaps

Risk heatmaps are often used in operational risk management and are especially beneficial for visually representing a company's risks and emphasizing those that need closer supervision. Typically, while analyzing operational risk, the risk manager will utilize a spreadsheet to record the company's important hazards and estimate their effect and likelihood (or probability).

Some entities still use spreadsheets to manage broader risks and display heatmaps, which are typically included in management information reports for senior management and other senior executives. Despite the fact that many companies have risk management systems that provide this functionality, some companies still rely on spreadsheets to manage broader risks and display heatmaps.

The total risk score is the product of the likelihood (or probability) and effect ratings. The formula for calculating the risk score is as follows:

Risk Score = Likelihood Score x Impact Score

When the list of risks is broad, often spanning many departments or business sectors, it is a significant difficulty for the risk manager to plot these risks on a heatmap, ensuring that all relevant hazards are shown appropriately. The hazards will be shown on a heatmap based on their respective scores. According to their individual scores, the hazards on the heatmap will be colored **red, amber, or green** (**RAG**).

The first example demonstrates how a comprehensive variety of hazards may be displayed using Excel in an understandable manner (the data sheet feeding into this chart has more than 100 risks).

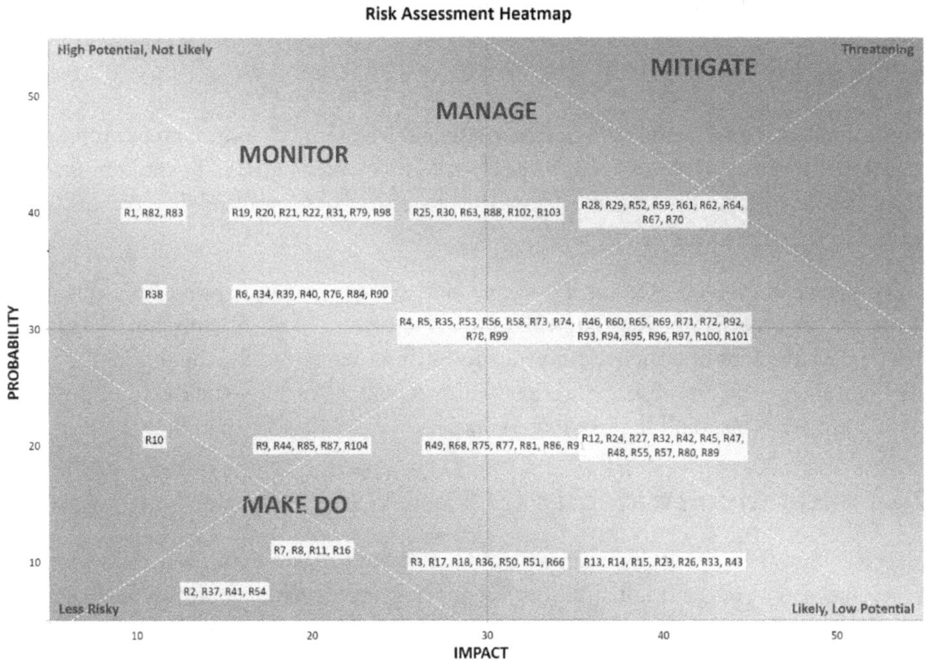

Figure 7.1 – Risk assessment heatmap

The second example illustrates a summarized heatmap in tabular format.

IMPACT \ LIKELIHOOD		10 Low	20 Medium	30 High	40 Very High
10	Low	4	1	1	3
20	Medium	4	5	7	7
30	High	7	7	10	6
40	Very High	7	12	14	9

NOTE

The figure shows the total number of identified risks per probability and impact score (e.g., P=10 and I=10, P=10 and I=20, and so on)

Figure 7.2 – Heatmap in tabular format

Well, now that we have defined how much a risk is *hot*, we need to find a way to take care of these risks, or, using the proper jargon, to *mitigate* them.

Risk mitigation

Risk mitigation refers to the methods to decrease risk and lessen the chance of an event happening. Risk mitigation is ensuring that your organization is completely safeguarded, which necessitates a continual focus on your main risks and concerns. The processes that govern and direct an organization are sometimes referred to as *controls* or *mitigation activities*.

To further comprehend this, let's examine it in connection to the overall **Enterprise Risk Management (ERM)** process. The objective of your controls is to avoid certain hazards from materializing. This results in the development of policies and procedures designed to reduce the probability of risks materializing, remove the possibility that they will materialize, or raise the likelihood that your processes will protect you should the risk materialize.

Best risk mitigation strategies

At any one given time, every firm confronts a plethora of hazards. They incur more risks when doing anything new (such as a project or initiative) or experiencing any form of organizational change. These inherent hazards are often related to the procedures involved in achieving the final objective. However, there are ways to reduce the likelihood (possibility) of occurrences that may be used to identify and guide better risk mitigation plans.

Consequently, the four most prevalent strategies are as follows:

- **Risk acceptance**, an idea that can be reduced to *taking the chance*. This means accepting that the danger exists and that there is nothing you can do to lessen or alter it. Instead, it involves comprehension of the likelihood of its occurrence and acceptance of the potential repercussions. This is the optimal method when the danger is low or the risk is unlikely to occur. When the cost of minimizing or avoiding risk is greater than the cost of accepting and leaving it to chance, it makes sense to accept the risk.
- **Risk avoidance**: If the risk associated with initiating a project, introducing a product, relocating your firm, and so on is too great to take, it may be preferable to forgo it. In this instance, risk avoidance involves avoiding engaging in the risk-causing behavior. Managing risk in this manner most closely resembles how individuals manage personal hazards. Despite the fact that some individuals are risk-seekers and others are risk-averse, everyone has a tipping point at which things become too hazardous to undertake.
- **Risk mitigation**: When evaluating risks, it is preferable not to avoid or accept certain hazards. In this case, risk minimization is investigated. Risk mitigation refers to the activities and techniques used to manage and mitigate risk. When risk and its likelihood are identified, management resources can be allocated appropriately.
- **Risk reduction**: Businesses may choose an acceptable degree of risk, known as the residual risk level. Risk minimization is the most prevalent method since there is often a means to minimize risk. It entails taking actions to mitigate the effects of outcomes. An example of risk reduction is risk transfer, such as purchasing insurance.
- **Risk transfer**: As previously stated, risk transfer includes transferring the risk to a third person or institution. As is the case of leasing property, risk transfers might be outsourced, transferred to an insurance company, or provided to a new organization. Not often do risk transfers result in decreased costs. A risk transfer is preferable when it can be utilized to mitigate future harm. Therefore, insurance may be costly, but it may be more cost-effective than experiencing the risk and being fully liable for repairs.

Tip – What is the most effective risk management strategy?

Obviously, the optimal technique depends on the risk you want to avoid. A solid rule of thumb for deciding which strategy to pursue is to undertake a risk assessment first. This will allow you to detect policy and activity gaps. Based on this input, you may effectively rank your efforts.

Just remember: there is no *one size fits all* formula here. 99.9% of the entities I have consulted for use the preceding strategies in conjunction with each other, according to their business needs.

How to establish risk mitigation strategies

All risks and benefits are evaluated differently based on your company's particular objectives. To effectively create risk reduction measures, you must engage in the following:

- **Understand the user's requirements**: Understand your clients' wants. Consider their needs while evaluating risks, since they are the foundation of your organization.
- **Seek out and use experts**: Risk need not be addressed in isolation. There are both software systems and subject matter experts available as resources.
- **Recognize risk that arises**: The worst thing you can do as a company leader is to ignore the existence of risk, since this is neither practical nor useful. When you are able to identify, define, and handle risk, you may better train your team and management to cope with its many varieties.
- **Encourage risk-taking**: Sometimes, taking risks is the best course of action. If your firm is capable of handling risk, promote risk-taking. Have backup plans and explain them so that everyone is on the same page to make this less intimidating.
- **Recognize possibilities**: Taking a risk may lead to the discovery of new opportunities. If you frame the discourse around risk in this manner, you may foster a problem-solving mindset that is adept at managing risk.
- **Promote consideration of mitigating strategies**: Consider comments from your team and include everyone. Everyone may have a unique risk mitigation strategy or approach. You can utilize data and analytics to evaluate alternatives and choose the optimal course of action.

Not every risk requires a mitigating strategy: as stated previously, it is occasionally preferable to take risk. Recognize that this is an option, and that some risks need no strategic response at all.

I tried my best here to give you all the basic (and non-basic) notions, but if you want to continue exploring the interesting world of risk management, you will find a plethora of books in your favorite bookstore that can help you to dig into the matter. For us, it's time to move on to data classification.

Data classification

We started this chapter talking about assets, and data classification is the process of organizing data assets, so it's worth a mention here.

Data classification involves building a classification scheme and defining one or more taxonomies for the whole organization. A categorization system facilitates the efficient determination of data action priorities and intensities. Data classification depends on characteristics such as criticality, security, access and usage, privacy, ethics, data quality, and storage needs.

Why is the classification of data important?

Classification of data offers businesses with an interface for implementing rules and processes across data types, structures, and storage systems. Classified data enables an organization to create and apply a single handling policy for sensitive data across numerous systems and data items. Defining many rules for each sort of data item is impractical in contexts with plentiful data today.

The categorization of data provides a corporate context to applications and processes. On the basis of data categorization, for instance, an organization might identify apps that handle sensitive data and specify stronger security criteria for such applications:

- **Compliance**: Data categorization makes it simpler to comply with regulatory frameworks such as GDPR, CCPA, HIPAA, and PCI, and also demonstrates compliance
- **Security**: Data categorization makes the organization aware of the data's sensitivity, both as a whole and each time new data is presented, and enables the organization to apply the appropriate degree of security control based on this context
- **Governance**: Data categorization facilitates the mapping, monitoring, and management of data

What are the four levels of data classification?

In information security, there are commonly four categorization levels for data:

- **Public**: Data that may exist in the public domain and can be freely shared with anybody outside the organization, a flyer outlining the company's goods and services, for example
- **Internal**: Company-wide data that is retained inside the organization and should not be shared outside, while not being sensitive, for instance, instructions on how to contact the company's IT support
- **Confidential**: This is information is domain-specific data, may be shared with particular individuals or teams, and includes sensitive corporate information; a pricing list for one of the company's goods, for instance
- **Restricted**: Highly sensitive information that should only be accessible on a need-to-know basis is *restricted*, for example, employment agreements

What are the various types of data classification?

While data is categorized depending on the requirements of each organization, there are a few typical methods of data classification:

- **Data-based**: A classification that explains the characteristics of the data. A credit card number or an email address are examples.

- **Context-based**: Classification that describes the business context of the data, for instance, sensitive information or earnings data.
- **Source-based**: Categorization that identifies the data source, for instance, consumer information gathered through a webinar registration form.

Difficulties with data classification

While data categorization is necessary for performing a variety of operations, information security focuses primarily on sensitive data. In the majority of businesses, sensitive data is categorized into various sensitivity levels and then mapped to distinct sensitive data categories (e.g., personal information).

Typically, companies confront the following obstacles when categorizing data:

- **False positives**: The same data may appear in several forms and circumstances. False classifications are more likely to be produced by classification algorithms that disregard the format and context of the input. As classification efforts often entail enormous volumes of data, even very low false positive rates might prohibit an organization from classifying properly.
- **False negatives**: According to different regulatory requirements, data may be deemed sensitive in one circumstance but not another. For instance, a name may be deemed non-sensitive by itself, but sensitive when paired with a medical record. Oftentimes, inaccurate categorization results from classifying data outside of its use context.
- **Big data**: Data lakes and data warehouses represent ever-expanding dynamic data stores, posing a formidable challenge for categorization methods that are not continuous.
- **Cost**: For the majority of classification tools, the cost of adopting and maintaining a data categorization strategy is contingent upon the quantity of data and the number of rules imposed. This procedure limits a company's ability to categorize massive datasets with rigorous access rules.

Effects of compliance standards on data classification

Many legislation and compliance requirements mandate that enterprises classify their data. Depending on the kind of data used, processed, collected, sent, and stored by an organization, each compliance standard may have varying requirements.

Here are several common compliance standards and their data classification requirements:

- **GDPR**: Under GDPR, organizations that handle the personal data of European data subjects must categorize all the kinds of data gathered. As mentioned in the previous chapters, GDPR classifies as *special* data pertaining to race, political beliefs, healthcare, ethnic origin, and biometrics. This information needs greater security.
- **PCI-DSS**: Entities are required by PCI DSS Requirement 9.6.1 to *classify data such that the sensitivity of the data may be assessed.*

- **SOC2**: Trust Services (SOC2) Entities are required by SOC2 criteria to show that they routinely identify and manage sensitive information in accordance with their specific confidentiality goals.
- **HIPAA**: **Protectedthanks health information** (**PHI**) is a high-risk asset under HIPAA. The HIPAA Security Rule mandates that businesses and related **business associates** (**BA**) to whom the law is applicable identify PHI and adopt protections to assure its availability, confidentiality, and integrity. The HIPAA Privacy Rule restricts the uses and disclosures of **protected health information** (**PHI**) and requires those applicable businesses and business partners to implement data categorization methods.

Preciousness of data is heavily dependent of the value we attribute to it.

Let's use an example to better understand this concept: let's suppose there is a country named XYZ and their king wants to conquer the adjacent country of ZYX. He calls all his counselors, ministries and advisers and prepares a war plan and puts it in the safe. This plan, as you may imagine, has enormous value. But, for some reason, the king never decides to use this plan and, instead, he agrees a long-lasting peace agreement with the other country. When his successor (or an opponent, or a revolution, you name it) ascends to the throne and finds the attack plan, what will the plan's value be then?

The answer is *I don't know*, and you probably don't know either. But for sure its value will be different than in the past because of the successful peace agreement, because the old king is dead, and many other different reasons. Data classification is the technique of ascribing value to some information.

Data classification levels

Data sensitivity levels assist in establishing how to handle each form of classified data. For instance, the **Center for Internet Security** (**CIS**) proposes three information classes:

- Public
- Business Confidential
- Sensitive

With seven categories of data sensitivity, the US Government has a more comprehensive categorization system:

- **Controlled Unclassified Information** (**CUI**)
- Public Trust
- Confidential
- Secret
- Top Secret

- Code Word Classification
- Restricted Data/Formerly Restricted Data

Using more than three layers might complicate data categorization and make it difficult to monitor and maintain. Using less than three tiers is deemed too basic and may result in inadequate protection and privacy. As recommended by the CIS, the majority of enterprises employ three categorization levels.

Here is a simplified version of the CIS classification definitions that you can use in your efforts to classify data:

- **Low-sensitivity data**: This consists of publicly available data that does not require access restrictions, such as web pages, blog posts, and job postings.
- **Medium-sensitivity data**: This is intended exclusively for internal use, and a breach might have a significant effect on the business, for instance, company strategies, client lists, and anonymous personal data.
- **High-sensitivity data**: This consists of information that is protected by rules or compliance requirements, necessitating tight access restrictions and security measures. The data, if compromised, might cause serious damage to people or the company, as well as incur compliance penalties or fines.

Developing a policy for data classification

A data categorization policy outlines the manner in which your business manages its information life cycle. The objective is to guarantee that sensitive data is handled according to the amount of risk it presents. A data categorization policy should handle access and authorization, taking the data structure and its typical business applications into consideration.

Here are numerous important aspects that your policy should address:

- **Objectives**: The rationale for applying data categorization and the desired outcomes, together with quantifiable **key performance indicators** (**KPIs**).
- **Workflows**: Clarify how the whole categorization process should be structured and coordinated. Explain how this procedure will affect all workers and how they should handle various degrees of sensitive information.
- **Location**: Identify where the data is kept, such as on site, in the cloud, on backup systems, in databases, files, and so on.
- **Schema**: Determine and describe the data classification categories.
- **Data owners**: Clarify the roles and responsibilities of all stakeholders participating in the categorization management process. Describe how each position should organize and allow access to data.

- **Compliance**: Clearly identify what information is governed by compliance standards and what steps are necessary to achieve compliance.

Data classification procedures

Here are a few recommended practices that may help you enhance your organization's data categorization:

- **Conduct a data risk assessment**: A full awareness of all data needs, including those connected to corporate rules and compliance standards, may be attained via a data risk assessment. You should also identify the contractual obligations for privacy and confidentiality. Define goals for data categorization in collaboration with all stakeholders, including IT, security, and legal teams.
- **Create a data inventory**: Before you can categorize data, you must identify it using methods and tools for data discovery. Once all sensitive data has been found, it must be identified and classified to ensure that each category of data is adequately secured. To make the procedure faster and more precise, you may mark any item containing sensitive data. This may considerably enhance the enforcement of your data categorization rules. You may manually or automatically label data.

  This procedure may be automated via the use of intelligent categorization systems. Using specified criteria, for instance, a data classification system may automatically recognize and categorize data, and then tag it with the relevant categorization label. Throughout the entire data lifespan, these systems may continually monitor data to ensure that it is always appropriately categorized.
- **Establish data security measures**: Each level of data categorization needs a unique degree of protection. To guarantee that each level is adequately secured, standardize your security methods. Define the policy-based controls for each label categorization.
- **Maintenance and supervision**: Data is dynamic and must be continuously monitored and maintained. It may be copied, generated, edited, removed, and transferred regularly. Due to the fact that data undergoes several transformations during its existence, classifying it may be a time-consuming endeavor. Identifying which data actually needs to be safeguarded and focusing classification efforts there is a crucial step in reducing classification time. Automated categorization systems are an additional method for reducing workloads and expediting the identification and processing of newly produced sensitive data. Lastly, verify that your data categorization standards are adaptable enough to accommodate changes in data structure, the introduction of new data kinds, and an increase in data volume.

Now that we have exhaustively dealt with data and its classification, it's time to move to ISO 27001 controls and why they are so important.

ISO 27001 controls

The ISO 27001 standard is comprised of the standard itself, plus a second part, called Annex A, where all the controls (114 divided into 14 categories) exist:

- Information Security Policies
- Organization of Information Security
- Human Resources Security
- Asset Management
- Access Control
- Cryptography
- Physical and Environmental Security
- Operational Security
- Communications Security
- System Acquisition, Development, and Maintenance
- Supplier Relationships
- Information Security Incident Management
- Information Security Aspects of Business Continuity Management
- Compliance

Each of the 14 categories provide you with a clear explanation of the primary objective(s) of that category.

Control Category A.5 – Information Security Policies (1 objective and 2 controls)

This category's aim is to give management guidance and assistance on information security in accordance with the organization's needs and applicable laws and regulations. This is accomplished by the documentation of a set of information security rules that must be authorized, publicized, disseminated, and reviewed at certain intervals.

Control Category A.6 – Organization of Information Security (2 objectives and 7 controls)

The first purpose is to develop a management structure that starts and regulates the implementation and operation of information security. This involves ensuring the following:

- Information security roles and responsibilities are explained and understood
- Segregation of duties is recognized and maintained
- Appropriate contact information is created and maintained with authorities, including the ICO, and special interest organizations, such as ISACA

No matter the kind of project, information security is developed and handled in project management. The second purpose is to protect the security of mobile devices and remote work.

This is accomplished by developing and executing a policy and supplementary security measures to control the risks associated with the usage of mobile devices and to safeguard information remotely accessed, processed, or stored.

Control Category A.7 – Human Resource Security (3 objectives and 6 controls)

The primary purpose is to ensure that employees understand their obligations and are qualified for the positions for which they are being evaluated. This is accomplished by completing adequate background checks on all applicants and including information security duties in employment contracts.

The second purpose is to ensure that employees are aware of and comply with their information security duties. To do this, they must implement information security in accordance with organizational rules and procedures. The organization is responsible for ensuring that personnel get proper training and frequent updates.

A structured and disclosed disciplinary procedure must also be developed so that any person who violates information security may be punished. The end purpose of this category is to safeguard an organization's interests when employees change jobs or leave the organization by defining, communicating, and enforcing restrictive covenants.

Control Category A.8 – Asset Management (3 objectives and 10 controls)

The first aim requires the identification of information assets and the assignment of suitable protection tasks. This is accomplished by developing an asset inventory that identifies asset owners. Document and execute rules on the permissible use of these assets. When recovered, assets must also be secured and maintained. The subsequent purpose is to guarantee that data is adequately safeguarded.

To do this, it is necessary to develop a categorization system and classify the assets properly. Therefore, all electronic and physical assets must be labeled in line with the categorization system, and procedures for managing assets must also be designed and executed. The final purpose is to prevent unauthorized disclosure, alteration, deletion, or destruction of information stored on media. This can be accomplished by employing removable-media management methods. These processes must address the safe disposal and transit of storage media holding sensitive information.

Control Category A.9 – Access Control (4 objectives and 14 controls)

The primary goal is to restrict access to information and data processing resources: this is accomplished in part by developing and enforcing an access control policy and limiting user access to just the systems and network regions they require to execute their jobs.

The second goal is to guarantee authorized user access and prevent unauthorized access.

The following controls are used for this purpose:

- A structured procedure for user registration and de-registration
- A structured procedure for user access provisioning
- Restriction and management of the assignment and use of privileged access rights
- A structured method for managing the distribution of passwords, PINs, and so on
- The examination of access rights
- Users' access privileges are revoked when they leave an organization or switch positions

The third purpose is to hold users responsible for protecting their passwords, PINs, tokens, and so on. As a result, it is necessary to adhere to prescribed procedures for the usage of secret authentication information. This category's end purpose is to prevent unauthorized access to systems and applications. To fulfill this purpose, controls must limit access to information and systems and, where applicable, implement secure login processes. In addition to restricting utility applications that may circumvent system and application constraints, access to program source code must also be controlled. For this purpose, password management solutions are often used.

Control Category A.10 – Cryptography (1 objective and 2 controls)

This category's purpose is to guarantee that cryptography is utilized properly to safeguard the confidentiality, integrity, and validity of information.

This is accomplished by creating and implementing a cryptographic policy that includes information on the usage, protection, and lifespan of cryptographic keys.

Control Category A.11 – Physical and Environmental Security (2 objectives and 15 controls)

The primary purpose of this category is to prevent unauthorized physical access to, damage of, and interference with data- and information-processing infrastructure.

Controls used to achieve these aims include the following:

- Defining and utilizing physical boundary security
- Ensuring that physical access controls are installed and used
- Protecting offices, rooms, and infrastructure
- Safeguarding against external and environmental dangers
- Developing and enforcing protocols for working in secure environments
- Securing delivery and loading locations regardless of location

The second purpose is to avoid the loss, theft, compromise, or destruction of assets and the disruption of activities.

Controls to achieve this purpose include the following:

- Equipment placement and protection, to prevent information from being neglected or equipment from being harmed by the environment
- The administration and safeguarding of supporting utilities, including **uninterruptible power supply** (**UPS**), electricity, gas, and water
- Guarding against inadvertent or deliberate damage to power and communication connections
- Regularly maintaining and servicing equipment, including **heating, ventilation, and air conditioning** (**HVAC**) as applicable
- Managing the removal of assets from the organization's premises in an efficient manner
- Protecting valuables that are removed from the property
- Reusing and discarding equipment in a safe way
- Ensuring users adequately safeguard unattended equipment
- Implementing a policy for a clean desk and screen

Control Category A.12 – Operations Security (7 objectives and 14 controls)

The first objective is to guarantee that information processing facilities are properly and securely managed.

To do this, operational procedures must be recorded and made accessible.

Change management is included in these procedures to govern modifications to business processes, information processing facilities, and systems.

Capacity management must also be used to monitor and forecast capacity requirements.

Additionally, it should be highlighted that the development, testing, and operational environments must be segregated in order to decrease the danger of unauthorized access or modifications to operational environments.

The following purpose is to safeguard information and information-processing facilities against malware. This is done by implementing anti-malware software to identify, prevent, and recover from attacks.

Users must be aware of the organization's anti-malware software and its guidelines on permissible and undesirable use.

The third objective is to defend against data loss by ensuring that frequent backups of information, software, and systems are performed and tested in accordance with an established backup strategy.

The subsequent aim involves documenting occurrences and producing proof. This is achieved by generating, storing, evaluating, and preserving user activity logs, including those of administrators and ordinary users, exception reports, and information security event logs.

All pertinent information-processing system clocks must be synchronized to a single reference time source, such as the **network time protocol** (**NTP**).

The fifth objective is to ensure the integrity of operating systems.

Implementing and using control processes to oversee the installation of software on operating systems accomplishes this objective.

The following purpose is to avoid the exploitation of technological flaws and may be achieved by collecting data about technological vulnerabilities, assessing the dangers they may cause, and implementing corrective measures.

Additionally, regulations controlling software installation must be defined and enforced. This category's end purpose is to minimize the effect of audit operations on operating systems.

In order to minimize interruptions, strategies must be agreed upon regarding audit requirements and actions requiring verification of operating systems.

Control Category A.13 – Communications Security (2 objectives and 7 controls)

The second purpose is to preserve the security of both internal and external information transfers, and this may be accomplished by creating formal transfer rules, processes, and controls to secure information being transmitted across all kinds of communication facilities, including electronic messaging via email, communications platforms, and social media.

Therefore, information transfer agreements must include provisions for the safe sharing of business information.

Control Category A.14 – System Acquisition, Development, and Maintenance (3 objectives and 13 controls)

The primary purpose is to guarantee that information security is an intrinsic component of information systems throughout their entire lifespan, including the requirements for information systems that provide services via public networks. This implies that information security needs must be included into the specifications for any new or upgraded information systems.

Protecting data involved in application services that traverse public networks is a further control that may assist in achieving this purpose. Information involved in application service transactions must also be safeguarded to avoid incomplete transmission, misrouting, unauthorized message modification, unauthorized message disclosure, unauthorized message duplication, and unauthorized message replay.

The subsequent purpose is to guarantee that information security is established and executed within the development life cycle, which is closely related to design and development activities.

The following controls may assist in achieving this goal:

- Rules for software and system development must be developed and implemented
- Changes made to systems throughout the development life cycle must be governed by established change control processes
- When operating systems are modified, mission-critical applications must be examined and verified for negative effects on operations and security
- Software package modifications must be discouraged
- If modifications are needed, they must be confined to those that are essential and rigorously governed
- Any information system implementation activities must define, record, and use secure system engineering principles
- Establishing and adequately protecting secure development environments
- Any outsourced development operations must be managed and monitored
- During development, security functionality must be evaluated
- Programs and criteria for system acceptability testing must be created for new information systems, upgrades, and new versions

The final objective is to ensure the security of data used for testing by carefully choosing data, encrypting or otherwise safeguarding it, and restricting access to only authorized employees.

It is necessary to create and apply guidelines for software and system development. Changes made to systems during the lifespan of development must be managed by defined change control methods.

When operating systems are updated, mission-critical applications must be analyzed for adverse implications on operations and security. It is necessary to discourage software package change. If alterations are necessary, they must be limited to the bare minimum and strictly regulated. Any operations involving the development of an information system must define, document, and execute secure system engineering principles.

Creating and appropriately safeguarding secure development environments

Any outsourced development activities need management and oversight. Security functionality must be examined throughout the development process. For new information systems, updates, and new versions, programs and criteria for system acceptability testing must be devised.

The ultimate goal is to secure the data used for testing by selecting data with care, encrypting or otherwise protecting it, and limiting access to only authorized personnel.

Control Category A.15 – Supplier relationships (2 objectives and 5 controls)

The primary purpose of this category is to safeguard supplier-accessible assets. To achieve this, information security standards to limit risks associated with suppliers having access to assets must be exhaustively specified in a policy for supplier management.

As a result, written agreements must be negotiated and executed with each supplier, including all pertinent criteria outlined in the supplier management policy. Information security risks linked with information and communications technology services and the supply chain must be addressed in these formal agreements.

The second goal is to maintain an established degree of information security and service delivery in accordance with supplier contracts. To do this, suppliers must be watched, examined, and in certain instances audited on a regular basis. Changes to supplier services must also be handled, along with the maintenance and improvement of current information security policies, procedures, and controls; taking into account the importance of corporate information, systems, processes, and reassessment of risks.

Control Category A.16 – Information security incident management (1 objective and 7 controls)

This category has a single aim, which is to establish a uniform and effective approach to the management of information security incidents, including communications on security events and vulnerabilities.

The following controls may assist in achieving this objective:

- For a prompt, effective, and systematic reaction to information security events, management responsibilities and processes must be developed and executed
- Information security incidents must be promptly reported via the proper management channels
- Employees and contractors are required to disclose any identified or suspected information security vulnerabilities
- Information security incidents must be evaluated carefully to determine their classification as occurrences
- Deficiencies or occurrences, i.e., missing occurrences
- Information security issues must be addressed in accordance with established processes
- Utilize the knowledge acquired from analyzing and resolving information security events to lessen the possibility or effect of future occurrences
- Documented processes must outline the identification, gathering, acquisition, and preservation of information that may be used as evidence

Control Category A.17 – Information security aspects of business continuity management (2 objectives and 4 controls)

The initial purpose of this category is to prevent violations of legal, legislative, regulatory, or contractual information security duties and security requirements.

To achieve this purpose, it is necessary to identify the needs for information security and the continuity of information security management under bad scenarios. Processes, procedures, and controls must then be created, documented, implemented, and maintained. Once in place, these arrangements must be frequently evaluated and validated to guarantee their efficacy.

The second purpose is to guarantee that information processing facilities are available. This is performed by establishing redundant information-processing facilities to satisfy availability needs.

Control Category A.18 – Compliance (2 objectives and 8 controls)

The primary purpose of this category is to prevent violations of legal, legislative, regulatory, or contractual information security duties and security standards. Identifying and recording pertinent legal, statutory, regulatory, and contractual requirements, as well as the strategy for satisfying them, are examples of controls that might assist in achieving this purpose:

- Implementing processes to assure compliance with legal, statutory, regulatory, and contractual obligations for intellectual property rights and the usage of proprietary software products

- Protecting records against loss, tampering, falsification, unauthorized access, and unauthorized disclosure, in accordance with legal, statutory, regulatory, contractual, and corporate requirements
- As required by applicable laws and regulations, ensuring the privacy and security of personally identifiable information
- Utilizing cryptographic controls in accordance with all applicable international and national agreements, laws, and regulations

The second purpose is to guarantee that information security is established and managed in compliance with the rules and procedures of the organization. This is accomplished by conducting independent evaluations of the strategy for managing information security and its execution at predetermined intervals or in response to substantial changes.

The compliance of information processing and processes within their areas of responsibility of given managers must also be routinely reviewed by them; finally, information systems must undergo frequent compliance reviews, which may be accomplished via penetration testing.

Who is charged for implementing Annex A controls?

There are two essential considerations for addressing this question.

Less than forty percent of ISO 27001 Annex A controls are technology-based. Information security vulnerabilities are often caused by human behavior. Therefore, contrary to popular belief, IT cannot and should not be the only answer.

Information security is, in reality, about constructing a system of mature, resilient rules. The present Annex A framework applies the following percentages to control locations inside an organization:

- 37% – Technology
- 36% – Organizational/documentation
- 13% – Physical security
- 5% – Supplier and buyers
- 5% – Human resource management
- 4% – Legal protection

Consequently, applying the controls stated in Annex A is and must always be the responsibility of a number of persons and departments within an organization, the number of which is dependent on the size and complexity of the organization.

Using the ISO 27001 controls

The controls outlined in Annex A of ISO 27001 are a vital component of risk treatment and must be chosen based on a comprehensive analysis of an organization's information security threats.

Typically, chosen controls must be justified by one of the following:

- Risk assessment
- Business need or best method
- Legal or contractual requirement

Once controls have been identified, organizations must submit a **Statement of Applicability (SoA)** that must contain, at a minimum, all 114 controls listed in Annex A of ISO 27001, along with reasons for inclusions and, preferably, concise descriptions of how they have been implemented. The SoA acts as a tool for providing senior management with accurate information on the degree of risk to which their organizations are exposed and the status of risk treatment efforts.

Identification of ISO 27001 controls to implement

Only after a thorough evaluation of an organization's inherent information security threats can it be determined which measures should be adopted. Once the risks are known, the appropriate countermeasures may be determined. Possibly, the greater the number of controls adopted, the greater the likelihood that the organization can minimize or at least mitigate exposure to recognized risks.

Nonetheless, Annex A controls may be omitted if deemed irrelevant. An example of this would be a company that does not produce software.

Obviously, there would be no need for a strategy of secure growth. If a control is to be omitted, a complete rationale must be included in the SoA.

Summary

This chapter was very discursive, but we talked about risk management, data classification (still, as part of risk management) and all the controls within Annex A of ISO 27001.

In the next chapter, we will discuss preparing foolproof policies and procedures to avoid internal risks. We will examine security systems and devices, cybersecurity vulnerabilities, social engineering, common pain points, and critical success factors.

8

Preparing Policies and Procedures to Avoid Internal Risk

In the previous chapter, we've been through the main principles for deciding what to use and how to use it in terms of controls and risk management related to our entity. As already explained, if we buy off-the-shelf software, there is no need to implement controls related to software (just remember to keep them beside our Statement of Applicability) and so on. However, once we decide to use some controls, we will need to prepare (or update) our policy and procedures accordingly.

In this chapter, we will go through all this, with a hands-on flavor: in fact, my aim is to also give you a good amount of practical tips on how to write down policies (and procedures).

We'll have a (one-way, of course) conversation related to the following topics:

- Company policies
- Policy writing instructions
- Company procedures

Company policies

The purpose of company policy is to create define standards of behavior within a business, detailing the duties of both workers and employers. The administration of corporate policy and procedures seeks to safeguard both the legal rights of employees and the economic interests of employers. Depending on the demands of the company, diverse policies and procedures define regulations for employee behavior, attendance, dress codes, privacy, and other aspects of the terms and conditions of employment.

How do you determine the appropriate policies for your business?

In the following scenarios, a company should develop and apply policies:

- Company-wide guidelines on the proper way to conduct oneself (dress codes, email, internet policies, or smartphone use)
- Guidance for dealing with typical situations (standards of conduct, travel expenditures, or purchase of company merchandise)
- Legal aspects of the organization (charges of harassment or discriminatory hiring and promotion practices)
- Adherence to government regulations and agencies (the Family and Medical Leave Act, the Disabilities Act, the Equal Employment Opportunity Commission, or minimum wage regulation)
- Establishing uniform work rules, regulations, and standards (progressive discipline, safety rules, and guidelines on breaks and smoke breaks)
- Offering workers equitable treatment (eligibility for benefits, paid time off, tuition assistance, bereavement, or jury duty exemption)
- There may be other reasons to adopt a policy, but don't allow one employee's terrible conduct to be the impetus for implementing a regulation that will affect others

To maintain compliance and a healthy corporate culture, employees require consistent company policies to guide them in their tasks and responsibilities, as well as the organization's underlying business values, ethics, and beliefs. Additionally, written rules and procedures shield your business from any legal action.

Creating written rules may seem like a daunting undertaking, particularly if you are also managing other responsibilities, but here are a few policies to get you started:

- **Personnel policies** – Clearly specify business hours, codes of behavior, employment conditions (in terms of hiring and termination), earnings or salary (and bonuses, if applicable), insurance and health benefits, paid versus unpaid vacation days, sick leave, and retirement.
- **Disciplinary action policies** – Address concerns of honesty, performance, safety, and misbehavior, as well as identifying what constitutes a breach of corporate policy and how workers will be penalized if they break particular regulations.
- **Security policies** – Create rules describing what safe conduct at work looks like, how to utilize safety equipment, how to report safety risks, and so on using industry best practices and applicable local, state, and federal regulations as guidelines.
- **Technology policies** – Establish standards for acceptable and unacceptable internet, email, and social media use for personal reasons in the workplace.

- **Privacy policies** – Protect your staff, your organization, and your customers by implementing a policy that promotes openness and trust with your customers.
- **Payment policies** – Determine the conditions for consumers and suppliers to do business with your organization. Set an appropriate payment period and define penalties for late or non-payment.
- **Policies on confidentiality** – Protect sensitive information and make sure to include vendor, customer, and other supplier ties.
- **Whistleblower policy** – Ensure you have a policy against retribution to safeguard your workers and your business.
- **Policies on employee performance** – Define the job of each employee, including their degree of responsibility, decision-making power, broad objectives, and particular duties. Identify explicit mechanisms for performance monitoring and personnel development via training.
- **Document and record retention rules** – Develop organized policies for document retention and storage in accordance with local, state, and federal regulations. Please be extremely careful with this one, as it may involve the GDPR retention policy as well.

Policy writing instructions

When establishing a new policy or updating an existing one, you should adhere to the following writing tips:

- **Keep things simple** – Policies need to be expressed in straightforward terms, not legalese. The policy should be simple for all employees (from the CEO to the cleaning personnel) to comprehend.
- **Keep it generic** – Policies cannot foresee all conceivable circumstances. Policies should be drafted with enough specificity to be applicable in a variety of situations. Thorough assistance can be offered in the form of frequently asked questions or detailed process rules or standards.
- **Make it relevant** – The policy should explain to the audience why it exists, who it impacts, the most important rules and constraints in it, when and under what conditions it applies, and how it should be implemented. *Terms of…* should be explained explicitly for the reader under *Definitions*.
- **Verify correctness and conformity** – Ensure that the proposed policy conforms with all outstanding policies already in place (if any) to guarantee conformity. At the same time, verify that these policies won't go against any current national, federal, or state laws, regulatory requirements, or industry standards.

- **Ensure that the policy can be implemented** – A policy should not be developed if it is not intended to be enforced or if it makes commitments without securing enough resources.
- **Clearly specify who is responsible for what** – Define the roles and responsibilities of departments and people with precision. Ensure that the policy specifies who is permitted to make particular choices and who is accountable for carrying out certain responsibilities.
- **Less is more** – A policy does not need to be long. In many cases, shorter is preferable. The purpose of the policy is to communicate vital information simply and clearly. Longer policies may be harder to comprehend, implement, and interpret.

So far, we've defined policy as a collection of rules or instructions for an organization and its personnel to follow in order to accomplish a certain objective (i.e., compliance) and they have to respond to what workers must or must not do, as well as provide directives, boundaries, principles, and decision-making guidelines. Policies respond to inquiries such as "*what?*" and "*why?*"

What about procedures, then?

Procedures are the antithesis of policies; they specify how a policy should be implemented. A policy outlines a rule, whereas procedures specify who is expected to follow the rule and how. Procedures address queries such as "*how?*," "*when?*," and "*where?*"

Without examining their objective, far too many businesses perceive rules and procedures as a necessary evil. It's not about best practices or becoming a soulless corporation; the objective of policies and procedures is to describe what management wants to occur and how it should occur.

I've come to feel that the key different between a small and medium-sized organization is whether or not management has taken the time to design, execute, and maintain policies and procedures.

Companies with mature policies, processes, and systems are simpler to audit, have a better grasp of their security posture and risk, and seem to operate much more sustainably than those that have paid little attention to governance.

The importance of policies and procedures versus their pain

Once management knows the definitions of policies and procedures, they cease asking, "*What are policies and processes?*" and "*What is a policy's purpose?*," and ask, "*Why am I required to develop policies and procedures?*" Small firm management often has the same set of obstacles to documenting policies and procedures, all of which relate to the complexity, corporate culture, and time constraints involved. However, let's not forget: the benefits of policies and procedures exceed their disadvantages. The aim of policies and procedures extends much beyond the simple documentation of regulations. Typically, my description of these advantages sounds like this.

It is difficult to draft policies and procedures, but it's not that difficult. If the majority of organizations lacked developed rules and processes, they would not be in business. It's obviously simpler to specify security from the outset, but that doesn't imply it's impossible to begin with what you're doing today and then tweak it later.

Occasionally, the main argument is not how difficult it is to document rules and processes, but rather how terrified most people are of documenting how they're doing things incorrectly. Begin with where you are and then be realistic about where you want to go. In certain instances, you may not meet the best practice level, but if you allow that shame to prevent you from documenting your rules, you are missing the point. Knowing precisely what you are doing in the now allows you to determine what you should be doing tomorrow. It's how you can create a genuine budget, detect real business risks, and react effectively when anything goes wrong.

If your practice isn't *right*, but you're honest about it, it's far less of an issue than if you have nothing documented.

One of the best examples on how to write a privacy policy, for instance, comes from Twitter. As one of the biggest and most popular social networking platforms in the world, Twitter's privacy policy is an excellent example of a comprehensive but easily accessible policy. Utilizing color coding, hyperlinks, and highlighting, it is well-organized and straightforward to explore. However, the length of this privacy policy is a significant drawback. Observe the scroll bar: this makes it more difficult for the user to quickly comprehend how Twitter collects, uses, and protects user data (you can check here: `https://twitter.com/en/privacy`).

Policies and procedures will not change your company, but they'll probably change your perspective! Writing everything down, implementing formal procedures, and establishing expectations will require you to surrender some flexibility. These new features may need adjustments to the corporate structure, business culture, revenue funnel, or *informal but excellent* procedures to satisfy the criteria you have outlined. Depending on your current organizational structure, you may realize that you require extra personnel to undertake new duties, or that some procedures may move more slowly.

For instance, with the implementation of new rules and processes, your network engineer must now get management approval before making a firewall adjustment. Your team may not be able to simply pick up the phone and request access to an extra network segment. Isn't it going to add some time and maybe some irritation to the process? Alternatively, how much would you lose if you lost the person who knew precisely why your firewall was configured the way it was? Without documenting these procedures, you create enormous vulnerabilities. People, training, standards, and apps – how much is that small bit of overhead worth if it guarantees that you have a firm grasp on what's happening inside your organization, networks, and enterprise?

However, you may reduce the magnitude of the transition by incorporating your company's culture into its rules and processes. Nowhere does it state that rules and procedures must be excruciatingly formal, tedious to read, and packed with legalese. What are the factors that attract potential employees? Adapt your rules and processes to your company's culture, operations, and interpersonal dynamics. This will reduce the difficulty of applying them and assist protect your organization's identity.

Do you remember the White Rabbit in Alice in Wonderland – that bizarre rabbit wearing a huge clock stating that "*There's no time*?" Well, that's the case. I've never heard so many times "*There is no time*" as an excuse for not writing policies and procedures. In a world of lean personnel, quick turnover, and a focus on accomplishing more with less, it may be incredibly difficult to find time for governance. Therefore, it does not matter. I can offer you management book after management book, essay after essay, and white paper after white paper on how following set rules and procedures will benefit your organization at every level.

If you can commit to implementing and enforcing your rules, you will be astounded by the short-term win of how much easier audits become and even more astounded by the long-term benefits you will get. Your operations will be less stressful, your employees will have more direction, and, if done correctly, you will finally understand precisely what you are managing and why.

The benefits of policies and processes exceed their disadvantages. The rewards of committing to the process are substantial.

How to physically write a policy?

Use a template: establishing a consistent policy template ensures that each policy paper is ordered and comprehensible. It establishes the baseline for how all future regulations will be written and arranged so that they are simple to read and navigate.

Even if you produce a number of additional regulations in the years to come, the format will be simple to duplicate since you have established this standard today. This will also facilitate the writing process and save a substantial amount of time.

> **Tip**
>
> If your entity has not established any policy yet, a good idea could be to create a policy on how to draft a policy.

Here are some suggestions for things to put in your draft policy:

- Information regarding the policy, such as the policy's title, the dates for when it becomes effective and is revised, the approver's signature, and the department(s) it applies to
- Introduction or statement of purpose: what is it about? Why is it necessary?
- What is the organization's stance on the subject?

It's vital to clarify terminology as you go, particularly words and phrases with various meanings and industry- or job-specific terms. This makes rules simple to comprehend and might save you from having to argue over terminology in the event of litigation.

Define employee conduct guidelines and limits. What are the repercussions for violating a rule?

How are incidents and violations to be reported? What is the method for reporting?

Basically, think before writing. Once a policy is approved, it can take time to retire it, get approval from the management again, and so on.

Selecting a method for managing the process

You could create all the regulations in your preferred word processor, but then you'd have to distribute the document so that everyone may annotate their own copy, resulting in many copies of the same page.

Alternatively, you can upload it to a cloud-based word processor, therefore reducing the number of versions you need to manage. Everyone is able to edit the same document and all changes will be saved. However, you still want a solution that provides version control and can match your rules to your accreditation and licensing requirements.

Establishing a policy management group

Depending on the size of your firm, you may need assistance in writing your policies and procedures. It also facilitates more buy-in from stakeholders within the firm. Plus, it assures you don't overlook vital facts.

Since your rules will affect everyone in the firm, you should enlist the assistance of individuals from diverse departments. Consult the subject matter experts on the operation of a certain department or function. Include those who understand and can assist you in adhering to any applicable local, state, and federal laws affecting the operation of the group.

> Tip
>
> Let's suppose you write an HR policy, including all the steps related to hiring, termination, and so on, and maybe some national, regional, or other laws apply. Therefore, it's imperative to collaborate with your HR team to elaborate on a better and more definitive policy.

Now that you have management support, an organized team, a framework, and a technological solution, you are prepared to begin writing. Here is how it should function.

Prioritizing a policy list

You cannot write every policy at once and some policies are more significant than others; thus, make a list of policies that must be completed first. Prioritize your new regulations and amendments based on their relative significance and establish a schedule and sequence for their completion.

Consult with your policy team (if there is one) to determine what needs to be addressed. Defining these priorities with your ultimate objective in mind can help you remain on track.

Conduct exhaustive research. Examine your present processes to determine how things are currently carried out. Additionally, you will need to evaluate any compliance concerns that may have caused your policy review.

There are many approaches to analyzing and studying existing processes:

- Interviewing people responsible for day-to-day activities
- Observing colleagues to determine existing practices
- Interviewing internal and external specialists
- Finding the most recent legislation, rules, and accreditation standards
- Identifying overlapping rules to ensure uniform terminology and standards

Creating a preliminary draft

Writing policies and procedures is an ongoing process. The first draft will need many modifications. It makes sense to get input from stakeholders and colleagues and you should edit your copy depending on their comments.

Having someone other than the policy owner produce the original draft may promote an outsider's viewpoint, making your processes eventually more transferrable to everyday operations.

This might also assist to clarify the wording and eliminate any unnecessary technical jargon from your work.

Avoid using a large number of industry-specific words, particularly if your company spans many licensing groups, roles, and sectors. The same acronyms and words may have different meanings to various employee groups; thus, you need to prevent misunderstanding.

Additionally, limiting technical jargon can make it simpler for new workers who may be unfamiliar with the business to comprehend your rules and processes.

Verifying the processes

To guarantee the validity of your methods, you must see them in operation; it is generally a good idea to have the workers who conduct the daily job execute the processes.

Remember that this only applies to the Procedures section of your handbook and not to the policies and forbidden activities sections.

Sending a draft out for review

Now that you have a draft, it is time to evaluate it; if a non-specialist authored the first document, you should have a specialist examine it. This is the key to the success of your policy. You will have to walk a tight line between the requirement for thoroughness for your subject matter specialists and the need for clarity and simplicity for your non-experts.

Obtaining final approval and signatures

Typically, a member of the executive team must approve any new policy. Because they are ultimately responsible for the policy, they must formally endorse the final document. This should always be carried out by the highest level of leadership for each policy.

For instance, you do not need the CEO's approval for new spill cleanup measures, but you must for workplace harassment and the handling of confidential information. Equally, the IT manager should not approve an employee conduct code; that responsibility lies with the CTO or CIO, who is ultimately accountable.

Employee Code of Conduct example draft

The Employee Code of Conduct is one of the most essential components of the employee handbook. We prepared a code of conduct template to help you convey your expectations to your staff straightforwardly and sensitively.

Remember that this template is not a legal document and may not comply with all applicable local and national regulations. Please request that your attorney evaluates the finished policy papers or handbook.

Template for the Employee Code of Conduct

You are accountable for behaving correctly at work as an employee. Here, we outline our expectations. We cannot cover every possible situation of behavior, but we have faith that you will always use sound judgment. Contact your human resources department if you have any concerns or questions.

The dress code

The official dress code of our company is business/business casual/smart casual/casual. This consists of slacks/loafers/blouses/boots. However, a worker's position may also influence their attire. If you often meet with clients or potential clients, please dress more formally. We want you to arrive at work clean and avoid wearing unprofessional attire (e.g., workout clothes).

As long as you adhere to our aforementioned criteria, we have no special expectations about your attire or accessories.

We also allow and respect how religious views, ethnicity, or disability influence grooming styles, dress styles, and accessories in the workplace.

Internet security and electronic gadgets

This section concerns everything digital in the workplace. To maintain security and safeguard our assets, we wish to establish standards for the use of computers, phones, our internet connection, and social media.

Internet use

Our company internet connection is largely used for business purposes. However, you may occasionally use our internet connection for personal reasons, so long as it does not interfere with your job duties. If requested, we also expect you to temporarily cease personal activities that slow down our internet connection (such as picture uploading).

You are prohibited from the following:

- Using our internet connection to download or upload vulgar, offensive, or illegal content
- Transmitting sensitive information to unauthorized parties
- Invading the privacy of another individual and obtaining access to sensitive information
- Downloading or uploading pirated movies, music, material, or software
- Visiting potentially harmful websites that may damage the security of our network and PCs
- Carrying out unauthorized or unlawful acts, such as hacking, fraud, or the purchase or sale of illicit items

Cell phones

We permit mobile phone usage at work. However, we also want to guarantee that your gadgets will not distract you from your job or disturb the office environment. Please adhere to the following very basic rules:

- Use your mobile phone for work-related purposes (business calls, productivity apps, calendars)
- Use an empty conference room or common area for personal calls so as not to disturb your coworkers
- Avoid playing mobile games and texting excessively
- Never use your cell phone while operating a work car
- Do not record personal information on your phone
- Do not download or post improper, unlawful, or obscene content while using our business internet connection
- Additionally, you may not use your phone in locations where it is expressly forbidden (e.g., laboratories)

Corporate email

Email is crucial for our business. You should use your workplace email mainly for business purposes, although we permit occasional personal usage. Guidance on how to use business email at work:

- Use for work-related purposes. There are no restrictions on using a corporate email for work-related activities. For instance, you may subscribe to publications and online services that will benefit your career or professional development.
- Personal usage. You may use your email for personal purposes so long as you maintain its security and avoid sending spam and releasing sensitive information. You may, for instance, send emails to relatives and friends and download e-books, manuals, and other information for personal use.

Our general expectations

Regarding how you use your business email, we want you to avoid the following:

- Registering for unlawful, untrustworthy, disreputable, or questionable websites and services.
- Sending unsolicited commercial emails or material.
- Registering for a competitor's services without permission.
- Sending offensive or discriminatory communications and information.
- Sending unsolicited emails, even to colleagues.
- In general, use robust passwords and be alert when detecting malicious or phishing emails. Ask our security specialists if you are unsure whether an email you received is secure or not.

Social media

We want to give some recommendations in order to avoid irresponsible usage of social media in the workplace. We will discuss both the usage of personal social media at work and the use of social media to represent our organization.

Personal use of social media at work

General guidance on how to use social media at work:

- You are authorized to access your personal accounts at work. However, we want you to behave responsibly and productively in accordance with our rules. Specifically, we request that you exercise self-discipline and avoid being distracted by social media networks.
- Ensure that people are aware that your personal account or claims do not represent our organization. Use a disclaimer such as "*These are my personal thoughts.*"

- Refrain from divulging intellectual property (such as trademarks) or sensitive information. Before sharing unannounced corporate news, consult your boss or the public relations department.
- Avoid any information that is libelous, insulting, or disparaging. You may be in violation of our company's anti-harassment policy if you send this kind of material to coworkers, clients, or business partners.

Representing our business through social media

Guidance when managing social media through a company:

- If you manage our social media accounts or represent our firm in public, we expect you to safeguard its image and reputation. Specifically, you must exhibit respect, courtesy, and patience.
- If possible, avoid discussing topics beyond your area of expertise.
- Comply with our standards on confidentiality and data protection, as well as the laws regulating copyrights, trademarks, plagiarism, and fair use.
- Coordinate with our PR or marketing department before sharing any material that could have a significant effect.
- Avoid removing or disregarding comments without justification.
- Correct or delete any misleading or inaccurate material as fast as feasible.

Competing interests

When you are suffering a conflict of interest, your own aims and duties to us are no longer aligned. For instance, holding shares with one of our rivals is a conflict of interest.

In other instances, you may encounter an ethical dilemma. Accepting a bribe, for instance, may be financially advantageous, but it is unlawful and against our company code of ethics. If we become aware of such conduct, you will be fired and may face legal consequences.

Conflicts of interest are therefore a big concern for all of us. We anticipate that you will be cautious in identifying situations that constitute conflicts of interest for yourself or your direct subordinates. Follow our rules and always behave in the best interests of our firm. Whenever possible, avoid allowing personal or financial concerns to interfere with your work. Discuss any ethical problem with your manager or HR and we will do our best to assist you in resolving it.

Employee interactions

We aim to guarantee that all staff interactions are suitable and amicable. Please adhere to our principles and conduct yourself professionally at all times.

Fraternization

The term *fraternization* refers to dating or befriending coworkers. In this policy, *dating* refers to romantic relationships and consensual sexual encounters. Relationships that are not consensual constitute sexual violence and we expressly ban forbid them.

Dating coworkers

If you begin a romantic relationship with a coworker, we want you to retain your professionalism and keep personal conversations outside of the office.

You must also respect your coworkers who date one another. We will not accept sexual jokes, nasty rumors, or inappropriate remarks. Please notify Human Resources if you come across this kind of conduct.

Dating managers

To prevent charges of favoritism, misuse of power, and sexual harassment, supervisors are prohibited from dating their direct subordinates. This limitation applies to all employees reporting to managers.

Additionally, if you are the recruiting manager for your team, you cannot employ your spouse. You may recommend them to other teams or departments where you do not have management or recruiting power.

Employees who work together may develop friendships either inside or outside the workplace. This connection between peers is encouraged since it may facilitate communication and collaboration. However, we expect you to prioritize your job and leave personal issues outside of the office.

Employment of relatives

Everyone in our organization ought to be employed, acknowledged, or promoted on the basis of their abilities, character, and work ethic. We do not want to witness nepotism, favoritism, or conflicts of interest and thus, we impose employment limitations on relatives of workers.

To our organization, a *relative* is somebody connected by blood or marriage to an employee within the third degree. This comprises the following: parents, grandparents, in-laws, spouses or domestic partners, children, grandchildren, siblings, uncles, aunts, nieces, nephews, step-parents, step-children, and adoptive children.

As an employee, you may suggest family members to our organization. Here are our only limitations:

- You may not have a supervisory or subordinate relationship with a relative
- You are ineligible for transfer, promotion, or employment if you report to a relative

- You cannot serve on a hiring committee if a relative of yours is being interviewed for that post
- If you become connected to a manager or direct report after joining our organization, we may be required to transfer one of you

Company visitors

Please get authorization from our HR manager/security officer/workplace manager before inviting a guest to our office. Additionally, please notify our reception/gate/ front office of your guest's arrival. Visitors are required to sign in and provide identification. They will be given passes and requested to return them to reception/the gate/the front office at the end of their visit:

- You have obligations when you have office guests. You must always attend to your guests (especially when they are underage).
- Keep your guests out of places containing hazardous machinery, chemicals, private documents, or sensitive equipment.
- Prevent your guests from attempting to convert your coworkers, soliciting gifts, or seeking participation in events while on our property.
- Whoever brings orders, mail, or deliveries to our personnel must wait at the building's reception or gate. If you are awaiting a delivery, front office staff/security guards will tell you so that you may collect it.

Distribution and solicitation

Solicitation is demanding any type of money, support, or involvement for unrelated items, individuals, organizations, or causes (e.g., religious proselytism or asking for petition signatures). Distribution refers to the act of spreading materials for commercial or political goals.

Non-employee solicitation and distribution are prohibited in our workplace. You may solicit from your colleagues as an employee only when you ask colleagues to assist arrange events for another employee (such as the adoption or birth of a child, promotion, or retirement).

You may solicit support for a cause, charity, or fundraising event that is sponsored, supported, coordinated, or approved by our organization.

You may invite coworkers to employee events for permissible non-business purposes (e.g., recreation or volunteering).

You may invite coworkers to join legally protected employment-related activities or organizations (e.g., trade unions).

In all circumstances, we urge that you refrain from disturbing or distracting coworkers from their work.

Cloud hosting policy

This policy is very specific and it has been planned to be available worldwide.

> Tip
>
> This is a policy sample.

1. **INTRODUCTION:**

   Information security exists to further the mission of ACME. ACME comprises diverse populations with evolving needs related to information technology resources and data. ACME management is committed to safeguarding those resources while protecting and promoting business and behavioral freedom. Although intrinsic tension exists between the free exchange of ideas and information security and this can manifest itself in some circumstances, the following framework has been identified to promote the best balance possible between information security and academic freedom.

   This policy describes the requirements for the appropriate and approved use of externally hosted ACME platforms and services.

2. **PURPOSE**:

   To ensure adequate protection of protected data stored on ACME-owned, leased, or personally owned hardware and software; this policy establishes the requirements for the implementation, transfer, removal, and disposal of all hardware housing this kind of information.

3. **SCOPE**:

   This policy also applies to all users who have access to ACME resources, including all employees, contractors, guests, consultants, temporary employees, and other users. Determining the level of sensitivity applicable to a given form of data is the first step in establishing the safeguards that are necessary for that type of data.

4. **DEFINITIONS**:

   Cloud hosting of systems and/or data can be categorized as the following models:

   - **Software as a Service** (**SaaS**) is a software distribution paradigm in which consumers can access applications via a network, usually the internet, that is hosted by a vendor or service provider.
   - Renting hardware, operating systems, storage, and network bandwidth online is possible with **Platform as a Service** (**PaaS**). Customers can rent virtualized servers and related services using the service delivery model to run their current apps or create and test new ones.

An organization can outsource the hardware, software, servers, and networking components necessary to support operations using the **Infrastructure as a Service** (**IaaS**) provider model. The equipment belongs to the service provider, who is also in charge of housing, operating, and maintaining it.

For the purpose of this document, the term cloud computing services is used to encompass SaaS, PaaS, and IaaS.

For cloud-hosted systems (SaaS, PaaS, IaaS, and similar) or data, each system owner must ensure the system protections described in the Information Classification Policy. *So, it's important here to define a protected system and the kind of protection given.*

EU-GDPR: The **General Data Protection Regulation** (**GDPR**)

ISO/IEC 31010: A standard concerning risk management

ISO/IEC 27001: Specifies a management system that is intended to bring information security under management control and gives specific requirements

HIPAA: The **Health Insurance Portability and Accountability Act** of 1996

HITECH: The HITECH Act set guidelines on the adoption and meaningful use of interoperable **Electronic Health Records** (**EHRs**)

FISMA: The **Federal Information Security Management Act** of 2002

PCI/DSS: Payment and Credit Card Industry Data Security Standards

FERPA: Gives parents access to their child's education records

PIPEDA: The **Personal Information Protection and Electronic Documents Act** (Canada)

Data custodian/data protection officer: The one in charge of a company's written or electronic records while safeguarding the data in accordance with the company's security policy or accepted IT practices.

5. **POLICY**:

If sensitive data and/or confidential data is stored using cloud computing services, the contracts for those services must be approved by ACME Procurement Services, and the applicable Information Security Officer must evaluate the system's security measures both before and after implementation, depending on the risk level.

In addition to other ACME policies, the following requirements must be followed in the use of cloud computing services:

5.1 – Pre-requisite Requirements

Consult with appropriate data owners, process owners, stakeholders, and subject matter experts during the evaluation process, or with the applicable Information Security Officer for guidance.

5.2 – Contractual requirements

- 5.2.1 – Both ACME and the vendor must declare the type of data that they may transfer back and forth because of their relationship. A contract must have clear terms that define the data owned by each party. The parties also must clearly define data that must be protected.
- 5.2.2 – The contract must specifically state what data ACME owns. It must also classify the type of data shared in the contract according to ACME's data classification policy requirements. Departments must exercise caution when sharing sensitive or confidential data (as defined by ACME's Information Classification Policy) within a cloud computing service.
- 5.2.3 – The contract must specify how the vendor can use ACME's data. Vendors cannot use ACME's data in any way that violates the law or this policy.

5.3 – Ensure a **Service Level Agreement** (**SLA**) with the vendor exists that requires the following:

- 5.3.1 – Clear definition of services
- 5.3.2 – Agreed-upon service levels
- 5.3.3 – Performance measurements
- 5.3.4 – Problem management
- 5.3.5 – Customer duties
- 5.3.6 – Disaster recovery
- 5.3.7 – Policies on the termination of the agreement
- 5.3.8 – Protection of sensitive information and intellectual property
- 5.3.9 – Definition of vendor versus customer responsibilities, especially pertaining to backups, incident response, and data recovery

5.4 – Cloud computing services should not be engaged without developing an exit strategy for disengaging from the vendor or service while integrating the service into normal internal business practices and/or business continuity and disaster recovery plans. ACME must determine how data will be recovered from the vendor.

5.5 – A proper risk assessment must be conducted by the applicable Information Security Office prior to any third-party hosting or cloud computing service arrangement.

6. **INTELLECTUAL PROPERTY AND COPYRIGHT MATERIALS (APPLICABLE ALSO TO PRIVACY AND DATA SECURITY)**

Information that has been classified by ACME as *Unclassified Public*, *Proprietary*, *Client Confidential Data*, or *Company Confidential Data* may be used only in accordance with the policy related to the classification of information that can be found in the Information Classification Policy.

7 – **Personally Identifiable Information** (**PII**) may only be used in compliance with information protected by federal, state, or local laws and regulations or industry standards, such as the GDPR, HIPAA, HITECH, FERPA, PIPEDA, and PCI-DSS.

7. **DATA AVAILABILITY AND RECORDS RETENTION:**

   8.1 – Ensure that all academic, administrative, or research-related data is retained according to the records retention and EU-GDPR requirements.

   8.2 – Back up data regularly to ensure that records are available when needed, as many providers assume no responsibility for the data recovery of content (for further information, please consult the ACME Business Continuity and Disaster Recovery Policy).

8. **ROLES AND RESPONSIBILITIES:**

   9.1 – Security and data security will be in charge of the operations, with support from the legal and ERP departments.

9. **OTHER APPLICABLE POLICIES:**

   - P001: Information Security Policy
   - P002: Permanent change of where equipment is located within the ACME office
   - P003: Sale and disposition of equipment
   - P004: Equipment donations and transfers to other entities (e.g., charities)
   - P005: Equipment deletion from ACME assets
   - P006: ACME **Acceptable Use Policy** (**AUP**)

These are just examples: you can customize them according to your needs, find other templates and samples through the internet, and still buy some decent packages at a decent price online. Of course, my suggestion, as usual, is to involve a third-party consultancy to do the job, and then you can update them on your own.

Company procedures

Would you wish to undergo a complex process to get an additional pen or pad of paper? Of course not!

Procedures and their near relatives, policies, may be a genuine pain in the you-know-what. Sometimes, they are excessively stringent and limiting, while other times they are too general and missing specifics. However, if a colleague calls in ill and you are suddenly responsible in case of an emergency, you should substitute that sick colleague just by reading and understanding a procedure. Therefore, it is helpful to have a well-written, clear protocol to follow.

Procedures may have a significant impact on an organization if executed properly. When stated clearly and correctly, they may improve the functionality of systems and individuals. If your employees know what to do, when to do it, how to do it, and how to avoid making mistakes, you may decrease aggravation and save a great deal of time and energy.

Procedures are the company's workhorses. Procedures detail "how to" complete a job or process, while policies outline how individuals should make choices.

Procedures emphasize action. They describe the actions to be performed and the sequence in which they must be taken. They are often instructive and may be used in training and orientation. Typically, well-written processes are solid, accurate, truthful, brief, and direct.

Writing an accurate, concise, and understandable method is not always simple. However, with a little bit of information and experience, you may develop good procedure-writing abilities and recognize many possibilities to enhance the quality of your work.

> Tip
>
> Numerous procedures seem *black and white*, with distinct phases and a single method: "*Complete A, then B, and then C.*" Occasionally, though, it is necessary to be less precise and allow for individual discretion. When a method is too restrictive, it might lead to misunderstanding. Since life is not always straightforward and uncomplicated, some methods must allow for subjectivity and individual choice.

When is a procedure necessary?

If you design processes for fundamental jobs, they will be disregarded since they are unnecessary. The first guideline of creating procedures is to ensure that they serve a purpose: perhaps individuals forget to complete particular activities, perhaps they continue to make mistakes, or perhaps jobs are so lengthy and complicated that a checklist is required for success.

A documented procedure is only required if the problem is severe or if there is a substantial advantage to clarifying a method. Before you begin, consider whether people really need or want to know something.

When a process requires a procedure

To a certain extent, a process works on its own. But then, your company needs to write it, to put it clear:

- Is extensive (for example, a year-end inventory)
- Is complicated (for example, benefits administration)
- Is routine, yet everyone must rigorously adhere to the guidelines (for example, a payroll)
- Requires consistency (for example, handling a refund request)
- Involves documentation (for example, disciplining a staff member)
- Involves considerable alteration (for example, installing a new computer system)
- Has severe implications for error (for example, safety guidelines)

In a normal business, many tasks are performed without formal processes. Unwritten norms and informal processes exist. Occasionally, though, these unwritten principles must be codified by a process. Here are some examples of when this may need to occur:

- Similar questions are constantly posed
- People seem perplexed
- There are too many possible interpretations of the technique

How to write a procedure

Not only what readers desire to know but also what they must know should be communicated in procedures. They may need to know how to do the task accurately, more quickly, or with less waste. They may also want to know why they must do a task in a specific way, where they may get assistance, and what happens if anything goes wrong. Whenever required, ensure that your processes address both technical and subjective factors.

It is also essential that your processes have the appropriate amount of information. Here are some questions to consider:

- Do users have sufficient information to act?
- Does it contain sufficient information to assist users in exercising sound professional judgment?
- Is the degree of information suitable for the topic?
- Is the degree of detail suitable for the audience?
- How familiar are readers with the topic?

Step 1: gathering information

Before you begin writing, you should collect extensive information on the technique you are creating.

Talk with subject matter experts as well as those who hold essential knowledge, including long-time employees, stakeholders, technical personnel, and process users.

Take copious notes and then organize the material at your leisure. As the process author, you should have a comprehensive grasp of what is occurring. From there, reduce the information just to what the end user needs to fully comprehend the procedure (a mind map is a fantastic tool for arranging information. This may assist you in ensuring that you have included and linked all the necessary components).

Step 2: beginning to write

When writing the initial draft of your method, you should not be concerned with perfect terminology and structure. The primary objective is to provide the necessary information. After that, you can concentrate on the wording and arrangement.

Here are some helpful guidelines:

- Record activities in the sequence in which they occur
- Begin with the first action and conclude with the last action
- Avoid excessive wordiness
- Just be explicit enough to ensure clear communication
- Use bullets and lists
- If you are too brief, you risk losing clarity
- Explain your assumptions and ensure that they are accurate
- Utilize jargon and slang with caution

Step 3: evaluating design elements

You may discover that words alone are insufficient to describe the technique. Occasionally, additional features might enhance a presentation. Here are a few prevalent formats.

Flowchart

This is a schematic of a process. You may outline and simplify a process by using a sequence of symbols and arrows to show the flow of activity. Make sure that your chart does not include too many strange symbols or too much text. If necessary, divide it into many smaller flowcharts.

Playscript

This seems to be a theatre script with many characters. In this instance, though, you list the staff members with varying duties. Scripts may be particularly beneficial when several people are participating in a process:

Person in charge	**Action**
	Gathering information
Writer responsibility	Writing the process
	Sharing the draft with stakeholders
	Reviewing a draft
Stakeholder responsibility	Submitting comments and corrections
Writer responsibility	Creating the final draft
Manager (business unit)	Approving the final version

The department head must approve the final version.

Question and answer

Match frequent procedural questions with the appropriate responses. This style is beneficial when methods are unclear or there are several variants. It also helps in addressing "what if" concerns.

Example:

Q: What happens if the columns are not balanced?

A. Initially, do not panic. Start with the most basic explanations and move backward. Calculate each column again. Then, search for faults in transcribing. If this does not resolve the issue, examine how you obtained your figures. If you were uncertain about any points, verify those numbers again. Then, methodically review each figure until the problem is discovered.

Matrix

The table links one variable with another. Where variables intersect, the cell displays the corresponding action. Matrix tables are very useful for reference reasons since they minimize the need for repeated searching. You can utilize them for a variety of purposes, including determining what activities to do and when, assisting users in making choices, and determining which forms or reports to use:

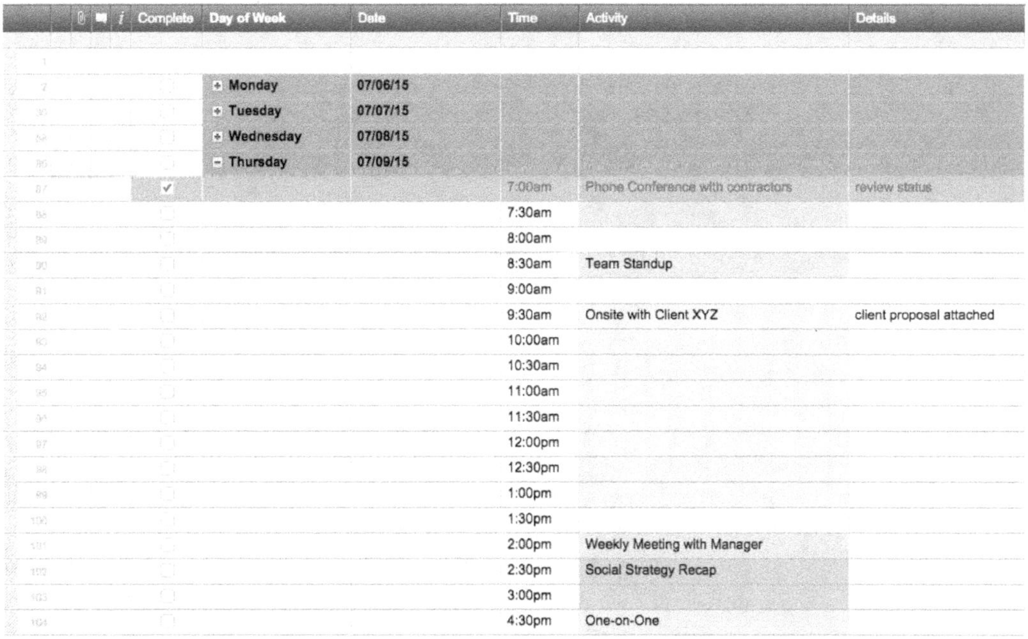

Complete	Day of Week	Date	Time	Activity	Details
	+ Monday	07/06/15			
	+ Tuesday	07/07/15			
	+ Wednesday	07/08/15			
	− Thursday	07/09/15			
✓			7:00am	Phone Conference with contractors	review status
			7:30am		
			8:00am		
			8:30am	Team Standup	
			9:00am		
			9:30am	Onsite with Client XYZ	client proposal attached
			10:00am		
			10:30am		
			11:00am		
			11:30am		
			12:00pm		
			12:30pm		
			1:00pm		
			1:30pm		
			2:00pm	Weekly Meeting with Manager	
			2:30pm	Social Strategy Recap	
			3:00pm		
			4:30pm	One-on-One	

Figure 8.1 – Another kind of example, using a matrix approach this time

Summary

So, in this chapter, we had a conversation concerning policies and procedures, with a lot of tips and recommendations. Hopefully, they are (or will be) useful!

Now, you should be able to write a proper policy or procedure by understanding all the requirements around the document. Practice makes perfect, but a good starting point is always helpful.

In the following chapter, we will cover social engineering.

9

Social Engineering, Password Guidance, and Policy

While in the previous chapter we got an in-depth look into policies and procedures, now we are going to understand the most powerful attack vector: social engineering. Why is it the most powerful? Mainly because it attacks the weakest link of the security chain: humans. While a machine (software) is intended to execute commands and orders, we use our intelligence, feelings, and so on to interact with others. But it's the interaction with other human beings to make us behave differently and in a less secure way.

In this chapter, we will cover the following topics:

- The starting point
- Common social engineering attack methods
- Have you got a M.A.P.P.?

The starting point

The internet has become an integral aspect of modern business and personal life since it facilitates the acquisition of information. Businesses and people use the internet for a variety of reasons, including content surfing, social networking, communicating, purchasing, downloading……

There are now roughly 4.81 billion internet users worldwide. Today, it is common practice for a person to hunt for a certain answer on the internet and get a satisfactory result. Alongside the convenience of locating different internet services, social networking websites are one of the most significant and rapidly growing areas of general interest nowadays. It is fairly popular for individuals to utilize social networking sites to maintain frequent touch with their friends and family.

Intruders compromise systems for a variety of motives. Consequently, it is essential to comprehend how and why hostile hackers target and exploit systems. According to Sun Tzu's *The Art of War*, *if you know yourself but not the opponent, for every triumph you achieve, you will also suffer a loss*. It is the responsibility of system administrators and security experts to protect their infrastructure against exploits by understanding their adversary: the malicious hackers who want to utilize the infrastructure for illicit operations.

Social engineering is a wide category of malevolent operations carried out via human contact. It employs psychological manipulation to deceive users into committing security errors or divulging sensitive data.

Social engineering is the practice of manipulating, persuading, or misleading an individual in order to get access to their computer system. The hacker may get unauthorized access by phone, email, snail mail, or direct contact. Examples include phishing, spear phishing, and CEO fraud.

Social engineering assaults consist of several phases. A perpetrator initially analyzes the target victim in order to obtain background information, such as possible entry points and weak security procedures, required to continue with the assault. The attacker next attempts to acquire the victim's confidence and give stimuli for later acts that violate security norms, such as disclosing sensitive information or providing access to vital resources.

OSINT

Open Source Intelligence (**OSINT**) is the lifeblood of social engineering. Information is the foundation and support of every interaction. Because OSINT is so critical to us as social engineers, it is crucial that you be familiar with the many methods for gathering information on your targets.

No matter how you collect OSINT, you must have a clear notion of what you're searching for. That is not as simple as it sounds. You cannot just request all information about the target. Each type of information has a unique value, which might vary depending on the type of assault you want to execute.

Social scientist

So, who are these individuals who carry out social engineering attacks? It might be a hacker who intends to cause harm or disruption. It may be a member of a cybercrime syndicate from somewhere in Europe attempting to infiltrate your network and steal money from your online bank account

Common social engineering attack methods

Understanding the many assault vectors for this sort of criminal activity is essential for its prevention. The following subsections provide insight into how cybercriminals operate.

Pretexting

To improve the likelihood that a prospective victim will bite, an imagined scenario is employed to interest the victim.

It is a bogus purpose that often involves some actual knowledge about the victim (e.g., date of birth or social security number) in an effort to get further information.

Let's have an example: Imagine that Mr. White is a middle manager of a company and goes to the same bar every morning to have an expresso coffee before going to work. Let's suppose that I am a Social Engineer who wants to hack that company. I'll go to the same place at the same time everyday. After a couple of weeks, I'll wish him *good morning* before leaving, and he will answer politely. Within a few months, I'll be able to talk to him, maybe about the weather, or briefly commenting on a strike or some local news. Another few weeks and he will (possibly) give me relevant details about his private life and I can be lucky enough to get parts of the passwords of his account (name of his sons, son's or wife's birthday and so on).

Misdirection theft

This is an example of fraud perpetrated by experienced criminals, often against a transportation or courier firm. The purpose is to deceive the firm into delivering the package to a different place than originally planned.

Phishing

This is the act of trying to collect sensitive information, such as usernames, passwords, and credit card information, by posing as a trustworthy company sending out bulk emails, attempting to avoid spam filters. Emails appearing to be from well-known social networking sites, banks, auction sites, or IT administrators are often used to deceive the public. It is an instance of false social engineering.

Targeted phishing

This is a limited, concentrated, and targeted email assault against a specific individual or organization with the intent of penetrating their defenses. After doing research on the target, a spear phishing assault is launched with a tailored component aimed to induce the target to act against their own best interests. The following subsections provide further information on the methodology.

Water-holing

This strategy makes use of websites that are frequently visited and trusted by users. The attacker at first will introduce a malware, then he will collect information on a certain set of users in order to determine which websites they frequent and will subsequently test those websites for weaknesses. Over time, one or more members of the target group will get infected, granting the attacker access to the protected system, via e-mail for instance (we always tend to trust legitimate websites, especially from those we are subscribed) .

Baiting

Luring a person into action by hanging something in front of them is known as baiting. It might be in the form of an (x-rated movie download from a peer-to-peer or social networking site, or it could be a *Q1 Layoff Plan*-labeled USB drive placed in public for the victim to locate. After using the device or downloading the malicious file, the victim's computer is infected, enabling the criminal to seize control of the network.

Quid pro quo

Quid pro quo is a Latin phrase meaning *something for something*. In this scenario, the victim receives a reward in return for information. An excellent example is hackers posing as IT assistants. They will phone everyone they can locate at a corporation and claim they have a fast remedy to solve all the IT issues that requires disabling antivirus software. Whoever falls for it will have ransomware installed on their computer.

Tailgating

This is a technique employed by social engineers to obtain entry to a building or other secured location. A tailgater waits for an authorized user to open and pass through a protected entrance before following them through.

Honeytrap

This is a type of deception where the attacker poses as an attractive person and engages in a relationship with the victim to eventually persuade them to share sensitive information. This is taken from classic espionage techniques in which attractive women were used to obtain secrets

Usually the lady will somehow seduce the victim to tell more than allowed (passwords, insider news, and similar). This is taken from classic espionage techniques in which a genuine woman was used.

Rogue

Also known as a rogue scanner, rogue anti-spyware, rogue anti-malware, or scareware, rogue security software is a kind of computer virus that induces users to pay for the phony or simulated eradication of malware. In recent years, malicious security software has become a major and severe danger to desktop computer security. This application is quite popular, and there are practically hundreds of them.

Vishing

Vishing draws its name from the combination of two words: voice and phishing. A vishing assault is similar to phishing, only it occurs over the phone or voicemail. It is a cybercrime since fraudsters utilize it to get access to victims' money or personal information. For instance, an attacker may attempt to get access to a person's bank account, steal their credit card data, or convince the victim to make a wire transfer to them.

How does vishing function?

There is a particular reason why fraudsters are increasingly turning to vishing. This form of telephone scam makes use of social engineering, a set of strategies that exploit people's basic emotions, such as trust, fear, greed, or charity. The cybercriminal attempts to generate these sensations, inciting fear or other emotions that might impair the victim's judgment, and uses this to steal money or sensitive information. For instance, a con artist may attempt to persuade them to make a lucrative investment or donate money to someone else, as himself or some relatives. In this example, the social engineering technique employed induces you to behave hastily, as opposed to analyzing the matter rationally and carefully. This can happen on social networks, with the scammer pretending to be in love with the victim and then requesting money to meet him/her (this is called a *sentimental scam*).

The most prevalent vishing methods

Cybercriminals often pose as trustworthy individuals, such as bank employees, Internal Revenue Service officials, or insurance agents. These fraudsters believe that you will trust these individuals enough to grant them access to your accounts or your money. In addition, they are very competent at adapting what they say on phone calls based on your location, age, and other particular variables. Here are some of the most prevalent approaches:

- In one sort of vishing attack, fraudsters phone you to inform you that your account has been hacked and is at risk of a cyber assault. The attacker may next attempt to persuade you to move funds from your checking account to a *more secure* account, or request your login credentials in order to resolve the issue. A legitimate bank would never phone a client to urge them to do such an action, thus it is better to hang up immediately. Contact your bank if you have any doubts about the status of your account.
- Some con artists may phone you and offer you a loan, a reward, or a fantastic investment opportunity. In most cases, these offers seem quite advantageous, thus the desire to accept them is great. But don't be fooled: if a contest you've never entered requests personal information, you may safely hang up. Remember that not everything that glitters is gold; if an offer seems too good to be true, then it probably is.
- Tax scams are also popular. Some experienced vishing fraudsters pose as revenue agency officials or debt collectors and intimidate victims by discussing outstanding taxes and threatening severe penalties. These calls are very annoying but do not be afraid. Even if you have ongoing obligations, you should always confirm that the collection agency requesting payment is authorized.
- Social security scams are another common example. Cybercriminals pose as representatives of a social security or welfare institution in order to get benefits or pensions, or to steal money. Seniors are common victims of these scams because they often live alone and may be unaware of the perils of phishing. To protect your loved ones against these scams, have a conversation with them, explaining which types of fraud are most prevalent and encouraging them to never provide their private information to strangers, especially over the phone.

How to protect against and avoid vishing attacks

Vishing prevention is not very tough. Following these guidelines can help you avoid being a victim of a vishing assault:

- Never provide or confirm your personal information over the phone, especially if the caller claims to represent your bank. If the caller were from your bank, they would never ask for this sort of information. Simply getting this request should prompt you to assume a vishing effort and hang up the phone. Don't forget to notify your bank of the situation.
- Do not answer calls from unfamiliar phone numbers. Allow the answering machine to play, listen to the message, and calmly assess the situation. Alternatively, if you believe the call may be authentic, call the number again from a different phone number. If it was a fraud, there will likely be no response.
- Check whether your country has an opposition registry. By registering your telephone number in this register, you will warn sales and marketing companies that you do not want to receive so-called *cold calls* or calls made for commercial objectives without your consent. Thus, if you were to get cold calls, it would likely be an effort at vishing.
- Do not respond to social media, email, or text communications requesting your phone number. This is often how hackers get the details of naïve individuals they would later target with a vishing assault.

How to identify a vishing effort

To identify a vishing assault, you must be vigilant for certain warning indications. If you receive the impression that the caller is attempting to hurry, manipulate, or alarm you, it's likely a phone scam.

The first step in avoiding vishing is to hang up on anybody who requests personal information, such as your address, bank account information, debit or credit card number, or passwords. If someone unexpectedly requests this information, hang up. No reputable firm would attempt to get your information in this manner.

Smishing

The name *smishing* is derived from a combination of the terms *SMS* and *phishing*. It has all the primary features of phishing (particularly the tactics of deception and social engineering) but varies from similarly prevalent email scams by using only text messages. The attacker utilizes mobile phones as a platform to entice new victims, targeting the sensitive data of the user. Scammers invent a wide variety of schemes, but in most instances, they can be traced back to the following core objectives: stealing the victim's money or identity. In SMS scams, sophisticated social engineering methods are the most important factor in persuading the victim to click on the link at the bottom of the message or engage with it. To do this, they attempt to rush the assaulted subject, who will behave illogically due to panic and the urge to flee a dangerous situation.

Alerts telling the user that their bank account has been hacked or pressing them to pay a past-due payment are excellent examples of psychological manipulation. In both circumstances, the victim is pressured to act immediately by exploiting their fear. Usually, though, if you think about the situation logically, it doesn't make sense. How can you lose money from your bank account and face repercussions for non-payment of an invoice simultaneously?

Smishing and messaging applications

More recently, it has become common for computer scams to be carried out via WhatsApp and other popular instant messaging applications, such as Signal and Telegram. While not technically smishing, we are dealing with a related phenomenon because the attacker's goals are identical: to deceive the victim in order to steal personal or bank account information. Taking into consideration the proliferation of instant messaging, which, particularly with the introduction of smartphones, has almost completely supplanted SMS messages, we might even call it *smishing 2.0*.

How to protect against smishing

To increase the credibility of the fraud, the attacker will often misappropriate the name of a reputable institution or corporation, such as banks, debt collection agencies, insurance organizations, and fashion or electronics retailers. Therefore, the message is displayed as originating from one of these institutions, and the rationale for this is pretty obvious: it enhances the trustworthiness of the received information. Additionally, consumers are more likely to believe an SMS sent from a reputable and well-known sender than one received by an unknown sender. Smishing efforts are quite diverse; however, they may be categorized according to the goals they often accomplish. The sender or topic of the message may differ, but not its objective. In the following list, we have outlined the primary strategies used by cybercriminals to recruit new victims:

- **Click on a link**: In this instance, the message instructs the user to click on a link that should lead to a phishing website where they may enter sensitive information. Some recent examples of this are a false bank login page that directs the user to input their credentials in order to access their bank account. There are also examples involving Amazon, e-commerce sites, and insurance corporations.
- **React to a message**: In this instance, the SMS encourages the user to reply to the received communication, demanding the entry of certain personal data (such as a PIN code or banking credentials).
- **Download an app**: In this instance, the message pushes the user to download an external app – fraudulently connected to the company described in the SMS – that contains malware in the vast majority of instances.
- **Call the suggested number**: A classic example is asking the victim to call a number pretending to be the customer service of a reputable firm. Instead of settling a possible issue, the impostor will attempt to get your account details.

- **Download an attachment**: The relevant document that might be an attachment can be possibly found on the real company's website, while the attachment in the e-mail may contain malware.
- **Send money**: In this situation, the fraudster poses as an insurance or debt collection agency and asks the user to make a wire transfer to the bank account information provided in the same SMS, citing outstanding debts.

In conclusion, we are confronted with a wide variety of scenarios that have three characteristics: psychological coercion, dishonesty, and a request to provide sensitive information. It is always feasible to defend oneself against these cons; just don't panic, and employ some common sense. If there are any concerns regarding the validity of the communication, a simple phone call to the customer care department of the participating firm (the genuine one, this time) will clear them up. In addition, as every credit institution notes, consumers are never requested to provide personal access information through SMS, email, or telephone.

Have you got a M.A.P.P.?

What exactly is a **M.A.P.P.**? It is an abbreviation for **Mitigation and Prevention Plan**. Now, we will understand the meaning of M.A.P.P. We need one of these to prevent and prepare for social engineering attacks. You can easily set up a M.A.P.P. by following these four steps:

- Learn how to recognize social engineering attacks (by creating a team of professional and requesting a third-party company, able to simulate social engineering attacks, to create a real-world scenario)
- Develop realistic and implementable policies
- Conduct periodic real-world audits
- Implement applicable security awareness programs

Step 1 – learn how to recognize social engineering attacks

Although this first step seems obvious, it is not. How many individuals in your organization are able to define phishing, vishing, smishing, and impersonation attacks? How many people do you believe are aware of how risky it is for an attacker to get the identity of your trash vendor? How many of your employees do you believe are familiar with malware, ransomware, and Trojans?

Do not misunderstand; I am not suggesting that every employee must have advanced cybersecurity knowledge. Everyone in your company must simply comprehend that these *bad guys* could possibly attack your organization. Understanding what assaults are, what they may look like, and what they may do to you is an essential first step.

You may be wondering, *How can we accomplish this?* That is an excellent question. What many years (24, to be precise) of working in cybersecurity has taught me, and what you should anticipate from a social engineering specialist, is how to spot and withstand a social engineering *attack*.

This initial step of learning how to recognize and acknowledge the existence of these assaults will put your team light-years ahead of an ordinary organization. Help your employees understand the value of the information they possess—that emails can be used to breach the entire organization; phone calls are used to obtain passwords and other sensitive information; if their mobile device is compromised, it can be used to attack their home and work networks; and just because a person is smiling and friendly, it doesn't mean you can ignore the badge policy.

Your workforce may be made more vigilant by educating them about potential assaults. Because I deal with kind of menaces everyday, I sometimes forget that not everyone is aware of these assaults.

Just a few days ago, my ex-wife texted me that an older friend of hers was scammed by *General Eric Hill* on Facebook, who claimed he was in need of money and asked her for $3,000 and to take a safe deposit box from a bank where he would then deposit his portfolio through a UN diplomat. Of course, this was all a fabrication. My ex-wife's friend transferred the fraudster the money and retrieved the safe deposit box but didn't receive anything in return.

Learn from this situation. Do not presume that understanding these assaults is just common wisdom. If someone is a victim of social engineering, it does not always indicate that they are foolish, worthless, and doomed to fail. Instead, demonstrate compassion and consider, *Okay, we can do better next time. How can we I improve tomorrow?* That will greatly enhance the success of the following step.

Step 2 – develop realistic and implementable policies

In the realm of security, policy may seem like a dirty word. Most individuals dislike creating, enforcing, and/or adhering to rules. Policies often have a negative reputation because they are illogical or unclear in their aim. Occasionally, rules are so restricted that people simply ignore them.

Creating a safe workplace with a culture of security awareness requires striking a balance. Policies must be firm, but they cannot be monoliths, which are not simple at all. However, achieving this balance is vital for success.

What constitutes a good policy? It should not be too restrictive and be actionable and attainable. There are a few components of a fantastic policy that we will discuss next.

Remove the thinking from policies

Too often, policies are so broad that they place an excessive amount of thought or decision-making in the hands of an individual who has not yet been trained on these matters. Now, I'm not suggesting that you should treat your employees like idiots. Simply understand that the less time an employee needs to spend contemplating anything, the better. The simplest solution is the best one.

Here's one example: An organization performed vishing exercise or a significant financial institution, and more than 80% of the time, they were successful in obtaining very sensitive information about the targets. They exploited their targets using empathy and trust by playing on these qualities.

To the credit of this financial institution, they had incredibly pleasant staff, and the social engineering company didn't want that to change. How awful would it be if the mitigating suggestion was *make your staff more suspicious and mistrustful*? The social engineering testing firm came up with a reasonable solution. They established an actual, executable policy: *You may not disclose any information to unauthenticated people.*

And they continued from there. They established both what constitutes valuable information and how to properly authenticate people. Then, they did something else that made a tremendous difference: they blocked their employees' ability to advance in their career if they did not answer security related questions correctly.

Let's have an example: Assume that a pregnant consultant working in an IT company, carrying a box of devices, needs to get into the server room. If there is someone else nearby who has server room access, you can bet he or she will take the box and open the door, letting her into the room, without checking whether the lady is authorized by a badge or similar.

In this case, a policy stating that IDs must be verified at server room only can easily be bypassed, because empathy for a person in need exceeds any other aspect. So, without forgetting empathy, a company can state that ID check must be done at the reception, so the lady's identity can be verified in a proper way. Never forget that humans are filled with emotions, reasoning, education, and belief that causes them to mostly take decisions considering this.

Make policies practical and realistic

I have personally seen rules stating *do not click on harmful links*. How does that sound to you? If you are saying, *Yeah, that's great—I'm going to utilize that*, I want you to put this book down and slowly hit yourself in the face with the back cover.

This kind of policy is poor since it lacks sufficient clarity for the employee. How do they identify harmful links? Are they aware that `support-google.com` is distinct from `Google.com`?

The policy is devoid of an *if* clause. Upon clicking the link, what happens? This policy is missing a section that reads *Please contact xxxxxxx@company.com if you believe that an email, phone conversation, or in-person interaction did not go according to policy.*

However, there is more! Now, you must instruct your staff on how to properly report the incident, including forwarding the email and passing on the caller ID information. What specifics should be reported? What are the repercussions of reporting?

A realistic policy aids the employee in seeing the subject from all sides and leaves no room for doubt. At one organization I worked with, I assisted in the creation of a new phishing policy education program. It went roughly as follows.

Phishing is a hazard to your organization and to you individually. Email-based assaults are used by malicious attackers to get personal information. They may use malicious files with extensions such as

`.exe`, `.pdf`, `.xls`, or `.doc`. Or, they may give you links to websites that are not what they claim to be and that include malware or other malicious software.

If you get an email from an unknown source, forward it to `abuse@company.com` before taking any action by clicking **FORWARD** and entering `abuse@company.com` in the **TO** field.

Within 24 hours, someone from that department will let you know whether this email is secure.

If you've already clicked on a link or opened an attachment that you believe may have been malicious, it's not too late to remove it. Report the email to the department of abuse.

Obviously, the policy included further information and connections to internal training and other resources. You get the point, though. A good policy is based on reality and provides clear advice about what actions are important to take and what to avoid.

A good policy helps the individual understand not just the what, but also the why. Eventually, if done correctly, your workforce will develop muscle memory for these actions.

Step 3 – conduct periodic real-world audits

You have educated your people about the nature of these assaults. Your workers have received training on how to respond to these types of assaults. You have established rules to assist them in taking the optimal action in the event of an assault. Now, how well did you retain all of this information? Will the workers' muscle memory kick in when they are tested? The only way to determine this is to choose the best security consulting partner and work with them.

Selecting the right training partner is crucial. Remember that isn't important how cool is the company you choose, but their expertise and how they want to help to leverage the security posture.

How can you determine whether the prospective spouse is a good match? Here are some recommendations:

- Ask excellent questions.
- Don't be hesitant to inquire about past employment or how the organization suggests handling a certain scenario. Is the response consistent with your basic values?

It is necessary to teach individuals about their wrongdoings, retest them after education, and then evaluate whether they posed a danger to the business, but it is a horrible idea to routinely fire individuals for failing.

Clearly establish the regulations. As a customer, nothing is worse than assuming that a pentest would only go one layer deep, only to discover that the pentester got five levels deep and you must now explain what occurred to your boss. The easiest method to guarantee that there are no issues is to have a properly defined set of test criteria so that no limits are crossed. Clearly stated regulations are comparable to the protective gear used by boxers during sparring.

As a customer seeking a pentester, you may have more criteria for selecting a vendor, but these are a solid starting point to guarantee you get the ideal sparring partner.

After selecting a partner, you should begin testing and then use the findings to decide what services you need and how often you will be evaluated. A trustworthy partner can help you evaluate your requirements and will be straightforward about them (rather than basing them on dollar signs).

Some services, such as phishing testing, are best performed monthly. Other services, such as penetration testing, perform well as yearly or semi-annual services. But there is no one-size-fits-all solution; it depends on your demands and how you want to achieve your objectives.

Step 4 – implement applicable security awareness programs

Perhaps you're wondering, *Didn't you just discuss security awareness? Are you repeating yourself?* Actually, no; not at all. All prior phases are a component of your security awareness program, but this step focuses on how successfully you utilize the previous three steps to develop meaningful, practical, and relevant programs.

Some companies have a comprehensive strategy for both teaching employees about vishing and phishing and ensuring their vishing education was comprehensive. IT educates staff about assaults, provides them with realistic situations and true procedures, and frequently tests them in a secure environment, but can have weaknesses in other parts, such as a phishing program.

If you feel that your company needs assistance with your awareness program, do not look for companies that want to create a new program from scratch, but find a company that is able to adapt what you have already to make it updated and comprehensive, based on the preceding three steps.

Summary

In this chapter, we looked deeply into social engineering, including techniques, and for some of them, we gave you a deep understanding of how to avoid them; most importantly, we gave you some hints on how to implement a social engineering program and why your organization needs one.

In the next chapter, we will go through vulnerability assessments and pentesting.

10
The Cloud

There is no cloud; it's just someone else's computer.

Of course, the preceding sentence is a sort of nerdy joke but isn't really far from the truth.

While in the previous chapter, we delved into social engineering and checking various aspects of it, it's now time to understand how the cloud works, focusing on cloud security and privacy.

In this chapter, we will cover the following topics:

- How did the cloud emerge?
- The seven pain points of cloud computing
- Cloud and GDPR concerns
- The GDPR code of conduct for **Cloud Service Providers** (**CSPs**), that is, the companies offering services as storage over the internet

How did the cloud emerge?

Due to the proliferation of gadgets such as smartphones, tablets, and laptops, we can now access the internet from almost anywhere, with all the advantages and disadvantages that this may involve. Occasionally, you may create a file on your home computer but forget to bring it with you to the office the following day. Sometimes, though, you may find yourself with many copies of the same file and be unable to determine which copy is required. In a worst-case scenario, you may lose your smartphone, tablet, or laptop with all of your information, or even worse, your preferred gadget could suddenly cease to function. So, collaboration is the keyword here.

What exactly is the cloud? How does it work?

To solve these and other similar issues, the cloud was created. The cloud is nothing more than a personal storage space, sometimes referred to as cloud storage, which is accessible from any location with an internet connection. It should be noted, however, that in addition to cloud storage, the word *cloud* can also apply to various services provided by cloud computing.

From a compliance perspective, according to NIST, *"Cloud computing [is] a model for enabling ubiquitous, convenient, on-demand network access to a shared pool of configurable computing resources (e.g., networks, servers, storage, applications, and services) that can be rapidly provisioned and released with minimal management effort or service provider interaction,"* while the German government adheres to an attestation scheme (also roughly adopted in France) by the **Federal Office for Information Security** (**BSI**). The standard is named the **Cloud Computing Compliance Controls Catalogue** (**C5**). They claim that *"Cloud computing is a new paradigm in ICT (information and communication technology). It consists of IT services being adjusted dynamically to the customers need and made available through a network in a billable manner."* Also, new associations have appeared to support the cloud experience (in Europe at least), such as the **Cloud Security Alliance** (**CSA**) (`https://cloudsecurityalliance.org/`) and, more recently, the **European Cloud User Coalition** (**ECUC**) (`https://ecuc.group/`) which, with no costs, *"aims to promote a structured dialog between cloud users, providers, and other parties."*

Cloud storage just synchronizes all of your favorite data in a single location, providing the benefit of re-downloading, altering, deleting, and/or upgrading it without the need to carry external hard disks, a USB drive, or any other item that is generally susceptible to loss or forgetfulness. In addition, with cloud storage, you will have the option of creating backup copies and sharing all of your favorite files with anyone you want, for as long as you want, with undeniable benefits in terms of time and convenience. Of course, where there are benefits, there are also hassles; let's go a bit into detail now.

What is cloud security?

Cloud security refers to the set of technologies, protocols, and best practices that allow you to protect data and information in a cloud architecture.

Cloud security is a shared responsibility. On the one hand, cloud service providers must guarantee an adequate and protected infrastructure. On the other hand, users must also use it correctly and implement adequate measures, as they too are responsible for protecting the applications and data managed.

Cloud security can differ depending on the type of cloud service and the deployment model. Let's clarify immediately, seeing an overview of the main ones.

Types of cloud services

Cloud services consist of infrastructures, platforms, or software hosted by external providers, and the various services are made available to the user via the internet. The types of cloud computing can be mainly divided into three categories:

- **Infrastructure as a Service (IaaS)**: The service provider manages the infrastructure (i.e., the physical servers, networks, virtual machines, data storage, and operating systems) on behalf of the customer, via an internet connection. It is up to the customer to secure what is added to the operating system and to manage the access, devices, and networks of end users.
- **Platform as a Service (PaaS)**: This is designed for developers and programmers. With this service, a host is provided to customers who can create and host their own applications, without having to create and manage the infrastructure of servers, storage, networks, and databases.
- **Software as a Service (SaaS)**: Here, the customer is provided with access to software applications managed by the cloud service provider, without the need for a computer or server. The customer can access online services (without necessarily having to install an app on the computers of individual users) by checking the software configuration but without managing the infrastructure (examples of SaaS include Microsoft Office 365, Dropbox, iCloud, and apps by Google).

Distribution models

In addition to the type of cloud service, the cloud computing distribution model is then defined. In this case, the main distribution methods are as follows:

- **Public model**: Cloud services are made available by an external provider and are available to anyone, free or paid. Some examples include Microsoft Azure and Amazon Web Services.
- **Private model**: Cloud services are made available for access by a single organization, via the internet or a private internal network. The private cloud can be managed by an external provider or even internally by the company itself.
- **Hybrid model**: Cloud services are provided by combining private clouds (third-party or in-house) with public clouds as needed, taking advantage of the best of both infrastructures.
- **Other models**: These include community cloud, multi-cloud, poly cloud, and HPC cloud. Without going into detail, suffice it to say that – in addition to the aforementioned – there are also other less popular solutions that can be used as needed.

Cloud security – examples of measures that can prevent risks

Cloud security, as anticipated, concerns a set of strategies aimed at achieving multiple objectives. This includes archiving and network protection against cyberattacks, recovering any lost or stolen data, and generally reducing the impact of compromised systems or personal data breaches.

Too often, migrations to the cloud are carried out without first evaluating which data and processes to move and without having defined cybersecurity measures suitable for your specific case.

Everything must start, therefore, from the awareness of how data has been secured up until now, of the infrastructures used, and of the weak points on which it is necessary to intervene. Therefore, have a snapshot of the current situation to evaluate which cloud service offers adequate levels of security and plan an adequate migration strategy.

Depending on the case and the needs, there are different tools that a company can implement for solid cloud security. Here are some examples:

- An **Identity and access management** (**IAM**) system, for identity and access management
- Micro-segmentation, thanks to which the implementation of the cloud is divided into distinct segments, down to the level of a single workload, minimizing the damage of a possible attacker
- Next-generation firewalls – compared to traditional ones, they add advanced features, such as application-aware filters, deep packet inspection, and intrusion prevention systems
- Cryptography so that data can only be decrypted using a specific key
- Threat intelligence, monitoring, and prevention, or features aimed at analyzing traffic to identify, block, or at least mitigate a malware attack

The seven pain points of cloud computing

Security is an issue for all firms, regardless of whether they operate in the cloud. You will be exposed to threats such as denial of service, malware, SQL injection, data breaches, and data loss – all of which may severely affect your company's reputation and financials.

Moving to the cloud introduces a new set of hazards and modifies the nature of others. This does not imply that cloud computing is insecure. In reality, many cloud service providers provide access to very advanced security technologies and resources that you would not have otherwise.

It simply implies that you must be aware of changing hazards in order to manage them. Consequently, let's examine the particular security vulnerabilities of cloud computing.

Reduced visibility

The majority of businesses will access a variety of cloud services through numerous devices, departments, and geographic locations. Without the proper tools, this level of complexity in a cloud computing arrangement might lead you to lose awareness of access to your infrastructure.

Without the proper procedures in place, it is possible to lose track of who is using your cloud services, including the information they access, post, and download.

Just remember, an asset in the cloud may not be visible. And if it is not visible, it cannot be protected, increasing the likelihood of data loss and data breaches.

Of course, the same or similar controls that apply to on premises are applied to the cloud.

Compliance violations

With the expansion of regulatory oversight, you must comply with a variety of strict compliance criteria. If you are not cautious, migrating to the cloud might expose you to compliance issues.

Many of these requirements require your organization to be aware of the location of your data, who has access to it, how it is handled, and how it is safeguarded. Other requirements may say that your cloud service provider needs to possess certain compliance certifications.

Transferring data inattentively to the cloud or migrating to the incorrect provider might place your firm in a position of non-compliance, introducing the possibility of severe legal and financial consequences (we spoke already of data transfer and Schrems II sentences, in *Chapter 4, Data Processing*).

Absence of a strategy and architecture for cloud security

You can simply avoid this cloud security risk, but many do not. In their rush to shift systems and data to the cloud, many firms become operational before the security mechanisms and plans to defend the infrastructure are in place.

Ensure that you create a cloud-specific security policy and architecture before deploying your systems and data to the cloud.

Internal threats

Your most trusted workers, contractors, and business partners may pose the greatest security threats. These internal risks may bring harm to your organization, even without malice. In truth, the majority of insider occurrences are the result of inadequate training or carelessness.

Despite the fact that you now encounter this difficulty, switching to the cloud modifies the danger. When you transfer over management of your data to your cloud service provider, you create a new level of insider danger posed by the company's personnel.

Contractual violations

Any contractual relationships you have will have constraints on the use, storage, and allowed access of any shared data. Inadvertently transferring limited data to a cloud provider without authorization might constitute a contract violation and result in legal action.

Make sure you read the terms and conditions of your cloud provider. Even if you have permission to transfer data to the cloud, several service providers reserve the right to share any data uploaded to their infrastructure. You may accidentally violate a non-disclosure agreement due to ignorance.

Unprotected user interface (API)

When running systems on a cloud infrastructure, you can implement control via an API. Any API included in your web or mobile apps may be accessed both internally and externally.

An external API may create a security risk to the cloud. Any unsecured external API provides thieves with unauthorized access to steal data and modify services.

The Facebook–Cambridge Analytica scandal is the most notable instance of an unsafe external API. Cambridge Analytica gained extensive access to Facebook user data through Facebook's unsecured external API.

Errors in the configuration of cloud services

Another possible cloud security concern is cloud service misconfiguration. This is a developing concern as the breadth and complexity of services expand. A misconfiguration of cloud services may result in data being exposed to the public, altered, or even erased.

Common reasons include retaining security and access control settings by default for extremely sensitive data. Others include mismatched access management, which gives unauthorized users access, and twisted data access, in which personal information is left accessible without authorization.

Cloud and GDPR concerns

Although the GDPR takes a risk-based approach to data protection, it makes no mention of the cloud directly. The regulation, on the other hand, is technology-neutral in that it applies regardless of the method used to treat personal data. The fragmented processing environment of the cloud, where such standards may not always apply, makes it difficult to implement the GDPR. The challenges are broken down in some detail in the following sections.

Security concerns specific to the cloud

The **European Data Protection Supervisor** (**EDPS**) and the **European Union Agency for Network and Information Security** (**ENISA**) have stated that the specific features and processes linked to the different service and deployment models of a cloud infrastructure imply specific risks compared to a "traditional" on-premises data center.

NIST defines three service models (SaaS, PaaS, and IaaS) and four deployment models: public, private, community, and hybrid (a composition of the former three models) cloud environments. Each represents different models of outsourcing with disparate security and privacy risks.

Some of the security tasks (such as monitoring, patching, and incident response) are outsourced. Depending on the type of cloud service, some tasks remain under the responsibility of the customer, while other tasks remain under the responsibility of the provider. Division of responsibilities can sometimes be a major source of problems, as it is often based on assumptions and is poorly documented, leading to overlaps and gaps. For example, in IaaS/PaaS, the customers run their own code on top of the cloud service and often remain responsible for this (application) software. In SaaS, on the other hand, the application software is usually under the control of the provider.

Therefore, it is not uncommon for customers to be confused about their responsibilities concerning security – that is, which security tasks are outsourced to the provider and which security tasks remain under their own responsibility.

What effect is GDPR having on the cloud industry?

Businesses still struggle to comply with the GDPR regulatory criteria nearly 5 years after the rule was enacted. Additionally, it has become necessary for both organizations and cloud service providers to modify their business models as a result of the fast use of cloud services by businesses. In order to comply with the regulations, they must significantly alter their business practices. GDPR lays out specific requirements for data controllers and processors to adhere to in *Chapter 4, Article 24–43*. The regulation outlines the obligations, specifications, and guidelines that must be followed when handling personal data. Let's take a deeper look at the specifications listed in that section in order to better comprehend the effects of GDPR on data controllers and processors as they apply to cloud service providers.

Requirements for cloud service providers under GDPR

When a cloud service provider stores or processes data belonging to EU persons on behalf of the data controller, it is said to be *in scope*. A cloud service provider and a data controller can become joint data controllers depending on how and why the data is processed, which entails additional important duties and responsibilities for the data processor. To implement the essential controls and specifications for compliance, the cloud service provider must define its function in accordance with the regulations established by GDPR.

The function role must be identified to make it simple to find the GDPR rules that apply. Therefore, defining roles and duties is the first stage in creating a suitable data protection policy. Once roles have been defined, the development of a data protection strategy is needed for cloud service providers in order to execute and manage the relevant GDPR standards.

Normative requirements

The following is a list of specifications that would be applicable to cloud service providers, paraphrasing the language of the law:

- Establish guidelines for the handling of personal data
- Establish procedures for processing data and upholding the rights of data subjects, such as the right to information, the right to access, the right to revoke consent, the right to alter information, and the right to object to the processing activities carried out by the cloud service provider
- Establish privacy requirements from the start for anybody handling or controlling data
- Create and implement rules for data portability and ownership
- Implement security measures to protect data privacy
- Establish guidelines for the handling of personal data for third parties and foreign organizations
- Create policies and processes for handling violations and incidents
- Create policies for the creation of contracts, data retention periods, and other necessary needs

The regulations that apply to cloud service providers with regard to data security and compliance are summarized in the following outline:

- **Security control requirements**: Cloud service providers must offer sufficient assurances that the necessary organizational and technical safeguards are in place to ensure GDPR compliance. Both the controller and the processor must apply the necessary steps to provide a degree of security appropriate to risk, which may include the following:
    - Pseudonymization and personal data encryption
    - Continually ensure the privacy, accuracy, availability, and robustness of processing systems and services
    - In the case of a technical failure or physical attack, immediately restore access to and the availability of personal data
    - Create a procedure for routinely testing, analyzing, and reviewing the efficiency of organizational and technical safeguards for processing security

  - Adherence to a recognized code of conduct, as described in *Article 40*, or a recognized certification method, as described in *Article 42*, may be used as a component to show conformity with standards
  - Unless compelled to do so by union or member state law, the data controller and data processor must make sure that anyone operating on their behalf and having access to personal data does not handle it without the controller's permission

- **Contractual requirements**: The commercial service contract outlines specific responsibilities for cloud service providers' GDPR and that the following contract clauses be included:
  - The cloud service provider or its subprocessors may only follow instructions from the data controller when processing data
  - A guarantee from the cloud service providers about security precautions and how *Article 32* GDPR standards will be met
  - A list of the subprocessors that the processor uses, together with information on how updates to these are handled by the controller
  - Information required to prove the cloud provider complies with *Article 28* of GDPR, as well as how the processor will support the data controller's audits and inspections
  - The safeguards in place to ensure the security of personal data handled outside the European Economic Area
  - The allocation of responsibility between the controller and processor in the event of a GDPR violation or personal data breach, as well as how the controller should be informed of such incidents
  - How the processor is carrying out its responsibilities to uphold the rights of data subjects
  - How types and categories of personal data are handled at the beginning and during transfer, normal processing, and *end-of-life* – including return and deletion – as well as the subject matter, extent, nature, context, purpose, and length of the processing
- **Documentation requirements**:
  - **Data controllers**: Where applicable, each controller shall keep a record of processing actions as well as a record including the following information:
    - Name and contact information for the controller, joint controller, controller's representative, and data protection officer, if applicable
    - Purpose of the processing
    - Categories of data subjects and types of personal data are described

    - Receivers in foreign nations or international organizations are among the categories of recipients to whom personal data has been given or will be given
    - Transfers of personal data to a third country or an international organization, including the name of the third country or international organization and the evidence of appropriate safeguards, as per *Article 49*
    - Predicted time limits for erasing the various categories of data, whenever possible
    - A general overview of the technical and organizational security measures mentioned in *Article 32*, whenever possible

- **Data processors**. The following information must be included in each processor's record of all categories of processing actions performed on behalf of a controller, when applicable:
    - Name, address, and phone number of the data protection officer and any other processors
    - Categories of processing activities performed
    - Transfers of personal data to a third country or an international organization, including the mention of the third country or the international organization and the proof of the necessary protections, as outlined in *Article 49*
    - A general overview of the organizational and technical security measures mentioned in *Article 32*

The GDPR code of conduct for CSPs

Cloud service providers and processors are required by GDPR to adopt approved codes of conduct or take part in certification or seal programs that have been authorized by supervisory authorities, in order to demonstrate compliance with GDPR standards. This assists in demonstrating conformity with the regulation, offering guarantees and assurances of cross-border transfer safeguards. The creation of codes of conduct that support the correct implementation of GDPR is encouraged under *Article 40*. The rule makes it clear that the proposed code of conduct must include particular elements related to how GDPR must be applied. The following ought to be mentioned:

- Fair and transparent processing – controllers' legitimate interests
- Gathering of personal information
- Anonymization of personal information
- Data made available to the general public and data subjects
- Exercising data subjects' rights
- Information given to children, their protection, and the process of obtaining approval from those who have parental responsibility for them

- Processes and policies mentioned in *Article 24* and *Article 25*, as well as the security-related procedures and policies mentioned in *Article 32*
- Notification of breaches of personal data to supervisory authorities and dissemination of such information to data subjects
- Transfer of personal data to international organizations or third nations
- Resolution of processing-related issues between controllers and data subjects through out-of-court actions and other dispute resolution processes, while upholding all protections for data subject rights under *Article 77* and *Article 79*

The regulation's enforcement has made it very clear that no company can shirk its obligation to process customer data safely. As previously mentioned, we can take into consideration associations such as ECUC (an interest group for **European Financial Institutions in Cloud** (ECUC) related questions `https://ecuc.group/`), **BSI – Cloud Computing Compliance Criteria Catalog** (**BSI C5** of the German Federal Office for Information Security, `https://www.bsi.bund.de/EN/Themen/Unternehmen-und-Organisationen/Informationen-und-Empfehlungen/Empfehlungen-nach-Angriffszielen/Cloud-Computing/Kriterienkatalog-C5/C5_Einfuehrung/C5_Einfuehrung_node.html`), or **Cloud Security Alliance** (**CSA,** a cloud computing environment, `https://www.cloudsecurityalliance.org`) for references. Every organization involved directly or indirectly in data processing or that has access to the personal data of an EU citizen will be required to comply with the legislation, regardless of whether it is outsourced to a third party or done in-house. Businesses, particularly data controllers and data processors, may incur significant fines for negligence or misunderstanding of these regulations. Cloud service providers must be aware of their individual responsibilities and tasks under GDPR and keep in mind that compliance with the law and the dangers of not doing so must be given top priority.

Summary

In this chapter, we spoke a lot about the cloud, talking about security, risk management, the types of cloud, and all the pain points related to it, concluding with GDPR. As a consumer, even if you use the cut-down versions of these services, usually for free, you'll find that the main players in the market comply with the main standards. From an entity perspective, you could be involved either in the adoption of a cloud platform or with a cloud company to create and improve a cloud governance program.

The realm of US privacy will be explored in the next chapter, along with the Federal Trade Commission (Section 5) and a review of local privacy laws. Finally, we'll look at two distinct yet related phenomena – **Bring Your Own Device** (**BYOD**)- and remote working.

11
What about the US?

In this final chapter, we will enter the world of US privacy, including the Federal Trade Commission (including Section 5), and check the status of local privacy laws, while looking at other laws that are relevant to data protection and trying to understand whether they can, sooner or later, lead to a national law. Finally, we will look at two different but similar phenomena: bring your own device and remote working.

In this chapter, we will cover the following topics:

- The US status of privacy
- **The Federal Trade Commission** (FTC)
- An overview of Section 5 of the FTC Act
- How NIST and FTC interact
- **Bring Your Own Device** (BYOD)
- Remote working
- What privacy rights are available to employees?

The US status of privacy

Customers are largely unaware of the data economy that supports everyday products and services. Their data is shared with a greater number of third parties, which not only increases the number of businesses that may make money from it but also increases the likelihood that their data can be breached or leaked in a way that results in actual harm. Just this past year, a news organization exposed a priest using pseudonymous app data that was purportedly leaked from an advertiser connected to the dating app Grindr. According to another report, the US government purchased location information from a prayer app. Apps for treating opioid addiction have been identified by researchers to share sensitive information. Additionally, a recent data breach at T-Mobile affected at least 40 million customers, some of whom had no prior connection to the company.

Consumer data privacy regulations can give people power over their data, but if they're executed poorly, they can also serve to protect the status quo.

What the current national privacy laws (don't) do

At the moment, privacy laws are a confusing jumble of many sectoral regulations. Historically, the US has a variety of inconsistent federal (and state) regulations that look at certain data categories, such as credit data or health information, or look at specific populations, such as children, and regulate within those areas.

The vast majority of goods that individuals use every day are unregulated in how they collect data. Unless a state has its own data privacy law, many corporations are essentially free to do anything they want with the data because there are no federal privacy rules governing them. Most states allow businesses to use, distribute, or sell any information they acquire about you without informing you first. No national legislation specifies when (or whether) a business must inform you whether your data is compromised or made available to unauthorized individuals.

Your data may be further sold or shared without your knowledge if a corporation distributes it with third parties (such as data brokers), including sensitive information such as your location or health.

Most US consumers think they are protected until they aren't. Sadly, customers are unable to observe and comprehend the flow of information because this ecosystem is largely opaque and concealed from view. Unlike the EU, with its **General Data Protection Regulation** (**GDPR**), the United States lacks a single legislation that protects the privacy of all kinds of data. Instead, it consists of a variety of regulations with acronyms such as HIPAA, FCRA, FERPA, GLBA, ECPA, COPPA, and VPPA that are intended to exclusively target particular categories of data in unique (and frequently outmoded) situations:

- Only communication between you and *covered entities*, such as physicians, hospitals, pharmacies, insurers, and other such organizations, is covered by the **Health Insurance Portability and Accountability Act** (**HIPAA**), which has little to do with privacy. People tend to think HIPAA covers all health data, but it doesn't. For instance, neither your Fitbit data nor the law's restrictions on who can inquire about your COVID-19 vaccination status are protected.
- Information in your credit report is protected by the **Fair Credit Reporting Act** (**FCRA**). It places restrictions on who can access credit reports, what data the credit agencies can gather, and how information is acquired.
- Who can seek student educational records is specified in the **Family Educational Rights and Privacy Act** (**FERPA**). This involves granting the right to view education records kept by a school to parents, qualified students, and other schools.
- Consumer financial products, such as loan services or investment advising services, are required to disclose how they share data as well as a customer's choice to opt out under the **Gramm-Leach-Bliley Act** (**GLBA**). As long as they declare such use in advance, the law does not impose

restrictions on how businesses utilize the data they acquire. It at least makes an effort to erect barriers to the security of some personal information.

- Government wiretapping of phone calls and other electronic signals is prohibited by the **Electronic Communications Privacy Act** (**ECPA**) (although the USA Patriot Act redefined much of this). Additionally, it establishes a wide range of guidelines for communication monitoring by employers. The ECPA was passed in 1986, and critics frequently point out how out of date it is. The ECPA does not defend against contemporary surveillance techniques, including law enforcement access to older material saved on servers, in cloud storage documents, and in search queries because it was written before the era of the modern internet.
- The **Children's Online Privacy Protection Rule** (**COPPA**) places restrictions on how much information businesses can gather about children under the age of 13 in their databases.
- The sharing of VHS rental records is prohibited by the **Video Privacy Protection Act** (**VPPA**). Although it may seem absurd now, this regulation was created as a result of a journalist retrieving Robert Bork's video rental history when he was a candidate for the Supreme Court. However, the VPPA hasn't prevented streaming firms from operating.
- A website or app that violates its own privacy statement may be targeted by the **Federal Trade Commission** (**FTC**) under the **Federal Trade Commission Act** (**FTC Act**). The FTC has the authority to look into instances of misleading users by claiming that video chats are end-to-end encrypted. This is what it did when it filed a complaint against Zoom. Recently, some organizations have urged the FTC to extend that authority to unlawful data practices.

It's understandable how people could become perplexed about the rights they have and do not have, given the variety of laws in existence. Additionally, there are a few state statutes in addition to these federal laws.

The **California Consumer Privacy Act** (**CCPA**) from 2018 and the **California Privacy Rights Act** (**CPRA**), which California voters approved in November 2020, are having a significant impact on the landscape of privacy and data security, alongside the **Virginia Consumer Data Protection Act** (**VCDPA**) and the **Colorado Privacy Act** (**Colopa** or **CPA**).

These three US states have three distinct, comprehensive consumer privacy laws. These laws only give their residents an extra layer of data protection, regardless of where a firm is situated.

Similar clauses in this legislation usually offer you some kind of notice and let you decide how to handle your data. In essence, a business operating under these standards is required to inform you if it is selling your data. You also have the option of agreeing or disagreeing with this, and you have the right to access, delete, correct, or move your data as you see fit. The permitted cure periods (the amount of time a business has to correct an error), the size or income level of businesses the law applies to, and whether you can use tools or *authorized agents* for opt-out requests are some other minor differences between these laws (such as a setting in your web browser that automatically opts you out of data sales on a web page, or a service where another person makes opt-out requests for you).

The privacy laws in California contain a limited *private right of action* – the capacity to bring a lawsuit against a company – against specific categories of data breaches, according to the experts, making them the strongest in the US. California also mandates a *global opt out* to stop data sharing across all devices or browsers, as opposed to being required to opt out on each website separately. At the same time, it's very difficult to establish the same purpose for the**VCDPA**; most professionals consider VCDPA a really weak law. Its foundation is opt-out consent. There are no safeguards for civil rights. No private right of action exists. Many of the provisions support various company models. The act essentially permits big data collection businesses to carry on as before. None of that should come as a surprise, given that Amazon had a significant influence on the creation of Virginia's statute.

At least four other states, including Massachusetts, New York, North Carolina, and Pennsylvania, are currently debating important, comprehensive legislation pertaining to the protection of consumer data. In the beginning, laws in other states differ. The International Association of Privacy Professionals offers a tracker that displays which states have privacy legislation in development and where those laws are in the process to be issued. It can be challenging to keep track of the status of all these proposals. At least 14 of the ideas are identical (or almost identical) to Virginia's laxer statute.

There are state-level laws that specifically protect certain facets of data privacy, similar to how there are regulations at the federal level. Missouri has laws governing e-book privacy. People have privacy rights over their biometric information, such as fingerprint or face scans, thanks to the Illinois **Biometric Information Privacy Act (BIPA)**. Knowing your rights when it comes to data-breach notifications is particularly difficult because there are at least 54 distinct regulations that differ by location.

Such state regulations are nevertheless helpful, despite the fact that they can be difficult to understand. While the idea is to raise the privacy bar, it's worth noting that when regulatory requirements are raised, businesses frequently decide to apply the tougher, more protective norm across the board for everyone.

Additionally, there is a chance that having too many state rules may make things confusing for both businesses and customers. A nationwide law would simplify things for everyone. In fact, to ensure that customers are aware of and have reasonable expectations regarding their rights over their data, there has to be federal legislation that takes a much more consistent approach to problem-solving.

The FTC

The FTC is an independent body of the US government whose main duties include promoting consumer protection and upholding civil (non-criminal) US antitrust law. Together with the Department of Justice Antitrust Division, the FTC is responsible for overseeing federal civil antitrust enforcement. The Federal Trade Commission Building in Washington, DC, serves as the organization's headquarters.

In reaction to the monopolistic trust crises of the 19th century, the Federal Trade Commission Act, which became law in 1914, formed the FTC. Since its founding, the FTC has enforced both the provisions of the FTC Act, 15 U.S.C. 41 et seq., as well as the provisions of the Clayton Act, a significant antitrust act. The FTC has issued a number of regulations and has been given authority to enforce more company regulation laws over time.

The FTC currently has the broadest federal authority over safeguarding customer privacy. Through the FTC Act of 1914, Congress initially established the agency to enforce antitrust laws. However, in 1938, Congress expanded the agency's authority under Section 5 of the FTC Act to include the prohibition of *unfair or deceptive acts or practices*, adding consumer protection issues to its purview. Since then, through laws like the Fair Credit Reporting Act and the **COPPA**, Congress has also granted the FTC greater statutory authority to protect privacy.

Despite these extra regulations, the FTC's scope of authority is constrained, which makes it difficult to trust the organization to protect privacy. The agency is not only underequipped to enforce privacy laws, but it also lacks a track record of doing so. It is uncertain whether tougher enforcement would result from Congress giving the agency more power and funding to protect privacy.

An overview of Section 5 of the FTC Act

Consumer privacy has been compromised by unfair data-gathering methods and spying, and this constant and unwanted observation causes consumers significant harm. This paper makes the case that the FTC ought to use its Section 5 unfairness authority to create a data minimization rule that would forbid all secondary data uses with a few exceptions, ensuring that people can use apps and online services without fear of being tracked without taking additional precautions. A right to opt out of secondary data use, including worldwide opt-out controls and databases, is also mandated. The FTC is allowed to decide whether to restrict certain secondary data uses, such as behavioral advertising or the use of sensitive data.

The FTC should also adopt data security requirements, access, portability, correction, and deletion rights, as well as obligations for data transparency for initial data use and civil rights protections over discriminatory data processing. These additional provisions would supplement the data minimization rule. Additionally, the FTC ought to forbid the use of dark patterns in data processing.

The FTC has a broad ability to enact prescriptive regulations in an effort to prevent commercial practices that could harm consumers. These privacy laws are likely to withstand First Amendment examination because the courts typically accord expert agencies wide deference when interpreting their substantive statutes.

NIST and FTC

The five core functions of the NIST Cybersecurity Framework can be used by businesses to establish or enhance a data security program, examine current data security procedures, or communicate data security requirements to stakeholders. The Framework's five core functions can also be used as a model by businesses of all sizes to conduct risk assessments and mitigation. And as the FTC's enforcement actions demonstrate, businesses might have better protected the information of their customers if they had adhered to basic security procedures, such as those outlined in the Framework.

Additionally, given that the FTC's enforcement actions are in line with the core functions of the Framework, businesses should read *Start with Security*, a publication from the FTC that outlines the lessons learned from the agency's data security cases and offers helpful advice for lowering cybersecurity risks. The nation's cybersecurity standard will be raised, and more comprehensive consumer data protection will result from executing the risk management strategy outlined in the Framework with a reasonable amount of rigor, as businesses should do.

Positively, the FTC acknowledges that the NIST Cybersecurity Framework is consistent with the organization's long-standing approach to data security and that it might be a helpful tool for businesses creating and assessing a data security program. There is no silver bullet to create acceptable data protection, as an old FTC blog post reiterates (`https://www.ftc.gov/business-guidance/small-businesses/cybersecurity/nist-framework`). In the end, solid policies and practices must be carefully designed, put into practice, and enforced in order to lessen the effects of cybersecurity events and intense regulatory scrutiny.

BYOD

You have probably wondered what BYOD is. The technology trend known as BYOD enables employees to execute work-related tasks on their personal mobile devices while also connecting to a corporate network and resources.

Employers are increasingly allowing employees to use their personal mobile devices to do work-related tasks and connect to the corporate network and resources (BYOD).

As a result, many businesses allow their employees to access the corporate network from home or to concentrate all company information on their personal smartphones, eliminating the need for them to carry two mobile devices.

There are several disadvantages associated with BYOD as well, including the risk that inadequate security measures pose to sensitive data.

BYOD is a notion that has many consequences for how a workplace is run and is not just about bringing your own gadgets to work.

And how did this phenomena become more widespread? The most frequent situation up until a few years ago was when users were less technologically advanced than businesses. For instance, a lot of people didn't have a computer at home but did have one at work, and the majority of people who had a mobile phone or a laptop had them because their employer had given them to them. Consumer technology advancements have bucked this trend, and today it is more typical for users to have technology that is more sophisticated, effective, and efficient than that provided by the business itself.

Like every form of working, BYOD has advantages and disadvantages. Let's examine the benefits and drawbacks of this trend.

Benefits of BYOD

If it weren't for the numerous benefits it offers, the BYOD phenomenon would not have taken off in the business world. Increased employee productivity is the biggest advantage; employees perform better and collaborate with coworkers more effectively because they feel more at ease using the apps and devices they choose for themselves, based on their personal preferences.

The second benefit mentioned by IT managers is that BYOD increases job satisfaction because employees can use the same terminals they typically use at work, which makes them happier and more content with their jobs. Another advantage, especially for those in control of European IT departments, is that BYOD reduces the cost of purchasing technology. Employees may pay the entire or partial cost of their mobile devices, and cloud-based software is available for them as well.

BYOD offers a lot more benefits. On one hand, it gives workers the freedom to choose when and where to do their work, giving them more flexibility. Additionally, since a worker frequently carries their smartphone, they are available to work anytime they need to, which enhances customer service.

Disadvantages of BYOD

BYOD is not entirely beneficial, and improper BYOD deployment can lead to a number of annoyances for both employers and employees.

The risk that BYOD poses to the security of a business network and the protection of sensitive company data is the main issue with its widespread adoption. Without adequate security measures or a remote data deletion system, the finder of, say, a lost employee's smartphone could have access to confidential company data.

Also, the entire business network may get contaminated if a user connects to it using a device that has malware on it.

Another disadvantage is that it uses up more network resources, necessitating an increase in those resources in order to support the connection of all devices. Additionally, since the most widely used applications incorporate multimedia components, more bandwidth is used.

Finally hand, the expansion of all kinds of terminals and applications necessitates the strengthening of IT support and maintenance teams, who must deal with the issues of a wide range of hardware and software.

Managing mobile devices

It is crucial to have a **Mobile Device Management** (**MDM**) system to control and monitor the devices that connect to a corporate network and ensure the security of the network and the company's data.

These apps, among many other things, enable remote application installation, file syncing, and device tracking.

These are MDM applications' most typical features:

- The extensive installation of applications on network-connected terminals
- Control over the available apps
- Device access management
- A device's location and tracking
- Lock file synchronization as a functionality
- The restriction of telephone and data usage
- Setting a lock password from a server and remotely deleting data from any terminal

In conclusion, these are the crucial features that ensure corporate network management and business security.

Criteria and recommendations

The risks associated with BYOD are mitigated by a sound security policy. The majority of large businesses now have a policy of access to a corporate network by devices owned by third parties, the issue being that many businesses are not ready to implement mobile initiatives.

To ensure BYOD's safety, a number of factors must be taken into consideration. First, corporate network services and access must be secured. All devices that connect to the network also require an extra layer of protection.

Finally, it's critical to protect data transfer by encrypting the data. Giving employees the information they need to utilize a company network safely is a highly recommended practice.

Remote working

The last few years have seen a rising trend of employees wanting to work remotely. This idea expands the idea of *merely* working from home or a co-working place (the use of an office or other working environment by people who are self-employed or working for different employers) and allows you to work from anywhere.

Gig workers and digital nomads have become accustomed to this; according to data from 2020, about 5 million Americans identify as such. With the COVID-19 epidemic demonstrating the effectiveness of remote labor and several locations opening their doors to digital nomads, the idea seems certain to gain traction in the next few years.

Security issues

As more people started working remotely during the epidemic, cybersecurity incidents significantly rose, as thieves tried to profit from the pandemic's stress and disruption as well as the larger *attack surface* they could now target.

Due to the epidemic, most industries shifted to remote work; however, this offered new attack surfaces for cybercriminals to exploit, such as the use of personal devices for work.

The pre-pandemic environment, when work was mostly carried out in a physical workspace, did not necessitate forcing employees and security teams to think about security in this way.

To set up safe and secure remote-working environments, companies require employees to be much more conscious of things that they wouldn't need to be aware of when they're working in the office. Who, for example, is standing behind us? Am I neglecting to watch my device? How well-protected is the network I'm using? Do I allow my family to use my device?

Important ramifications

The so-called *insider danger* that firms face has significantly increased as a result of a remote workforce. Insider risks have become more frequent and expensive during the COVID-19 era, as you can see by glancing at the statistics.

While we might imagine insider threat concerns as the domain of a disgruntled employee behaving deliberately, the vast majority of leaks and breaches are merely the result of carelessness and incompetence.

The results are consistent with those of a recent study by the University of Central Florida, which discovered that stressed-out personnel are far more prone to violate security rules and procedures. In fact, the researchers discovered that the most frequent type of violation occurs when observing the rules slows down employees and they break the rules to maintain their productivity.

However, the costs of such negligence have been estimated at up to $500,000, while major firms (those with 75,000 or more people) spent an average of $22.68 million to resolve insider-related problems.

Keeping a remote workforce secure

To do this, some steps are absolutely easy to implement that organizations can adopt right away, such as requiring more secure passwords, implementing two-factor authentication, making sure all devices are fully patched with the most recent software updates, and training staff members on secure practices, particularly in recognizing the types of phishing attacks that continue to make up the majority of cyberattacks today.

In an effort to provide secure remote access connections between employees and their private corporate network, **virtual private networks (VPNs)** are also frequently used. While VPNs can be very useful, they can also pose a lot of hazards, particularly if the network is not configured properly. Indeed, a standard VPN was used to carry out the Colonial Pipeline attack.

With stronger security than Wi-Fi or even VPNs, 5G promises to provide distant workers with more robust connectivity. With remote workers having the choice to use unlimited data alternatives as their primary connection to the workplace, 5G is expected to be a viable alternative to Wi-Fi thanks to the reduced latency it promises.

Through the use of anti-tracking and anti-spoofing capabilities, 5G technology has encryption built in. It also makes use of network slicing, which enables the splitting of a network into a number of virtual networks, each with its own set of security safeguards. This would make it possible to assign significant individuals inside organization-specific controls in an effort to fend off whale phishing, which occurs when such VIPs are targeted by criminals because of their importance.

A multifaceted strategy

The improved capabilities of 5G mean that many more devices are likely to be connected, and IoT devices increase the number of potential vulnerabilities within your network. However, 5G is not without its own concerns. An expanding number of non-business IoT devices are now connected to corporate networks, such as pet feeders, coffee makers, and fitness equipment. These applications, or at least the majority of them, are dependent either on Wi-Fi or 5G. The latter provides greater authentication, so I can't pretend to be you and you can't pretend to be me, as you could in the past. However, from the perspective of corporate security, 5G technology might not be distinguished from other forms of connection because no technology should be trusted a priori

Following COVID-19, it appears that remote work will continue to be popular, thus businesses must master cybersecurity to prevent their remote workforce from becoming easy prey for hackers. Although 5G can play a role in this, the best security is likely to result from a mix of other network features that go beyond the connection method itself.

The majority of security teams don't do care if you are working from office or home. They assume that connections outside your workplace are suspect and the workplace environment will be vulnerable to attack. Because of this, the great majority of assaults can be avoided by making sure passwords are safe, software is patched, and staff have a fundamental understanding of cyber hygiene and phishing awareness so that they don't put themselves in vulnerable positions.

In order to give remote workers the flexibility they want while keeping the security that is so important to the modern organization, there is an entire program available that consists of policies, tools, training, and other elements.

Assisting the transformation

We now live in a society where workers are progressively demanding more flexibility; organizations shouldn't rush to resume regular programming (I mean, working from office on a daily basis, but at least a hybrid model is desirable). What makes sense for hybrid models today could not be as effective in 6 months; therefore, this is an opportunity to reconsider our strategy for hybrid working.

Remote workers value *third spaces*, such as cafes, bars, and even pubs, where they can work remotely. The pandemic has seen much of the cybersecurity focus on making sure that home environments are as secure as possible.

Working in a third space raises the stakes, since these spaces, while giving workers the flexibility they seek, also significantly raise the risk from a cybersecurity standpoint. At the same time, every organization can see flexibility as a business requirement, so they have to find out how to make it work.

Computer safety

Fortunately, attaining adequate cyber hygiene to thwart the vast majority of intrusions doesn't necessitate cutting-edge equipment or a highly qualified security group. Organizations must just make sure that the fundamentals of cyber hygiene are followed. This comprises the following:

- A **two-factor authentication** (**2FA**) process. Most credential-based assaults are thwarted by **multi-factor authentication** (**MFA**) or 2FA. With the kind of passwordless technology that is becoming more and more common in contemporary software, this is simpler than ever. Wherever it is feasible, MFA should be enabled.
- Least privilege accessibility. Using MFA to protect login to vital accounts is important, but it's also crucial to make sure that each account has access to only the systems they actually require. In fact, researchers contend that different accounts should be used for email and internet browsing than for accessing privileged systems.
- Maintain device updates. Having the most recent patches and updates from a manufacturer is a fundamental necessity for every device connected to a network. Using endpoint management software, you can help make sure this occurs throughout the network.
- Install malware-detecting software. Ensuring malware protection software is installed and used in addition to more conventional antivirus software is another easy measure to take. This software frequently offers both protection from assaults and alerts that an attack is being attempted.
- Safeguard data. All of the aforementioned measures can prove to be quite efficient in protecting crucial organizational data, but it's also crucial that businesses have a clear awareness of the data they possess, as well as its relative sensitivity and significance. In fact, this is frequently required by laws such as the GDPR and supports a risk-based approach to data governance.

The integration of cyber hygiene training into employee onboarding is going to be a vital component to ensure that a diverse workforce is a secure workforce, as we become more accustomed to a hybrid way of working.

What privacy rights are available to employees?

Because there are typically few employee privacy rights at work, employees have very few electronic privacy rights when working from home. Employers have the right to observe how you use company-provided technology and computer networks, including how you type, save your data, access websites, and use your work email, in accordance with federal law and legal precedent.

Email privacy rights only apply to personal accounts; they do not apply if you are using company hardware or a network. Additionally, if someone forwards a post you create to a password-protected social media site on your own time on a company laptop, your employer may still take legal action against you.

What exemptions exist to worker monitoring?

There are a few exceptions to worker monitoring. Generally speaking, it is against the law for companies to record employees in break rooms or restrooms; however, it's unclear how this applies in the age of virtual meetings. Genetic information and union organizing-related messages cannot be legally read by employers, and union contracts may completely forbid monitoring.

While in the EU the situation is different, in the US barely half of the states prohibit companies from requesting employees' social media passwords, while Connecticut and Delaware state laws compel employers to declare that they are monitoring employee email. Selective employee monitoring based on race, gender, or other demographics might be against the law.

And it's unclear how closely businesses can watch what employees do on personal devices such as smartphones or PCs that they own but use for work, as there have been no legal precedents.

Do employees know what information employers can access?

The simplest method of preserving your right to digital privacy may be to learn what your employer is watching and refrain from doing any sensitive business through that channel.

The most crucial factor is to prevent your information and habits from being tracked. Choosing sites where your employer doesn't have access to your information, as well as knowing exactly who has access to it, can be crucial for your peace of mind.

To learn what information a company can access, you might have to ask your employer, or you might find an explanation in the employment agreement or the company's privacy policy. Unfortunately, most employers are not required to respond honestly, and refusing to give your permission could result in your termination. According to the workers' rights charity Workplace Fairness, at least one instance saw a judge finding that a company had the right to monitor employees' email, even when it explicitly stated it wouldn't.

Should employees bring personal equipment to work?

The best approach to preserve your privacy is to conduct all personal business using technology that you individually own; however, some workplaces might not allow this. Anytime you utilize an employer's hardware, email system, or software, it risks being exposed to your employer, and using, for instance, a BYOD device isn't ideal if you're looking to change jobs. Therefore, it's even more crucial that you are cautious of the gadget you use, especially while you're at home.

You shouldn't be signed in to any workplace networks. When you are, if your computer is connected to a company's network, your employer can see what you're doing even when you're not actively using the connection, as for background services.

There aren't many straightforward legal issues. However, it's safe to assume that unless you log on to your boss's network, you are completely safe from intrusion by your boss when you use your personal computer for anything. The point is, since you are somehow using company infrastructure, company VPN, for instance, the company can check what you are doing.

However, when telecommuting becomes the norm, employees might be increasingly resistant to surveillance.

Employing these kinds of tools makes your staff more stressed. Additionally, it lowers employee morale. Therefore, it may not be an optimal company plan.

Summary

In this chapter, we looked at the status of US privacy, including FTC Section 5 and all the relevant bills (HISPAA, FRCA, FERPA, GLBA, ECPA, COPPA, VPPA, CCRA, CPRA, VCDPA, and ColoPA), trying to understand whether the US will eventually have just one national law. Then, we discussed common topics such as BYOD and using a business laptop to *mind your own business*, mostly from a privacy perspective.

With this chapter, our journey into cybersecurity and privacy has ended. I sincerely hope you enjoyed the reading and learned new things (or old things from a different perspective).

Stay safe, and remember – humans are the weakest link in the cybersecurity chain.

Appendix

Due to framework and law changes, this appendix to the book is mandatory. I have also taken the opportunity to briefly introduce you to some quite relevant topics that I hadn't touched upon in previous chapters, such as **Vulnerability Assessment and Penetration Testing** (VA/PT). I decided to divide this appendix into different topics.

ISO 27002

The current version of ISO 27002 was issued in 2013 and is now hopelessly out of date. A great deal has changed in the last 8 years! Let's hope we won't have to wait another 8 years for the next edition.

As with the previous edition, ISO 27002 is meant to be independent in the sense that it may be utilized by organizations who are uninterested in ISO 27001 and just want a set of information security rules to implement inside their organization. In this regard, it is identical to other control frameworks, such as the CSA's NIST CSF. Choose your poison!

The new version will go out possibly in the upcoming months where the only significant change is that Annex A will match the new ISO 27002. This introduces 11 *new* controls, which are as follows:

- Threat intelligence
- Information security for use of cloud services
- ICT readiness for business continuity
- Physical security monitoring
- Configuration management
- Information deletion
- Data masking
- Data leakage prevention
- Monitoring activities
- Web filtering
- Secure coding

Note that the controls I've described previously are not the real ones. These are the controls' names. The control descriptions are included in ISO 27002 and will be included in the new Annex A when ISO 27001 is updated. ISO 27002 also provides implementation guidelines for these measures. For better understanding here, I need to clarify that all of the standards in the ISO 27000 series have a specific focus: while ISO 27001 is designed to build the foundations of information security in your organization and devise its framework; ISO 27002 is designed to implement controls named in Annex A of ISO 27001.

I have already read a great deal on the internet about these new regulations, and one of the most common assertions is that organizations will be required to adopt them. This is not true in my opinion for several reasons:

- ISO 27001 does not require the adoption of any controls. It is up to the organization to choose, based on a risk assessment, whether or not to apply these measures. In other words, these controls may not be required to handle one or more of the information security risks.
- Despite being labeled *new*, a number of these are already covered by current Annex A restrictions.
- In addition, it is quite probable that organizations are currently implementing at least some of these rules.
- It is absolutely useful to examine this list of new controls and ask, *should any of these new controls be required controls to assist in the management of one or more of my information security risks?* In this case, you must update your risk assessment and execute the control. When migrating to the new version of ISO 27001, you will have to conduct this inspection.

However, do not trust anybody who says you *must* implement these *new* controls.

What is different?

Each control is labeled in a variety of ways, such as whether it is preventative or remedial and whether it pertains to confidentiality, availability, or integrity. It remains to be seen whether this will be beneficial.

It features fewer controls (93 as opposed to 114), with some controls combined and others divided. In addition, it features a variety of additional *contemporary* measures, such as *cloud security*, *threat intelligence*, and *web filtering*; however, the fundamental concept remains the same. It is a collection of potential information security controls with implementation instructions for each control.

Is it superior to the previous version?

It depends; it attempts to cover certain current controls, such as those pertaining to the cloud. For the provided controls, some assistance is lacking, but the majority are superb.

Is it a standard set of controls for information security?

No, and this is due to the two primary causes listed as follows.

Reason 1: unbalanced coverage of the controls

There are 14 physical security controls, but only one cloud security control and 2 network security controls. There are further instances. This is just imbalanced.

Reason 2: controls are missing

Some of the most prevalent information security measures are buried in the extensive guidelines for other controls or are simply not addressed. There are no distinct controls for *Firewall*, *IDS*, *Email security*, *MFA*, *VPN*, *WAF*, *Cyber Insurance*, *Wireless access*, or *Third-party library/software management*, for instance. Some of them are not mentioned in the text.

Given the necessity of data validation in online applications, there are only a few controls and guidelines for validating data input.

There is just one control at a very high level for cloud computing, although I believe there should be numerous – for example, covering contracts, security obligations, tenant management, and service management. Yes, you may refer to ISO 27017; however, ISO 27002 should include at least the most typical cloud security rules on its own.

There are currently no adequate controls for business continuity management. There are some information security measures for business continuity planning, which are not the same thing. The lack of controls labeled *Business Continuity Plan* or *Exercise Business Continuity Plans* continues to perplex me. Yes, you may reference ISO 22301 for business continuity and disaster recovery management, but it makes no sense to me not to have these controls. Given the ubiquity of ransomware, there cannot be many organizations in the world that do not have at least one *Business Continuity Plan*, and this control is crucial from an information security standpoint.

Given that ISO 27002 is supposed to be utilized independently and fully apart from ISO 27001, it has relatively few governance rules, such as those pertaining to *risk assessment*, *information security committee*, and *competences*.

To be fair, ISO 27002 does state that organizations may need additional controls to enhance the ISO 27002 controls. Sadly, many organizations will not use ISO 27002 in this manner and will instead perceive it as a relatively complete collection of regularly used controls, which it is not!

Moreover, everyone will have their own opinions on what should be included in a list of *frequently used information security rules.*

What must you do at this time?

If you are just beginning to implement ISO 27001, it may be beneficial to get a copy and use it as a guide for implementing your controls. However, use with caution, even if throughout 2023 there will probably be no need to re-certify your company for the new release, but simply renew it, as usual, according to the certification-cycle of your company (usually 2 years). However, I am about to suggest you some strategies.

If you have previously implemented ISO 27001, you do not need to take any more action; nonetheless, you may find this updated version of ISO 27002 interesting since it contains valuable implementation strategies for various controls – that is, as a kind of quality control for your work.

What must you do when the new Annex A is released with the new ISO 27001 version?

Your certifying body or registrar will inform you of the transition arrangements to the new version, although you will likely have 2 years to completely transfer to the new version.

Depending on your circumstances and your desired strategy, there are two primary transition strategies.

Transition method 1 – do not modify the risk assessment

Why would you use this strategy?

This strategy is appropriate if you want to move to the latest version of ISO 27001 with little effort. In particular, you do not want to alter your risk assessment.

What is this strategy?

This strategy is predicated on continuing to use the previous ISO 27001:2013 Annex A rules. This is permissible since ISO 27001 enables controls to originate from any source, and you may pick the old Annex A controls as your source. Do not allow anybody to convince you that this is impossible. It can happen! The most important aspect of this technique is that it allows you to shift to the new edition of ISO 27001 without modifying your risk assessment.

To implement this strategy, you will need to do the following:

- Compare your controls with the new Annex A and record that you have done so – for example, in an email or as meeting minutes
- Make a few changes to the Statement of Applicability's format
- These modifications should not need more than a few days of work

Transition method 2 – "complete replacement"

Why would you use this strategy?

This option is appropriate if your risk assessment includes references to the old Annex A controls and you are willing to make all the required adjustments to your **Information Security Management System** (**ISMS**) and risk assessment to eliminate all references to the old Annex A.

What is this strategy?

This method eliminates any references to the old ISO 27001:2013 Annex A controls from your ISMS and replaces them with the new Annex A controls. This strategy is much more labor-intensive than the previous method.

Privacy

The **General Data Protection Regulation** (**GDPR**) Enforcement Tracker by CMS Law provides a summary of the fines and penalties that EU data protection authorities have issued as a result of the EU's GDPR. This list will be updated as often as we can. The software is alive on GitHub (to be compiled according to your needs) and all the explanations and linking are at `https://www.enforcementtracker.com/`.

The GDPR-CARPA, proposed last year by the Luxembourg authority, is a sort of certification for entities to prove that they are GDPR-compliant. The GDPR scheme sets the EDPB authority (European Data Protection Board) as the Central European authority for the whole GDPR process, and then every member state has its own local government authority. The compliance is done via an audit, and, even if at the moment, the certification is just a draft, it could be really interesting, because it would allow any certified entity to be chosen by another one (imagine a data processor). See more details here: `https://edpb.europa.eu/news/national-news/2022/cnpd-adopts-certification-mechanism-gdpr-carpa_en`.

The plethora of websites that use traffic monitoring services, such as AdSense Analytics (but also Google Fonts, if used in an online mode – i.e., if not downloaded and used offline) need to be, according to the European data protection board, set aside in favor of alternative services.

Some of these, using a nerdy metaphor, *call home* – I mean, send the requests to Mountain View (Google's home) without proper authorization.

US President Joe Biden has signed the long-awaited Executive Order that is intended to uphold the **Court of Justice of the European Union** (**CJEU**) earlier rulings, more than six months after an *agreement in principle* between the US and the EU. This aims to get around restrictions on data transfers between the EU and the US. The Executive Order from Biden appears to fall short of both requirements.

VA/PT

In past chapters, there were references to risk management and how to deal with vulnerability, among other things. What happens quite often, in terms of vulnerabilities in a company, is related to a technological gap, in which the most relevant (and therefore unsecure aspects, is related to missing updates. In this case, vulnerability management is the only thing you can do to have a clear view of the company perimeter.

VA

VA (short for **Vulnerability Assessment**) is a methodical analysis of an information system's security flaws. It assesses the system's susceptibility to known vulnerabilities, gives severity ratings to those vulnerabilities, and advises remedy or mitigation as necessary.

Among the risks that may be averted by VA are as follows:

- SQL injection, XSS injection, and more code injection threats
- The elevation of privileges as a result of flawed authentication techniques
- Software that comes with unsafe settings, such as guessable administrator passwords

Various forms of VA exist. They consist of the following:

- Host assessment – the evaluation of mission-critical servers that may be susceptible to assaults if they have not been thoroughly tested or created from a tested machine image
- Network and wireless assessment – the evaluation of policies and procedures designed to prevent unwanted access to private or public networks and network-accessible resources
- Assessment of databases and large data systems for vulnerabilities and misconfigurations, identification of rogue databases and unsecured development/test environments, and classification of sensitive data throughout an organization's infrastructure
- Application scans — the identification of security flaws in online applications and their source code using automated frontend scans or either static or dynamic source code analysis

Vulnerability identification (testing)

So, if you are ready to fire up your VA machine, it's time to go, even if I would strongly recommend you ask for help (either internal or external). In the case of external assessment, the company that you are dealing with must sign a **Non-Disclosure Agreement** (**NDA**), because they can see security issues that should not be divulged. I also suggest you give the testers all the information you can in terms of your company infrastructure: no one tells you clearly, but if they go blind, there's a risk that they can break some appliances and since they didn't know what kind of asset they were dealing with, it's your fault.

The purpose of this step is to compile an exhaustive list of an application's vulnerabilities. Security analysts evaluate the security of apps, servers, and other systems by scanning them using automated technologies or by manually testing and analyzing them. Additionally, analysts use vulnerability databases, vendor vulnerability notifications, asset management systems, and threat intelligence feeds to uncover security flaws.

Vulnerability analysis

The purpose of this phase is to discover the underlying cause and origin of the vulnerabilities identified in the first step.

It entails identifying the system components accountable for each vulnerability and the vulnerability's fundamental cause. For example, an outdated version of an open source library might be the underlying cause of a vulnerability. This gives a clear avenue for repair – the library's upgrade.

Risk assessment

The purpose of this phase is to rank vulnerabilities by importance. It entails security experts awarding a ranking or severity score to each vulnerability based on the following criteria:

- What systems are impacted?
- What data is in danger?
- Which organizational functions are at risk?
- The simplicity of assault or compromise
- The severity of an assault
- The potential harm caused by the vulnerability

Remediation

The purpose of this phase is to close security holes. Typically, security personnel, development teams, and operations teams collaborate to find the most effective method of repair or mitigation of each risk.

Specific corrective measures may include the following:

- Introduction of new security methods, technologies, or processes
- The implementation of operational or configurational modifications
- Development and deployment of a fix for a security flaw

VA cannot be a one-time occurrence. Organizations must operationalize and regularly repeat this process for it to be successful. DevSecOps, the practice of fostering collaboration between security, operations, and development teams, is equally crucial.

Vulnerability evaluation instruments

The purpose of VA tools is to automatically detect new and current threats that potentially attack your application. Examples of instruments include the following:

- Scanners for web applications that test and replicate known attack patterns.
- Protocol scanners that look for insecure ports, protocols, and network services.
- Network scanners that aid in network visualization and the detection of warning signals, such as stray IP addresses, faked packets, and unusual packet production from a single IP address.
- Schedule frequent, automated scans of all important IT systems as a recommended practice. The findings of these scans should be included in the organization's continuous process of VA.

PT

PT (short for **Penetration Testing**, or **Pentesting**) involves approved, simulated assaults undertaken to assess the security of a computer system. Penetration testers use the same tools, strategies, and procedures as attackers to identify and illustrate the commercial repercussions of a system's vulnerabilities. Typically, PT replicates a number of assaults that potentially affect a company. It can determine whether a system is resilient enough to survive assaults from authorized and unauthenticated positions, as well as from a variety of system roles. With the appropriate scope, PT may probe every facet of a system.

What advantages does PT offer?

Ideally, software and systems would be created with the intention of avoiding serious security vulnerabilities. PT gives insight into the extent to which this objective was met. PT may help a company do the following:

- Locate systemic vulnerabilities
- Assess the strength of the controls
- Support data privacy and security compliance (e.g., the PCI DSS, HIPAA, or GDPR)
- Provide management with qualitative and quantitative evidence of the existing security posture and budget objectives

How much access do penetration testers have?

Depending on the objectives of PT, testers are granted varying degrees of access to or knowledge about the target system. In certain instances, the PT team adopts a single strategy from the outset. Occasionally, the testing team modifies its approach as its understanding of the system grows throughout PT. There are three access levels for PT:

- **Opaque box**: The team knows nothing about the target system's core architecture. It behaves as would a hacker, searching for externally exploitable vulnerabilities.

- **Semi-opaque box**: The team is familiar with one or more credential sets. It is also familiar with the internal data structures, code, and algorithms of the target. The construction of test cases by penetration testers may be based on comprehensive design documentation, such as architectural diagrams of the target system.
- **Transparent box**: Penetration testers have access to systems and system artifacts, such as source code, binaries, containers, and occasionally even system servers. This method offers the greatest degree of certainty in the shortest length of time.

What are the steps of PT?

Penetration testers imitate assaults by adversaries with malicious intent. To do this, they normally implement the following steps:

- **Reconnaissance**: Collect as much information as possible from public and private sources on the target to guide the assault approach. Internet searches, domain registration information retrieval, social engineering, nonintrusive network scanning, and even trash diving are examples of sources. This data assists penetration testers in identifying the target's attack surface and potential vulnerabilities. Depending on the scope and goals of PT, reconnaissance may be as basic as placing a phone call to explore the system's functioning.
- **Scanning**: Utilizing specialized software, penetration testers investigate the target website or system for vulnerabilities, such as open services, application security concerns, and open source vulnerabilities. Based on what they discover during reconnaissance and testing, penetration testers use a range of tools.
- **Gaining entry**: The motives of an attacker may include stealing, modifying, or destroying data, transferring cash, or just harming a company's reputation. For each test scenario, penetration testers assess the most effective tools and strategies for gaining access to the system, whether via a vulnerability such as SQL injection, malware, social engineering, or another method.
- **Preserving access**: Once penetration testers obtain access to the target, their simulated assault must remain connected long enough to exfiltrate data, alter data, or abuse functionality. It is essential to demonstrate the possible effect.

What forms of PT exist?

An exhaustive approach to PT is required for optimum risk management. This requires testing every aspect of the environment:

- **Web application testers**: Evaluate the efficacy of security safeguards and search for vulnerabilities, attack patterns, and other possible security flaws that might lead to a web application penetration.
- **Mobile applications**: Using both automated and extensive manual testing, testers search for vulnerabilities in mobile application binaries and their accompanying server-side functionality. Typical server-side web service vulnerabilities are related to session management, cryptographic difficulties, and authentication and authorization concerns, among other things.

- **Networks:** This testing can find commonplace or significant security flaws in an external network and its associated systems. Experts use a checklist that consists of test cases for encrypted transport protocols, SSL certificate scope difficulties, and the usage of administrative services, among other items.
- **Cloud**: A cloud environment differs substantially from conventional on-premises setups. Typically, the enterprise utilizing the environment and the cloud services provider share security obligations. Due to this, cloud PT takes a set of specific skills and knowledge to examine the cloud's setups, APIs, databases, encryption, storage, and security controls, among other components.
- **Containers**: Docker containers often include vulnerabilities that may be exploited at scale. A frequent risk linked with containers and their environment is also misconfiguration. Both of these threats may be detected by a competent pentester.
- **Embedded apparatus/Internet of Things (IoT)**: Due to their extended life cycles, distant locations, power limits, regulatory requirements, and other factors, embedded or IoT devices such as medical devices, autos, in-home appliances, oil rig equipment, and watches have specific software testing needs. Experts conduct a comprehensive communication analysis as well as a client-server study to discover the faults relevant to the use case.
- **Mobile devices**: Penetration testers use both automatic and human analysis to identify vulnerabilities in mobile application binaries and the accompanying server-side functionality. Authentication and authorization concerns, client-side trust issues, misconfigured security controls, and cross-platform development framework difficulties are examples of application binary vulnerabilities. Typical server-side web service vulnerabilities include session management, cryptographic difficulties, authentication and authorization concerns, and others.
- **APIs**: Using both automated and manual testing methodologies, the OWASP API Security Top 10 list is covered. Among the security threats and vulnerabilities that testers search for are broken object-level permission, user authentication, excessive data exposure, lack of resources, rate limitation, and others.
- **CI/CD pipeline**: Modern DevSecOps procedures include intelligent and automated code scanning technologies into the CI/CD pipeline. In addition to static tools that identify known vulnerabilities, automated PT tools may be included in the CI/CD pipeline to simulate what a hacker could do to compromise an application's security. Automated CI/CD PT may uncover vulnerabilities and attack patterns that are not uncovered by static code scanning.

What are the advantages and disadvantages of PT?

As the frequency and severity of security breaches continue to rise, companies have never had a greater need for insight into their ability to resist assaults. For compliance with regulations such as the PCI DSS and HIPAA, frequent PT is required. Keeping these factors in mind, the following are the advantages and disadvantages of this sort of defect-finding approach.

Benefits of PT

- Identifies vulnerabilities in upstream security assurance procedures, such as automated tools, configuration and coding standards, architectural analysis, and other lightweight VA operations
- Identifies both known and undiscovered software faults and security vulnerabilities, including tiny problems that on their own aren't cause for alarm but might cause serious damage as part of a larger attack scheme
- Can attack any system by imitating the behavior of the majority of dangerous hackers, emulating a genuine opponent as closely as possible

Cons of PT

- Laborious and expensive
- Does not thoroughly prevent bugs and defects from entering production

Index

A

ACME 141
Action Plan (AP) 23-25
Advanced Persistent Threat (APT) 70
aggregate data 43
Annex A controls
  implementing, considerations 124
anonymization 43
APIs 198
asset management 117, 118
availability 6

B

Binding Corporate Rules (BCRs) 63
Biometric Information Privacy Act (BIPA) 178
Bring Your Own Device (BYOD) 180
  benefits 181
  criteria and recommendations 182
  disadvantages 181
  mobile devices, managing 181
BSI - Cloud Computing Compliance Criteria Catalog (BSI C5)
  reference link 173
business associates (BA) 113

C

California Consumer Privacy Act (CCPA) 177
  versus GDPR 42, 43
  versus LGPD 42, 43
California Privacy Rights Act (CPRA) 177
Center for Internet Security (CIS) 113
chief risk officer (CRO) 73
Children's Online Privacy Protection Act (COPPA) 177, 179
CI/CD pipeline 198
cloud
  concern 168
  emerging 163
  environment 198
  security concern 169
  working 164
cloud computing 166
  absence of architecture, for cloud security 167
  absence of strategy, for cloud security 167
  cloud services configuration errors 168
  compliance violation 167
  contractual violations 168
  internal threats 167

reduced visibility 167
unprotected user interface 168
Cloud Computing Compliance Controls Catalogue (C5) 164
cloud hosting policy 141, 142
applicable policies 144
data availability and records retention 144
intellectual property and copyright materials 143
personally identifiable information (PII) 143
purpose 141
requirements 142, 143
roles and responsibilities 144
scope 141
cloud security 164
risks measuring 166
Cloud Security Alliance (CSA) 164
reference link 173
Cloud Service Providers (CSPs) 163
using, in GDPR code of conduct 172, 173
cloud services, types 165
Infrastructure as a Service (IaaS) 165
Platform as a Service (PaaS) 165
Software as a Service (SaaS) 165
Colorado Privacy Act (CPA) 177
commitment 25, 26
Committee of Sponsoring Organization (COSO) 77
communication 94
internal communication, versus external communication 96, 97
plans 95, 96
techniques 95
communications Security 120
company policies 127
determining 128
disciplinary action policies 128
document and record retention rules 129
payment policies 129
personnel policies 128
policies on confidentiality 129
policies on employee performance 129
privacy policies 129
security policies 128
technology policies 128
whistleblower policy 129
company procedures 144
design elements, evaluating 147
guidelines, for writing 147
information gathering 146
necessity 145, 146
writing 146, 147
compliance 123
violation 167
confidentiality 6
confidentiality, integrity, and availability (CIA) 6, 7
context-based 112
controls 25
corporate governance 11, 12
Court of Justice of the European Union (CJEU) 63, 193
cryptography 118
Cybersecurity Framework (CSF) 15

D

data-based 111
data classification 110
categorization 111
difficulties 112
effects, of compliance standards on 112, 113
levels 111-114
need for 111
policy, developing 114, 115

- procedures 115
- types 111

data controller 53, 54, 171
- accountability 54

data controllers, accountability
- materials, training 56
- privacy dashboard 55, 56
- recommended documents 55

data custodian/data protection officer 142

data processor 54, 172
- mandatory documents 56-61

data protection
- dealing with 46-48
- warning 61

Data Protection Officer (DPO) 55

data security and compliance
- contractual requisites 171
- documentation requisites 171
- security control requisites 170

de-identified 43

Demilitarized Zone (DMZ) 9

Deming Cycle 85

design elements, company procedures
- flowchart 147
- matrix 148
- playscript 147, 148
- question and answer 148

Detect function 28

Distributed Denial of Service (DDoS) attacks 7, 70

distribution model 165

distribution model, methods
- hybrid model 165
- other model 165
- private model 165
- public model 165

docker containers 198

Documentation of Impact Assessment (DPIA) 60

documented information, ISO 27001 support requirements 97, 98
- developing and revising 98
- general 98
- recorded data management 99-101

E

Electronic Communications Privacy Act (ECPA) 177

Electronic Health Records (EHRs) 142

embedded apparatus 198

Employee Code of Conduct 135
- example draft 135
- template 135

employee privacy rights 186
- information access 186
- personal business 187
- worker monitoring exception 186

enterprise risk management (ERM) 72, 108
- versus traditional risk management 73, 74

EU-GDPR 142

European Cloud User Coalition (ECUC) 164

European Data Protection Board (EDPB) 62

European Data Protection Supervisor (EDPS) 169

European Union Agency for Network and Information Security (ENISA) 169

EU-US Privacy Shield 61-67

F

Fair Credit Reporting Act (FCRA) 176

Family Educational Rights and Privacy Act (FERPA) 142, 176

Federal Office for Information Security (BSI) 164
Federal Trade Commission Act (FTC Act) 177
Federal Trade Commission (FTC) 177, 178
overview 179
FISMA 142
Frequently Asked Questions (FAQs) 63

G

GDPR code of conduct
for Cloud Service Providers (CSPs) 172, 173
GDPR concern 168
cloud industry impact 169
cloud service providers requisites 169
normative requisites 170
General Data Protection Regulation (GDPR) 4, 22, 40, 112, 176, 193
aggregated information, need for 43
anonymous, need for 43
data access privileges 45, 46
de-identified, need for 43
fines 46
legal bases, for data processing 44
penalties 46
principles 48-51
Privacy Shield 61-67
pseudonymous, need for 43
territorial scope 41, 42
versus CCPA 42, 43
versus LGPD 42, 43
governance, risk, and compliance (GRC) 73
Gramm-Leach-Bliley Act (GLBA) 176

H

Health Insurance Portability and Accountability Act (HIPAA) 142, 176
heating, ventilation, and air conditioning (HVAC) 119
high-sensitivity data 114
HITECH 142
human resource security 117
hybrid model 165

I

Identify function 26, 27
categories 26
identity and access management (IAM) 166
incident management procedure 14
information security
concepts 8-11
definitions 8-11
information security aspects of business continuity management 123
information security incident management 122, 123
Information Security (IS) 17
information Security Management System (iSMS) 5, 21-23, 193
operating resource requirements 89, 90
structuring 85
information security policies 116
Infrastructure as a Service (IaaS) 142
integrity 6
International Organization for Standardization (ISO) 5
internet 151
Internet of Things (IoT) 198
ISACA
URL 12
iSMS, structuring
assessment 87
project development and documentation system 86

project development and risk analysis 87
project development and selection of controls 86
project objective and estimate 85
team building 86
ISO 27k
CIA triad 6, 7
standards 3-6
ISO 27001
mapping, with NIST SP 800 29, 34
operations 83, 84
standard 84
support requirements 88
versus NIST 14, 16
ISO 27001 controls 116
categories 116-124
identification, to implement 125
using 125
ISO 27001 support requirements 88
awareness 93, 94
communication 94-96
competency 90-93
documented information 97
ISO 27002 189, 190
controls 189
controls, implementing 190-192
controls, version updates 190
standard set of controls, for information security 191
ISO/IEC 27001 142
ISO/IEC 31010 142

K

key performance indicators (KPIs) 78, 114
key risk indicators (KRIs) 78

L

Lei Geral de Proteção de Dados Pessoais (LGPD)
versus CCPA 42, 43
versus GDPR 42, 43
low-sensitivity data 114

M

managed security service providers (MSSPs) 70
medium-sensitivity data 114
misdirection theft 153
Mitigation and Prevention Plan 158
applicable security awareness programs, implementing 162
periodic real-world audits, conducting 161
practical and realistic policies, developing 160
realistic and implementable policies, developing 159
social engineering attacks, recognizing 158, 159
thinking from policies, removing 159, 160
mobile applications 197
Mobile Device Management (MDM) 181
features 182
mobile devices 198
multi-factor authentication (MFA) 185

N

National Institute of Standards and Technology (NIST) 14-16, 180
service models 169
versus ISO 27001 14, 16

networks **198**
network time protocol (NTP) **120**
NIST Framework
  Detect function 28
  Identify function 26, 27
  Protect function 27, 28
  Recover function 29
  respond function 28
NIST SP 800
  mapping, with ISO 27001 29, 34
Non-Disclosure Agreement (NDA) **194**
non-identifiable **43**

O

opaque box **196**
Open Source Intelligence (OSINT) **152**
operations security **119, 120**
Organization of Information Security **117**

P

PCI/DSS **112, 142**
Penetration Testing (PT) **196**
  advantages 196, 199
  disadvantages 199
  forms 197, 198
  penetration testers, access 196, 197
  steps 197
phishing **153**
Physical and Environmental Security **119**
PIPEDA **142**
Plan-Do-Check-Act (PDCA)
  act phase 86
  check phase 86
  do phase 85
  plan phase 85
Platform as a Service (PaaS) **141**
policies **12**
  disadvantages 130
  significance 130, 131
policy **12**
  function 13
policy writing instructions
  cloud hosting policy 141
  draft, sending for review 134
  Employee Code of Conduct example draft 135
  final approval and signatures, obtaining 135
  general writing instructions 129, 130
  method, selecting for process management 133
  physical policy, writing 132
  policy list, prioritizing 133
  policy management group, establishing 133
  preliminary draft, creating 134
  processes, verifying 134
pretexting **153**
PRISM **62**
privacy **193**
privacy laws **38, 39**
Privacy Management System (PMS) **55**
Privacy Shield **62**
private model **165**
procedure **13**
procedures **12, 130**
  disadvantages 130
  significance 130, 131
project management **25, 26**
project risk management
  characteristics 105, 106
  elements 104
  evaluation 105
  fundamental notions 104
  heatmaps 107, 108

mitigation 108
Risk Management Plan 104
strategies 108, 109
strategies, establishing 110
protected health information (PHI) 113
Protect function 27, 28
categories 27
pseudonymous 43
public model 165

Q

qualitative risk analysis 79
performing, considerations 80
quantitative risk analysis 79
performing, considerations 80
versus qualitative risk analysis 80

R

Recover function 29
red, amber, or green (RAG) 107
reduced visibility 167
remote working 182
computer safety 185
multifaceted strategy 184
security 183, 184
security issues 183
threat 183
transformation, assisting 185
Respond function 28
components 28
risk analysis phases
risk identification 87
risk measurement 87
risk weighting 87
risk heatmaps 107, 108
risk management 69
benefits and challenges 76, 77
categories 72
heatmap 79
need for 73
program, implementing 72
qualitative risk analysis 79
quantitative risk analysis 79
security threats and challenges 69, 70
security threats, types 70
steps, for information security 75, 76
strategy, building 77-79
strategy, implementing 77-79
top-down approach 76
versus security threats 70, 71
risk mitigation 108
Risk Treatment Plan (RTP) 23-25

S

Safe Harbor 62
Schrems 53
Schrems II ruling 62
Section 5, of FTC Act
overview 179
security threat
versus risk management 70, 71
semi-opaque box 197
Service Level Agreement (SLA) 143
smishing 156
messaging applications 157
prevention 157
strategies, used for 157
SOC2 113
social engineering 152
Open Source Intelligence (OSINT) 152
social scientist 152

social engineering attack methods
- misdirection theft 153
- phishing 153
- pretexting 152
- smishing 156
- targeted phishing 153
- vishing 154

Software as a Service (SaaS) 141
source-based 112
standard contractual clauses (SCCs) 62
Statement of Applicability (SoA) 23-25, 125
supplier relationships 122
System Acquisition, Development, and Maintenance 121, 122

T

targeted phishing 153
- baiting 154
- honeytrap 154
- Quid pro quo 154
- rogue 154
- tailgating 154
- water-holing 153

template, Employee Code of Conduct
- business representing, through social media 138
- cell phones 136
- company visitors 140
- competing interests 138
- corporate email 137
- dating coworkers 139
- dating managers 139
- distribution 140
- dress code 135
- employee interactions 138
- employment of relatives 139
- fraternization 139
- general expectations 137
- internet security and electronic gadgets 136
- internet use 136
- personal use, of social media 137, 138
- social media 137
- solicitation 140

traditional risk management
- versus enterprise risk management 73, 74

transparent box 197
two-factor authentication (2FA) 185

U

uninterruptible power supply (UPS) 119
US privacy 175
- national privacy laws 176-178

V

Video Privacy Protection Act (VPPA) 177
Virginia Consumer Data Protection Act (VCDPA) 177, 178
virtual private networks (VPNs) 184
vishing 154
- functioning 155
- identifying 156
- prevalent approaches 155
- prevention 156

Vulnerability Assessment (VA) 194
- evaluation instruments 196
- remediation 195
- risk assessment 195
- vulnerability analysis 195
- vulnerability identification (testing) 194

W

web application testers 197

Other Books You May Enjoy

If you enjoyed this book, you may be interested in these other books by Packt:

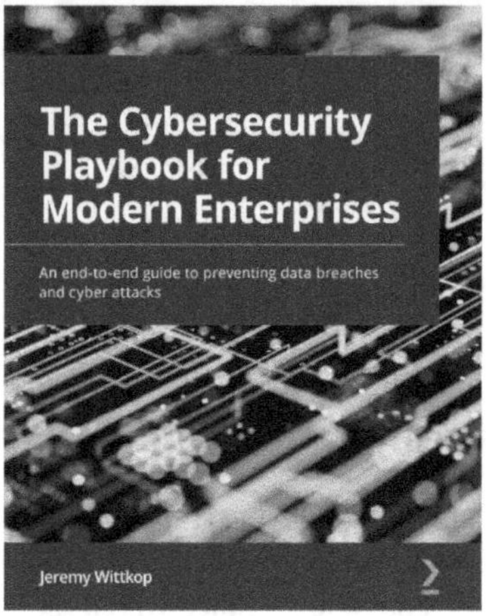

The Cybersecurity Playbook for Modern Enterprises

Jeremy Wittkop

ISBN: 9781803248639

- Understand the macro-implications of cyber attacks
- Identify malicious users and prevent harm to your organization
- Find out how ransomware attacks take place
- Work with emerging techniques for improving security profiles
- Explore identity and access management and endpoint security
- Get to grips with building advanced automation models
- Build effective training programs to protect against hacking techniques
- Discover best practices to help you and your family stay safe online

Hack the Cybersecurity Interview

Ken Underhill, Christophe Foulon, Tia Hopkins

ISBN: 9781801816632

- Understand the most common and important cybersecurity roles
- Focus on interview preparation for key cybersecurity areas
- Identify how to answer important behavioral questions
- Become well versed in the technical side of the interview
- Grasp key cybersecurity role-based questions and their answers
- Develop confidence and handle stress like a pro

Packt is searching for authors like you

If you're interested in becoming an author for Packt, please visit authors.packtpub.com and apply today. We have worked with thousands of developers and tech professionals, just like you, to help them share their insight with the global tech community. You can make a general application, apply for a specific hot topic that we are recruiting an author for, or submit your own idea.

Share Your Thoughts

Now you've finished *Cybersecurity and Privacy Law Handbook*, we'd love to hear your thoughts! Scan the QR code below to go straight to the Amazon review page for this book and share your feedback or leave a review on the site that you purchased it from.

https://packt.link/r/1-803-24241-8

Your review is important to us and the tech community and will help us make sure we're delivering excellent quality content.

Download a free PDF copy of this book

Thanks for purchasing this book!

Do you like to read on the go but are unable to carry your print books everywhere? Is your eBook purchase not compatible with the device of your choice?

Don't worry, now with every Packt book you get a DRM-free PDF version of that book at no cost.

Read anywhere, any place, on any device. Search, copy, and paste code from your favorite technical books directly into your application.

The perks don't stop there, you can get exclusive access to discounts, newsletters, and great free content in your inbox daily

Follow these simple steps to get the benefits:

1. Scan the QR code or visit the link below

   `https://packt.link/free-ebook/9781803242415`

2. Submit your proof of purchase
3. That's it! We'll send your free PDF and other benefits to your email directly